# Engraved:

## Canadian Stories of World War One

# Engraved:

## Canadian Stories of World War One

*Edited by Bernadette Rule*

Seraphim
EDITIONS

The publisher gratefully acknowledges the financial assistance of the Canada Council for the Arts and the Ontario Arts Council.

Library and Archives Canada Cataloguing in Publication

    Engraved : Canadian stories of World War One / edited by Bernadette Rule.

ISBN 978-1-927079-31-7 (pbk.)

    1. World War, 1914-1918--Canada.  2. World War, 1914-1918--Canada--Biography.  I. Rule, Bernadette, 1951-, editor

D547.C2E54 2014          940.3'71         C2014-905495-5

Editor: Bernadette Rule
Design and Typography: Rolf Busch

Published in 2014 by
Seraphim Editions
4456 Park Street
Niagara Falls, ON
L2P 2P6

Printed and bound in Canada

# Cold Front

*S.J. White*

First light, first thought
we thought the cold had
taken just your voice until
we touched you
on the shoulder
and you toppled
rifle at the ready
stiff as any statue
that they'd raise to you
on centre-ville, piazza
         city square.

I since have lived
ten-thousand
peaceful dawns
in heated rooms
in feather beds with
comfortable women
         and still
         I dream of you.

# Contents

# Foreword

Some years ago I bought a wristwatch from an antique dealer. It caught my eye because of its beauty, but it was the inscription on the back that sealed the deal. In the graceful cursive of 19th and early 20th century jewelry store engravers was written: *To Marjorie from Albert 1916.* The flowing script, the names, and especially that date set my imagination ticking. Albert, going off to the Great War, wanted to leave his love a token to wear at her pulse for measuring the hours until he returned. But the clerk told me it came from a Greensville, Ontario estate sale where they said it had been a brother's gift to his sister upon her graduation. Okay. Did he go to the war? She only shrugged, as if the question didn't particularly interest her.

In any case, they were close, this brother and sister. It seems feelings ran deep back in the day. People did things for keeps. Could Marjorie and Albert have imagined a day when watches would be rare? Could they have imagined a day when people their age would be unable to read cursive writing, let alone find someone to write their names in flourishing penmanship in a space the size of a quarter? For, make no mistake, the art *and* the import of that kind of engraving is virtually unknown in Canada today. Was it the war itself that changed all that?

When I was a child, at some point in the middle of the 20th century, I asked my mother why idealized scenes, like those depicted on calendars and Christmas cards, were always set in horse and buggy days, when everyone wore hats and the women carried muffs. I remember that she didn't hesitate. "They're set before World War One," she said, "before the world lost its innocence." She went on to explain that that war changed everything. People really had gone to it

9

believing it was "the war to end all wars", but it was the cruellest war in history, if such things can be quantified. It was state-sponsored slaughter. Then, a mere twenty years later, there was another one.

Today it seems war never ends. It is an industry – an immoral, polluting industry. Amazingly, there are still those who enter the military out of idealism, but most of us can no longer pretend that the government sees soldiers as anything but expendable fodder. We have heard too many heartbreaking stories, some from veterans about their unending struggle for support when they return. After one hundred years of "shell-shock" the military's resistance to understanding PTSD is extremely telling. Of course there was military and political corruption before 1914, but there was still room then for idealism about government, about something like a call to arms. World War One was a brutal lesson.

*Engraved* is a collection of stories and essays about Canadians during the First World War, with an underlying focus on how that war changed Canadian society. It was commissioned by Maureen Whyte, publisher of Seraphim Editions, in honour of the one hundredth anniversary of the start of what soon came to be called "The Great War".

There are many devoted siblings – many Marjories and Alberts – in these pages, as well as grandparents, parents, aunts, uncles, lovers, and friends – all of whose hearts are broken by the war. There are idealists and cynics, opportunists and martyrs, pacifists, patriots, and poets. Many of the stories are about ordinary men and women whose absence transformed their families. What also becomes clear is that even those who returned were never the same. Whether they gave one man or eight – as one writer's family did – whether they were fired by patriotism, pressured by society, or moved to resist, all were affected by the horrors of what is now known as the first modern war. Words like mud, trench foot, rats, lice, gasmasks, Ypres, Passchendaele, and Vimy Ridge can make us flinch even a century later. These stories give a context to those touchstones of suffering.

There are also stories here of extraordinary people: Georgina Pope, Canada's first military nurse, and the first Canadian ever to be awarded the Royal Red Cross Medal; John McCrae, the battlefield doctor whose iconic poem "In Flanders Fields" still shapes Remembrance Day ceremonies; and war artist A.Y. Jackson, whose vision was altered by the devastation he witnessed in France. That vision helped give birth to the artistic sensibility of Canada itself, through the Group of Seven. Details about field dentistry, the disastrous Ross Rifle, shell-shock, conscientious objectors, love, abandonment, and loyalty make it clear why that era remains engraved across the nation's collective memory and across our individual hearts.

The question that lingers is how, after living through such catastrophic and collective suffering – even after coming to understand the fallibility of our leaders – we can continue to participate in military conflicts. If only it *had* been "the war to end all wars."

Bernadette Rule
May 2014

# The Beaus

*Bruce Meyer*

Of all the wars that have touched my family, I consider World War One the hardest war to hold on to. It should have been, in both artefact and in fact, the one war that would stay with us. The four years of death cast a shadow on my family. It was the war of my grandparent's generation, the war of the lost. It is buried in the silence of family memories, in the depths of what was not said. The pain of it ran too deep to repeat the stories to a child. As I stood around the corners of doors, or in the November wind that rattled up Bay Street during the silence at Toronto's cenotaph, I snatched whatever fragments I could and tried to assemble them in my mind as if it was a jigsaw puzzle that had been passed to me with half the pieces missing. Whatever they called it before they waved off their conversation and hushed to silence because they thought I might be listening – the Great War, the war to end all wars, the First War – it was for me the War of the Beaus.

My grandfather came from a large family and I grew up surrounded by his sisters. The women presented themselves in every personality and shape. The one thing they had in common was that they were of the late Victorian generation, the generation that had lived and suffered through World War One. The women were the ones who stayed at home and waited. My grandmother would regale me with stories of the bandage rolling sessions, and the guessing games she and her friends would play as they turned the handles on the rolling machines they had bolted to the dining room table. My grandmother started going with my grandfather around the time the war broke out.

They courted for seven years, a long courtship that was prolonged by the uncertainty of the war. My grandfather was almost completely deaf. He was also frail, colour-blind, and flat-footed. Only when he was on his deathbed at the age of eighty-eight did his role in the war become known to us.

\* \* \*

The eldest of my grandfather's sisters, Beatrice, grew old with great enormity. I remember her as a large woman always seated in a chair. In her declining years, she seemed unmoveable to me, and she probably was. I would climb her body as she sat in a large easy chair that groaned beneath her, scrambling up her heights for a kiss.

Her husband, a former Toronto Harbour Commissioner, had been invited to join the fabled Princess Patricia's Light Infantry as a Captain. Benjamin Miller's connections must have been good, because he was offered an officer's commission and readily accepted. On his last leave home, he and my aunt were married. They had courted for years before the war, but had always found one way or another to put off the nuptials. When they married, many of her sisters and brothers and their friends and neighbours talked behind their hands, but who were they to stand in the way of true love when a war threatened the "Old Country"? Captain Benjamin Miller was her first cousin. She had bid him farewell at Union Station, a ritual that the sisters replayed over and over again throughout the four years of the war. As he hung his head out the window of the officer's carriage and doffed his cap to bid his city farewell, she had kissed his forehead.

He lasted a year and a bit more in the trenches. One day, the eldest aunt received a telegram informing her that her husband had been severely wounded at Mount Sorel. She feared that he would never see their child, and she waited for news to arrive from his regiment's commanding officer. Months passed. There was only silence. Then she received a letter from him explaining that he had been out of touch because of a bothersome piece of shrapnel that had entered his forehead, not far off the place where she had kissed him goodbye. The

13

good news, he added, was that they would never be poor. The doctor's had replaced the missing portion of his skull with a silver plate. Uncle Ben would hold his head and rock back and forth for hours on end. Eventually, he would simply give up fighting the pain and turn to the Scotsman's cure. He became a favorite on the party circuit of Toronto even during prohibition, and especially when he was Harbour Commissioner.

My grandfather told me this story one autumn afternoon when I was about five. It was my first encounter with the Great War, as the family called it. He had just come from helping his eldest sister sort out her husband's belongings after the funeral. She showed her brother a letter and said, "He was so brave, so brave." They laid aside the last item from his dresser and his closet, perhaps because both siblings knew it was the toughest thing to part with. It was his khaki officer's tunic. It lay on the bed, its arms spread as if to say "what now," and they stood and looked at it until my aunt decided it would have to go. "I'll send it to the Crippled Civilians," she said. My grandfather questioned her. "Won't they have seen enough of khaki battle dress, especially one with moth holes shot through it?" He reached down and rippled a button from the front of it. "Bruce will want this," he said.

The button was brass, and although it had tarnished from years of not being spit-polished and paraded, I could still see a beaver hunched over a protruding rock as if it had emerged from the still, dark, and mysterious waters. I think of those ripples in the insignia as the lacunae of what could be read as history or the private stories that soldiers never tell of what they have seen. Behind the beaver was a maple leaf, its arms spread out in announcement of surprise, as if it had never existed before. It reminded me of spring, its tips reaching for the very edges of the button and piercing the letters of the word Canada set as a blazon over the beaver. Above the scene sat the crown imperial.

The more I held the button in the palm of my hand, the more it shone and came to life. I took it to school and kept it in my pocket the way boys keep chestnuts or stones they find. I announced to my kindergarten class that it had "belonged to my Uncle Ben who had been in World War One." The teacher quizzed me: "What did your

Uncle Ben do?" I replied that he was the face on the box of rice. That day I was sent home with a note saying, "Bruce is fibbing to the class again." That same day a boy who was the older brother of a classmate asked to see the button. He put it in his pocket and walked away. I had lost my first contact with the war.

\* \* \*

The second beau, my Uncle Cliff, was a man I only met once or twice. He married my grandfather's youngest sister, Grace, before going off to join the Royal Flying Corps. She was just fifteen at the time. She followed the exploits of Lt. Clifford Riley as reported in the *Mail and Empire* and the *Toronto Star*. According to the stories she told me as she waited for the arrival of her own passing in a suburban nursing home, Cliff was dashing and brave. He had been given a Sopwith. "A camel?" I asked. "No," she replied as if I was stupid. "An airplane."

He had flown many missions. He was in a squadron that shot down balloons. "Do you know what I mean?" she quizzed me. "Balloon busters." I had heard about the balloon busters from my grandmother. Her best friend's only brother, a Lieutenant named Carleton Chrysler – on whose ancestral farm the final battle for Canada had been fought during the War of 1812 – had been a member of a balloon buster squadron. He, too, had been engaged. He, too, had a girl waiting at home for him. "Never ask my friend about her brother," my grandmother warned me. "She goes to pieces."

The average life expectancy of a balloon buster was three missions. Uncle Cliff, unlike Carleton Chrysler who only lasted two missions, was shot down following his fifteenth mission and had been credited with five balloons. Had he shot down airplanes rather than balloons, he would have been considered an ace. Balloons, however, did not count as official "kills."

I leaned into my aunt as she gazed out the window of her nursing home. "That would have made him an ace," I said.

"Would have, but he was never credited with the final balloon because he was badly injured. His plane veered back to the British

15

lines, fortunately, and when he crashed they took parts of his engine out of his body. He got the best care possible." With that she fell silent. My grandmother told me that Uncle Cliff never went swimming at family gatherings at Lake Simcoe. His lower body was too badly burned to be seen in public. That is where his story ends. Before she died, my grandfather's youngest sister set fire to her room in the nursing home by burning all the photographs of her husband, including their wedding photo.

* * *

The third of the many sisters, Hazel, was the one I was closest to during my childhood. She had been the beauty of the family. Each birthday she sent me a box of tin Highlanders. By the time I was nine or so and the toy soldiers were ready to march off into the closet, I had a very large brigade of them: bagpipers, drummers, marching men with their rifles shouldered. Every line in their tartan kilts was painted by hand, and when they were arranged in parade files, the kilts almost seemed to sway to the haunting spirit in their regimental march.

Aunt Hazel should have gone to university. She had the brains. The family wanted to send her, but they did not have enough money to do so. They told her that her childhood sweetheart – her intended whom she had met at Lord Dufferin School when they were seven or eight years old – would support her throughout her life. Her beau, Tom Kelly, was brilliant. He was an outstanding athlete who won all the Varsity competitions for running. My grandfather, who was very fast even into old age, claimed that Tom Kelly could beat him by a country mile in a footrace. Tom topped every class he entered. He was given a scholarship to University College at the University of Toronto where he stood first in his year. He entered the University of Toronto Law School at the old Osgoode Hall courthouse on University Avenue. He was destined for great things, everyone said, and Tom and Hazel would make the perfect couple.

Instead of pursuing her dreams – dreams that she was worthy of obtaining – she became a stenographer and worked her way up in a pharmaceuticals firm. Later in life she became the first woman to be vice-president of such a company in Canada. She never married and I always wondered why. Throughout her life she had educated herself by reading and attending public lectures. She gave my mother a set of the works of Joseph Conrad when her niece finished high school and was accepted into university. She told my mother, "Conrad is very special. He will lead you to adventure."

Conrad had been the favorite author of Tom Kelly. He had given her his own set of Conrad just before he departed for France as a Private in the Toronto Scottish. It is probably conjecture to think that he pictured himself as Lord Jim, though he was of that generation that had read the ripping yarns of such writers as G.A. Henty and Robert Louis Stevenson. Conrad seemed a down-to-earth option compared to the wild tales of valorous young men who spoke to Tom Kelly's generation.

On his arrival in France, Kelly was chosen to be the regiment's runner. His legs could carry him faster than just about any man. My grandmother once told me that Tom was a young Achilles. The enigma he was became part of my childhood one November day when I was five years old.

Remembrance Day was a school holiday. My mother was nursing my young sister and decided to drop me at my grandmother's house. The wind made my grandfather's hearing aids whistle, so he decided not to accompany us downtown to have chocolate milk and sandwiches at the Georgian Room of Eaton's department store. "But first," my grandmother said, "there is something we have to do." In the distance I heard bagpipes echoing off the walls of the office towers on Bay Street. "Let's go see the Highlanders," she said as we walked along Queen Street to the foot of the City Hall.

A crowd had gathered as the bagpipes fell silent and the 48th Highlanders took their position on the steps. A woman behind me pushed me to the front. "Let the boy get a better look." I turned and my grandmother nodded as we moved to the front row of the gathering. A minister in a flowing white robe began to speak. His voice was sad and hollow as he led us in prayer. Then a bugler started to play a very simple yet haunting song. "That is the Last Post," my grandmother whispered as she bent over me. Then a terrible silence broke out and out of that silence guns began to sound and the City Hall's bell tower chimed with a tragic sound that I have never heard since.

Startled, I looked up across the gathering and there, through her long, black veil fluttering in the cold wind, I saw my Aunt Hazel. Tears were running down her cheeks. I raised my hand to point but my grandmother caught my arm and moved it down, and she again bent and whispered in my ear, "Leave her alone. This is Aunt Hazel's moment." The startled pigeons circled from the clock tower and I heard their wings beating the air.

As we sat and ate our lunch, I asked my grandmother why we could not have gone over to greet Aunt Hazel after the ceremony and invite her along to lunch with us. "She lost her beau in the First World War. His name was Tom Kelly."

I could never get the family to tell me much about Tom Kelly, except that he and Aunt Hazel had been in love and that one day she saw his name on the list of those who could not be accounted for and her life fell into a widowed silence. He was a shadow that fell across the family, someone who haunted the life of the maiden aunt who each April 23 sent me a box of tin highlander toy soldiers.

* * *

The same sense of mystery surrounded my grandfather. On his deathbed after a very long and loving life, he called out, "Is that door tiled? Tile that door!" I asked my grandmother what he meant by that.

"Your grandfather was a Mason."

"Why was he not in the war?"

"He was deemed unfit for active service. He worked for a dry-goods firm. He worked for John McDonald, a senator, the man who built Oaklands, that huge house on the lip of the Avenue Road hill, that house that is now part of De La Salle School. The man immediately ahead of him in the firm, Walter Rumble, went down on the *Lusitania*.

"It sank in fifteen minutes after it was torpedoed off Ireland.

"Walter was on deck and was ready to get into a lifeboat when he said to someone that he had to go back to his cabin because of something Mr. McDonald had to have delivered. People thought Walter was carrying gold and he had gone back for it. He was never seen again. Your grandfather was ordered to take his place and had to go overseas."

"Why?"

"The story he told everyone was that John McDonald needed new suits from his Saville Row tailor. Your grandfather was sent from New York on a filthy tramp steamer, something not worth a torpedo. All the way over, he told me, there was a Bulgarian actress who kept following him around. His cabin was entered but your grandfather was cagey. He left his Bible opened to a particular passage and tied a piece of thread from a table leg to the door. When he came back the thread was broken and the Bible was turned to a different page. Your great-grandfather kept hearing about all the ships being sunk by the U-Boats. We didn't even know the name of your grandfather's ship. First he said he didn't know and then he said he couldn't tell us for safety reasons. His father paced up and down, wringing his hands, and repeating 'My poor boy, my poor boy.' When your grandfather arrived in Liverpool the police came on board and arrested the actress as a spy. Your grandfather was then chased through the dockland by several armed men, but he got away. When he arrived in London, the first night at his hotel, the Zeppelins bombed the city and took out the building next door. He slept through it because of his deafness. In the morning he carried to the tailor on Saville Row a large package of suits to be altered. He was taken into the back room and all the garments were counted and weighed. They had him unwrap the apparel and he noticed that there were bulks of papers sewn in the lining. That was all he would ever tell me."

If one is lucky, the past reveals itself after many years. For the most part, though, time buries things in its silence. I read an article a decade ago about how the first Canadian secret service during World War One had been made up of Scottish Rite masons – the only men Prime Minister Robert Borden would trust. He, too, was a Scottish Rite mason. So was Senator John McDonald. Had my grandfather been a secret courier? Why would someone cross the Atlantic in the middle of a war to deliver suits and pick up new ones? I had tried to ask my grandfather about the war during his final days. "It will all come out someday," was all he said. "It will all come out. I did my part." I am still waiting to find out what he did.

* * *

The story of Private Thomas Kelly, as I discovered in the process of writing this piece, is something that is far more clear and, in its own way, tragic. I found the file on Tom Kelly on the National Archives web site. Someone, perhaps descendants of his sister, posted newspaper clippings, pictures, and even a memorial notice sent out to students of Lord Dufferin School. In the photos he is a confident young man. His eyes, blue according to the records, have a penetrating look as if he is sizing up the scenario before him and working out a case to present in response to it. He has the look of someone who would have been a good lawyer, perhaps a judge. His hair is light brown and his complexion is fair. He was tall for his times, listed at 5'10." There is an athletic air about him.

Private Kelly marched into action as part of the Canadian Corps at the Second Battle of Ypres in April of 1915. It was the first major event of the war for Canadian troops. Our nationals had the French colonial "Zoaves" on one flank and some British troops on the other. As they fired at the oncoming waves of Germans – all of whom were high on medical ether from canisters they inhaled prior to going 'over the top' – the Ross Rifles issued to the Canadians jammed and overheated. The Canadians used them as clubs to beat the attackers back. Suddenly, the Germans receded and, in their place, a cloud of greenish mist drifted toward the Canadian lines. It was the first gas attack. The French colonials fled. The British fell back choking and gasping. The Canadians, who had gotten the bright idea of urinating on their handkerchiefs to buffer the chlorine, held their ground and stopped the second wave of the attack.

The Second Battle of Ypres took place on April 23, 1915. That was the day Private Thomas Kelly was listed as "Missing in Action." His body was never found. A report states that he was carrying a message from his commander to the commander of the British unit. He disappeared into a mist of gas and shells and was never seen again as he ran, not for his life, but for his duty. His name is inscribed on the Menin Gate – that haunting structure raised in memory of the fallen from the Battle of the Somme that poet Siegfried Sassoon called "the gravestone of those who have no graves." In a small tribute to her Highlander, her fallen beau among the all the beaus in the family who were disfigured and broken by the war, Aunt Hazel never forgot my birthday.

# For King and Country

*Katharine O'Flynn*

On August 4, 1914, King George V declared war on Germany. In our remote corner of his empire – Creston, British Columbia, Canada – we didn't hear about the declaration until the next day. Then the whole town went wild. People rushed uptown to find out what others knew and to share their excitement. When the train came in from Nelson with yesterday's papers, everyone rushed to the station to see what had been reported so far. Nothing much, except that Britain was at war, and so, of course was Canada.

The news was not unexpected; the politicians had been talking about readiness for the past month. And certainly the news was not unwelcome. Most of Creston's citizens were British born or of British descent, and their loyalty to the British cause was unquestioning. People reminded each other of the words of the old Prime Minister, Sir Wilfred Laurier: "When Britain calls, all Canadians will answer, 'Ready, aye ready!'"

Eager young men dashed around trying to find out where the deuce a fellow went to enlist.

The ladies stormed the Mercantile and plundered it of all soldierly brown and green yarns and material available. My mother carried off two yards of beige cotton, and began cutting out and hemming military handkerchiefs for the volunteers. Gran cornered a dozen skeins of brown wool and started knitting.

Half a dozen young men from Creston enlisted: Archie Murdoch,

Alphabetical Smith, Bill Mason, Bob Powers, the vicar with the patriotic name of John Bull, and the Hastings boy from West Creston. They were feted as conquering heroes.

It came as no surprise to us to learn that Mr. Mallandaine was already in the army, had been since the North West Rebellion. We were now to address him as Captain Mallandaine.

The rector at Christ Church preached on Sunday and on many following Sundays about the glory of war, the wickedness of the Hun, and the righteousness of the British cause. He told us that even those of us who were not going into battle ourselves could help win the war by showing support for our soldiers in every way we could. We took his message to heart.

Gran knitted socks for the gallant boys, setting herself a goal of a pair a week. She and Mum taught me how to knit too. Even though I was only seven years old, I could do my bit. As soon as I could make a four-inch square, with the rows even and no dropped stitches, I was entrusted with the knitting of a scarf in brown four-ply.

I worried that the war would be over by the time I got it finished.

The volunteers worried that the war would be over before they'd got themselves kitted up and trained and transported to England, and from there to France.

Patriotism swept through the country and through our little town. Union Jacks blossomed everywhere. Advertising got on the bandwagon. There were flags or military insignia or information about the armed services in ads and on packages of just about everything, so the consumer could feel patriotic by drinking Frye's cocoa or using a Gillette safety razor or putting True Blue blueing in the white wash.

Gran bought red, white and blue ribbon and tried, in vain, to include the colours in the new autumn models for her hat shop. In the end, aesthetics triumphed over patriotism in the millinery sphere. "If the war is still on in the spring," she reflected, "I could do the red, white and blue in boater styles, but it simply can't be done with felts. I won't have my ladies looking like the chorus in the pantomime."

"The war will be long over by next spring," everyone assured her. 23

"But never mind; you can use the ribbon to decorate the Odd Fellows Hall for the farewell party."

The only two people I knew who were not wildly keen on the war were Uncle Andy, and Dorothy Bacon.

Uncle Andy said the war was nonsense, a fool's game. This upset Mum, but Gran told her to pay no attention to him. "It's the Irish in him," she explained. "He says what he says to annoy you; he wants to lead you into an argument. I'm sure he doesn't really believe what he says. I would advise you to ignore him."

Dorothy Bacon, who came two afternoons a week to Gran's house and shop, Rosebank, to do the plain sewing for the autumn show, didn't like the war because it would take her fiancé, Bill Mason, away from her. "I wouldn't mind so much if it was only to Vancouver or Calgary he was going," she told us, "but England is so far away. And France farther. I'll miss him fearful bad."

"Away is away, whether it's two hundred miles or two thousand," Mum said. "You must be very proud that your future husband will be a hero. And don't worry; the war will be over and he'll be back before you know it."

"I suppose," Dorothy said, but there was still doubt in her voice and she got weepy when she tried to teach me songs like "Let me Call you Sweetheart" and "Love's Old Sweet Song" as she sat sewing ribbons.

Among the volunteers, Archie Murdoch was our special friend. During the weeks of preparation he often came round to Rosebank for afternoon tea. Mum and Gran were making him handkerchiefs and socks and gloves. "I'll be the best equipped soldier in the front lines," he said as he tried things on.

Often when he visited he brought his wonderful dog Bobby with him. Bobby was a border collie spaniel mix, a clever and patient dog, capable of performing a dozen tricks. While the adults had their tea, my brother David and I would get Bobby to do a special show of 'Roll over and play dead German,' or 'Chase the wicked Germans away' for their entertainment.

One afternoon when Mr. Murdoch arrived at Rosebank's gate with Bobby trotting at his heels as usual, he called out, "Olwen! David!

Could you keep Bobby from destroying Gran's borders while I talk to your mother for a few minutes?"

Sure we could.

Presently, Mum and Mr. Murdoch walked out to the garden. "Mr. Murdoch has a request for you children," Mum said in a very serious way.

A request? For us? I was puzzled. We were children. Adults told us what to do; they didn't make requests of us.

"What it is, children," Archie said, "is I was wondering if you would look after Bobby for me while I'm away at the war? Your Mother says she thinks you could manage it."

Would we? You bet we would!

Mr. Murdoch shook our hands, as if we'd concluded a serious business arrangement.

I felt immensely grown up and patriotic and happy. Looking after Bobby would be much more fun as war work than knitting that interminable scarf. There was no hope of its being finished in time to present to Mr. Murdoch.

A few days later, the volunteers were ready to leave. Everyone, absolutely everyone, even Uncle Andy, went to the station to see our boys off. David and me and lots of other kids had Union Jacks to wave. The brass band played and there was a holiday mood in the air.

Captain Mallandaine gave a speech and got everyone to stand at attention for "God Save the King" and our soldiers stood self-consciously, the straightest and the tallest and the most solemn men there. Then Gramps Little led hoorahs for our gallant boys and the holiday mood returned.

"Give the Kaiser what for!" people shouted. No one had scruples about expressing aggressive hatred of the foe.

The only people who cried at the station that afternoon were Mr. Hastings, the widower, saying goodbye to his only son. Poor old man, it was embarrassing for him, but still, he shouldn't have come to the station if he couldn't keep control over himself, was the general opinion. And Dorothy Bacon clung weeping to her fiancé Bill till the very last minute, "making an exhibition of herself," as Gran remarked.

At last the train puffed out of the station with the soldiers leaning out the windows and we ran along the platform as far as we could, waving our flags and shouting wildly until the train was out of sight.

"Those boys will have the war knocked into a cocked hat by Christmas," Mum said with satisfaction as we climbed back Fourth Street towards Rosebank.

Through the next months, news came back from our boys. They were training at Sam Hughes' great army camp at Valcartier in Quebec. They hoped to be sent overseas soon.

David and I put out a bowl of water for Bobby every morning. We fed him twice a day on leftovers and bones and scraps the butcher gave us. "It's for Archie Murdoch's dog. We're keeping him while Archie's away at the war," Mum explained so the butcher would be sure to give him good bones.

"Your master will be home soon," I told Bobby, stroking his thick black and white fur or rubbing under his chin, which made him close his eyes in ecstasy. "Just as soon as he gives the Kaiser what for."

My scarf progressed one sweaty row at a time.

In September, the Masons received news that their boy Bill was ill in hospital in Quebec. While they were deciding whether they should travel all that way to see him, a telegram came. He had died of pneumonia.

"And he didn't even get to the war," people exclaimed over and over, knowing what a disappointment that must be to the Masons and to Dorothy, his intended. "Perhaps she had a premonition," my mother speculated, "Remember the way she carried on at the station the day the boys left?"

She was taking the news of his death hard, her family said. Stayed in her room howling, for hours, they reported.

Gran and Mum and I paid a sympathy call. Dorothy was up in her room and wouldn't come down. "Why don't you go up to her?" Mrs. Bacon asked me. "She's fond of you. Maybe you could cheer her up a bit."

I liked Dorothy, even if she was a bit soppy. She had started to teach me how to crochet, and she was going to teach me how to do lace-making. I hoped all this howling wasn't going to put an end to her afternoons with us at Rosebank. I went upstairs.

I found Dorothy sitting on her bed, with piles of clothes and linens around her. She wasn't howling, but she was sniffling. "Is there anything I could do to help?" I asked. Mum had told me to say that.

"Yes. Go to the Mercantile and get me a roll of white tissue paper." Dorothy gave me a dime. "And come straight back."

I ran to the Mercantile and came back with the tissue paper. By then Dorothy had a large trunk ready in the middle of the floor. "Everything has to be wrapped in tissue," she told me. "To save it nice."

I cut the tissue into squares and she wrapped each item and packed it neatly into the trunk. There were fine lawn nightgowns with lace work on the collars, and linen sheets with drawn work hems, embroidered pillow cases, appliqued luncheon cloths and napkins, tea towels with smiling tea pots embroidered on them, and hand towels with wide crocheted borders.

"Bill died for King and Country just as much as if he'd been killed in battle," I said. That's what my Mum had said to Bill's mother.

"No, he didn't," Dorothy said. "He died of pneumonia because of sleeping in a damp tent. It was a stupid, stupid waste. He shouldn't have gone at all." And then she began to sob out loud.

I wasn't being much of a comfort about Bill, so I tried another subject. "Where are you sending all these things?" I asked. "To the Belgian refugees?" This didn't seem like the kind of stuff that went into packages for the soldiers.

"I'm not sending them nowhere," Dorothy said. "I'm just keeping them nice."

And she did. She kept them nice all her life long.

She showed up for work at Gran's again the next week, and she finished teaching me how to crochet, but we never got started on the lace making. There was no more singing, and of course she didn't talk about Bill any more. She didn't talk much at all, so it was no fun anymore sitting with her while she worked.

She lived on in the brown shingle house on Second Street and kept it neat as a pin. In due time she nursed her mother into her grave and then her father. She never married, and as far as anyone could see, she

27

never used those beautiful things she'd sewn for her hope chest and then packed away.

Meanwhile, in October the first contingent of Canadian boys was sent from Valcartier to England. Thirty thousand men went. Five thousand more than the Prime Minister had promised. They'd lick the Huns in no time.

Archie Murdoch wrote from Salisbury Plain in England. They were closer to the war, but not in it yet. Worse luck. It was cold and wet, and war would be a treat, compared with the endless marching through the mud they were doing just now. He hoped Bobby was well.

In February he wrote again. All the other Creston boys had gone off to France. Only he'd been kept on at Salisbury to do some stupid office job. "Just my rotten luck," he wrote. "How's Bobby?"

In March the Hastings boy was killed in action. The news came as a sombre shock. Hastings was our first casualty, not counting poor Bill, who was a sort of unfortunate accident. Everybody went to the memorial service at Christ Church. Crestoners began to realize that war wasn't just flag-waving and fine sounding speeches. Men were getting killed, even men we knew.

Christmas was long past and the war hadn't ended, as everyone had predicted it would, and now it looked as though it wasn't going to end for a while yet either.

I was sent down to the station with two cents every day at train time to buy yesterday's Nelson paper as soon as it arrived. Gran, and Gramps Little and Uncle Andy pored over the war news and maps and had long discussions about how the battles were being fought and what the generals were doing wrong and how they could improve. Gramps began to mutter about useless tactics and the waste of lives but Gran said she wouldn't have any of that kind of defeatist and disloyal talk in her house.

All over the country other people in other towns were realizing, like our war experts, that the Germans were a much more formidable enemy than they'd thought. Either that, or the British army wasn't as fine and efficient a fighting force as we'd been led to believe.

No one ever voiced doubts about the inevitability of Germany's defeat, but they began to talk about a prolonged war.

Attitudes hardened against the Germans. In England the King changed his German name to the English Windsor, and in Creston Mr. Lowenberg took his mother's maiden name of Constable. Thousands of enemy aliens were interned in camps across the country. Patriotic Canadians refused to buy from businesses with German names, and wouldn't give work to anyone of German origin. Under threat of boycott, the town of Berlin in Ontario changed its name to Kitchener. German was no longer taught in schools, and some musicians refused to play works by Beethoven or Wagner or other German composers.

My mother had a hard time with this. She didn't mind so much about Wagner but she loved to play Beethoven sonatas on the piano. Eventually she found the solution in the name Beethoven. Who had ever heard of any Germans named Beethoven, other than Ludwig van himself? Therefore it couldn't be a German name. Even if he had been born in Germany, the family wasn't German. They must have come from Belgium, Mum guessed. So it was all right, it was even patriotic, for her to play and enjoy Beethoven songs and sonatas and peasant dances.

Some bad boys threw stones at Mrs. Baker's dachshund. "That's going too far," Gran said. "Poor innocent dog! He's not German. Mind you," she added, "I've always thought those dachshunds are a ridiculous looking breed. I would never have one myself."

More soldiers were needed. Recruiting posters appeared in town. A few more men enlisted. We saw them off at the station, but there was less jubilation than there had been for the first contingent. These recruits didn't inspire admiration. We knew that they were unemployed miners or forestry workers; they were going to war more for the sake of a job than for the glory of the Empire. Our hoorahs had a forced and feeble sound to them. We didn't really believe in their gallantry, and they didn't care.

The war went on and on because it couldn't stop until one side won. Britain would win in the end, of course, but victory was taking much longer than anyone had imagined.

The knitting and the bandage rolling continued.

At last I finished the scarf. Mum helped me wrap it up and we took it to the Red Cross meeting and it was added to the Creston women's parcel for the war effort.

There were more recruiting signs, but no more volunteers. There was talk of conscription.

We got something called a field postcard from Archie Murdoch. "Going up to the front now," was scrawled in pencil. "Hurrah! Will write later."

Only a few days later the news reached us through a letter from Alphabetical Smith. Archie had been killed in action on his first day in combat.

Mum cried and wrote a letter of sympathy to his mother in Edinburgh.

"What will we do about Bobby?" I asked.

"We'll keep him," Mum said. "It's what Archie would have wanted."

Poor Bobby. I stroked his thick furry ruff. "Mr. Murdoch died for King and Country," I told him. I wondered if the dog knew his master was dead. Myself, I could hardly remember Mr. Murdoch by now. "Don't worry, Bobby. I'll look after you," I promised.

At the memorial service we sang,

"We by enemies distrest
They in Paradise at rest;
We the captives – they the freed –
We and they are one indeed."

I was sad about Mr. Murdoch's getting killed, especially on his very first day fighting. But now Bobby was going to stay with us forever. I couldn't help but be happy about that.

"Stop grinning like a Cheshire cat," Mum hissed at me.

On the way home we stopped at the Mercantile to buy wool for my next scarf. Would this war never end?

## Author's Note

"For King and Country" is one of many stories I remember my mother, Olwen Evans, telling me about her childhood in Creston, B.C. I've written it in her voice, more or less as she told it.

# Georgina Pope

*Anne White*

*An interview with Cecily Jane "Georgina" Fane Pope*

*Ardgowan, Charlottetown, Prince Edward Island, 1938*

*Miss Georgina Pope, 75 years old at the time, told me how her remarkable journey started. I wanted to talk to this exceptional woman because in the late '30s it looked like we might have another war. She had been a nurse not only in the Boer War, but also in the Great War at the site of the Passchendaele debacle that had 300,000 casualties. Miss Pope appeared frail, but proper, sitting very upright. She had all her faculties and only seemed to need to steel her emotions when talking about some of her memories of the First World War. It was as if they were too painful to remember. Nevertheless she tried, and her unforgettable story emerged.*

My mother, Helen Desbrisay Pope, raised eight children, all of whom one acquaintance described as strong, vigorous, intelligent and good looking. Hmm! Is that good? I suppose so, except that we were nonconformist and a bit of a handful. We were raised to be ambitious. My grandpapa was Governor of Prince Edward Island and my father, William Pope, even managed to bring Prince Edward Island into Confederation. He was, I am told, one of the most powerful, politically manipulative and ruthless men on the island. My brother Joseph was already working in Ottawa as secretary to Sir John A. Macdonald. Mama herself was not one to shrink from a challenge.

However nothing had prepared her for my request one afternoon in the summer of 1882, shortly after my father died.

"Mama, I know this will be difficult for you, but I wish to go to New York to the Bellevue Hospital to train as one of the Nightingale nurses." I was twenty years old, unmarried, with no desire to marry. I reached out to touch my mother's hand. "Papa was such a clever man. And with Joseph in Ottawa, well ... I feel unfulfilled. I am a woman, but I feel that I, too, should make a contribution." I looked my mother in the eyes and then glanced quickly downwards, not sure what to expect.

Helen Pope's husband had been the founding member of the Orange Lodge on Prince Edward Island. Yet, to Mama's credit, all the children were raised to be independent thinkers and two of us had already converted to Roman Catholicism in the face of strong paternal disapproval. Mama probably knew that she was going to fight a losing battle with me. She sank down into an overstuffed button-back chair with her hands clasped in her lap, sighed and then grasped my hand.

"Georgie, my dear, we had to delay your coming out because poor Papa died, but time is passing and you need to be presented to Canadian society. It will be expensive and truly, Papa – while always making sure we had the best – left us a little stretched financially. We need to make you a good match. Pope women don't work. Nursing? A nurse ...? Surely this is not an occupation for a young lady? Papa would not have approved."

This was the reply I had more or less expected. I could be quite persuasive and was certainly not easily deterred. "Mama, nursing has changed. Miss Nightingale has transformed nursing through her work in the Crimea. She believes that nursing is an art and a science, that a nurse needs a careful education. Patients need ventilation and a clean place in which to heal. They are to be put in the best condition for nature to be able to act on them. It is the responsibility of nurses to reduce noise, relieve anxieties and help them sleep. She says that health means not only to be well, but to be able to use every power we have to heal. Her methods are being taught in the United States now, but in only one hospital. It's in New York. Can you not see, Mama, that this is very different from the old perception of nursing, which – I grant –

was unbecoming? The ideas of Florence Nightingale are most exciting. I truly would feel privileged to be part of this new profession!"

A huge sigh from Mama betrayed her realisation that she had no arguments with which to rebut my enthusiasm.

Mama capitulated and I went to what came to be known as the "Mother of Nursing Schools in North America", graduating from Bellevue Hospital in 1885. First I became a junior nurse in a private hospital in Washington D.C. and then moved to Columbia Hospital for Women where I was Superintendent of Nursing. A quick rise, but there were few of us trained in this new field. At the risk of you thinking me boastful I can say my extreme work ethic, organisational skill and administrative abilities made me outstanding among my peers, some of whom were surely in it just for the adventure.

Over the next five years I worked to found a school of nursing. Unfortunately I had established a pattern that was to haunt me for much of my working life. I exhausted myself, became unwell and had to resign. After a little further nursing education I returned to work as the matron of St John's Hospital in Yonkers, New York.

By 1899 Mama was now nearly as old as I am now – ailing, my sister said – and I felt I should come back here to Ardgowan, the family home, to spend a little time with her. After a week back in Charlottetown, I was beginning to feel what the voyageurs called cabin fever. My sisters descended on the house with young nephews and nieces who tumbled around giggling, crying, squabbling, tormenting the poor dogs and always needing to be fed, cleaned or picked up. The noise was tolerable, though it could be irritating at times, but I felt there was no real function for me in the house anymore.

Then I received some news from Joseph in Ottawa that promised an exciting and useful role for me. The recently knighted Prime Minister, Sir Wilfred Laurier, had agreed to support the British in South Africa against the Boers by committing one thousand infantrymen to fight. Laurier had been placed in an embarrassing position when a telegram from the British Government had been leaked to the press thanking him for supplying troops, before any had been promised. An unpopular decision, especially in Quebec, and it is still unclear forty years later whether the leak was part of a British conspiracy and sending the forces was a result of this, or of Canadian patriotism.

*So you had to ask for your mother's blessing again to leave the family home? I know she was to live for another five years, but you must have had some concerns about leaving her?*

Mama was sat in the library in Papa's favourite wingback chair looking out the window at the still meticulously manicured grounds. The leaves were just beginning to turn that incredible deep red that so meant "home" to me when I was away. The edges of the vast lawns were circumscribed by a brilliant boundary of foliage dropped from trees that Papa had carefully planned for shade. It almost seemed as if the expanse of grass was weeping blood around the edges. I hoped not an omen of things to come. I was never a good Cassandra, so I dismissed my morbid thoughts.

Glancing at Mama with my nurse's eye I thought she looked far stronger than I had been led to expect from my sister's letter. I kissed her wrinkled cheek and lowered myself to the pouffé at her feet. Her apparent good health made it easier for me to ask her if I could leave again.

"Mama, I have heard from Joseph that Canada has promised a small contingent of troops to South Africa to assist in the Boer War. They speak of sending a small auxiliary of doctors and nurses. The Canadian military has never had a medical unit before, Mama, and I should dearly like to be part of something so innovative. I have the training and the experience, and it would be such an adventure."

She reached down, tilted my chin up with a light touch, looked directly into my eyes and answered," Georgina, I know that whatever I say, you will probably manage to get your brother to put in a word for you and be selected. I don't understand why you have this need to work. You have a life here that is comfortable and there are many young men who would still wish to marry you, even at 27. However, you have chosen a path. You are a nurse, and – for better or worse –

35

you should use your skills. Why you can't do this at home close to your family is unfathomable to me, but I suppose I shall have to give you my blessing."


*Did you have any idea what you were going to? South Africa and a war zone were not at all like New York. The nursing would have been quite different.*

You are correct. We thought it would be a grand adventure. I learned in the first few weeks that all of us, soldiers and medical staff, were in for a rude shock. We landed in Capetown on December first, 1899. Many troops were on deck to catch the brisk wind. We had forgotten it would be midsummer and most of the boys had never been outside their small Canadian farming towns. Those that coped with the rough seas off the Cape were shouting, pointing out puffs of fine smoke on the surface of the roiling sea. As we plummeted down into the trough of a wave, they would be jumping up to catch their first sight of a whale as we rose on the next upward surge.

The excitement of finally seeing the flat top of Table Mountain with its protective cloth of clouds was marred for many by nausea. They were white as sheets, knuckles gripped tight, clutching the rails and relieving themselves over the side of the ship. Their comrades were not too kind, laughing and telling them to make sure which way the wind was blowing. Poor souls, they were dehydrated because of the heat and their inability, for days, to keep anything down. They hadn't even been in battle yet, but some were already claiming they wanted to die.

We disembarked to a scene like nothing any of us had witnessed before. The dock was a seething hive of what the British Captain who met us called kaffirs. Muscular, but scrawny, scurrying, labouring – so many black people, lifting, pushing, sweating, being shouted at. "Stupid munt!" Then the bowed head. "Yes, baas." Some were even kicked and beaten. A mangy dog was snuffling in foul discarded fish entrails. He also was abused, but not as often as the kaffirs. The stench on the docks was not going to help the soldiers with *mal de mer*, who misguidedly thought they had finally reached salvation. Rancid sweat, vomit, stale urine, feces, oil, rotting fish – the smell of industry, subservience and poverty entwined.

On landing I was informed that I was to be the Superintendent of the Canadian Nurses and told we would be kept safely at Wynberg Hospital near Capetown. We had thought we would be with the troops who were advancing to the front. Not so. Women were to be protected from the horrors of the battlefront. They really thought we were delicate flowers and should leave the difficult work to the men in the field hospitals.

So, initially we stayed in the base hospital that had been built in the 1800's – a rather fortress-like building – waiting for the wounded to be transported to us. There were six nurses for a 600-bed hospital. Amazing that we coped, but we did. I still had the perception that war was, as Mr Kipling had described it, a great adventure. If I'd known then what I know now, I should have been grateful to be away from some of the carnage.

We had less than two weeks to get organised before what was later called "Black Week" occurred. The Boers savaged the Highland regiment in three separate battles. There were nearly 3,000 killed, wounded or captured. The floodgates opened and, as you can imagine, we were swamped. As Canadian nurses we had never had to deal with such terrible injuries. Young men with gaping holes in their abdomens, traumatic amputations with ragged edges – so hard for the surgeons to repair without removing even more of the limb – hair still matted with brain tissue. And the smell of rotting gangrenous flesh – indescribable. Did you know that, if you squeeze a gangrenous limb it may crackle because of the bubbles of gas in the tissues? It's most unnerving. It was overwhelming, trying to nurse so many young men, barely out of childhood, who screamed in pain for their mothers and who, despite all our efforts, often succumbed to infection.

*Miss Pope shook her head slowly and became very quiet for a while, maybe thinking of her brothers who – but for their position in society – might have volunteered for service. Or perhaps she was silenced by the waste of young life. But then, as she had done throughout her life, she*

37

*pulled herself together, took a deep breath, sat up straight and continued with her difficult story.*

After we had dealt with that slaughter, when intakes decreased, we were moved to Rondebosch Number Three General Hospital, where the Canadian medical staff came into their own. We had all manner of unpleasantness at Rondebosch: snakes, scorpions, Cape South Easter sand storms and torrential rains. Did you know that 14,000 men were killed by enteric fever in the Boer war – more than died from wounds? The British had not had to deal with typhoid or cholera epidemics for quite a few years. In Canada we were still getting regular outbreaks and were skilled at nursing these patients, to the amazement of the English medical people. It's all about getting fluids into the patient. So simple, but lifesaving.

By March thousands were getting sick at Bloemfontein and the Army finally moved us closer to the front at Kroonstadt, to cope with the men who were too sick to be moved. Winter was coming on and I should *never* have complained about Rondebosch.

We were now under canvas with hoar frost sparkling icy ferns on both the inside and outside of the tent in the mornings. We were short of water and had poor rations. Being in a tent, with water trickling down one's neck as one bent over the patient, or dripping into open wounds, combined with the humidity when the sun came out, made work quite difficult. No breeze moved the air inside the tents. The stench of purulent wounds, feces and fear, mixed with disinfectant carbolic, accumulated like a heavy suffocating blanket over us all. The soldiers, bless them, were so grateful and cheerful, bearing the loss of limbs with fortitude and with consideration for the presence of "the Sister", which was quite touching.

As things slowed down we were allowed to rest in Pretoria before returning to Canada after the year's deployment ended.

I returned briefly to Natal Stationary Hospital in South Africa in 1902, just before the war ended. To be quite honest, I wish that I hadn't. I might not have heard of the horrendous solution of the "Boer problem" by Lord Kitchener. I felt so frustrated by my impotence to aid the victims in any way. The British were herding the Boer women and children into concentration camps. I heard later that 35,000 died of starvation and disease and that the episode that was Britain's great shame was only ended in 1902 because of a persistent woman, Emily Hobhouse, who hounded the powers that be about the inhumane conditions in these camps.

*Before this interview, I was not aware of these camps, nor of the remarkable woman who challenged a well-established male system. In those days, men were expected to work for power and money, and a woman was expected to work to make a "good match" with one of these men and to live through him, not to challenge him or the system. Neither Miss Hobhouse nor Miss Pope is well known, unlike male participants in the Boer War, perhaps reflecting the extensive minimisation of women's contributions.*

*When Miss Pope returned to Canada, she was the first Canadian to be awarded the Royal Red Cross Medal. Despite being the most experienced military nurse in the country, Canada had no permanent place for her in the military. She remained active in the militia, but was only expected to turn up for duty two or three times a year.*

*In 1904, finally, the Department of Militia created an Army medical corps with a permanent nursing branch. Miss Pope was hired as matron and was one of the first fulltime military nurses. In 1908 she was promoted to Head of Military Nursing Services and stationed in Halifax. She supervised a staff of five and a reserve of twenty-five to eighty. She was responsible for managing nurses and teaching two annual classes of reservists each year. Much of her time over the next few years was spent creating the profession of military nursing in Canada. The Canadian Army valued these women so greatly that they were the first military in the world to grant officer status to a nursing branch. In effect, this meant that Canadian nurses were respected, treated as any officer would be, and expected to adhere to military rules and regulations. Through this, the status of nursing as a profession increased.*

*I asked Miss Pope about some of the changes in Canada, particularly for women, during this time and into the time of the Great War. She looked pensive and then made a wry smile.*

Well, yes, there were changes, but mostly they were changes of convenience to the men. We were still told not to worry our pretty little heads about politics and were not given the vote until late in the war, when they realised that women were able to comprehend complexities besides needlepoint and childcare.

One interesting power that women had at the opening of the 1914 war, which was taken away later, was that no married man was allowed to enlist to fight·in the war without his wife's signed permission. Because of this, women were targeted by propaganda: "When the war is over and someone asks your husband or your son what he did in the Great War, is he to hang his head because you wouldn't let him go?" Wives were shamed at meetings into getting their men to enlist. Women worked in farms, munitions factories, and in fact most jobs that men would have done, but now couldn't because they were away fighting. They were paid a quarter to half the wages men received, and worked extremely long hours. What was worse was that they were not respected by the men with whom they worked. In fact they were resented. Even when they were doing outstanding work, they were belittled and called incompetent.

By the way, speaking of wages, were you aware that something that we all take for granted now was started to help fund the war? We did not have income tax until Sir Robert Borden imposed a "temporary" tax in 1917. Temporary indeed!

*You must have wanted to resume active service when the war broke out in 1914?*

I did indeed. I was war-hardened, experienced, the Head of the Army Nursing Service – and *passed over*. I was fifty-two years old. My best friend, Margaret McDonald, was given the position. It was a bitter pill to swallow. I wrote to beg for field postings and, to my chagrin, Margaret wouldn't put in a word for me. I was told that I'd be more useful training nurses in Halifax. In fact, I must have trained a good proportion of the 3,100 nurses who were sent to Flanders and France.

It may have been a blessing that I stayed at home, as I became unwell and had to take a few months sick leave, although I must say I felt almost as if I'd been put out to pasture. However, in the mysterious ways of the military, in 1917, three years older and just recovered from a serious illness, I was cleared for overseas duty. It didn't make a lot of sense, but I was delighted to finally put my battlefield skills back to use. What I didn't realise was that I'd never been that close to a battlefield. My innocence set me up for one of the greatest shocks of my life. In the twelve years since I had served in Africa, war and the rules of engagement had changed radically.

I sailed for Britain and was stationed near Salisbury for a week or so prior to going to #2 Canadian Stationary Hospital near Outreau. Outreau was about twenty miles from the British lines in the Ypres salient. We arrived there in December, 1917, just six months before the sinking by torpedo off the coast of Ireland of the Hospital ship *Llandovery Castle*. All fourteen nurses on board, many of whom I had trained, succumbed to the sea. But this tragedy was yet to come.

The tragedy from home that greeted us on our arrival in France was the news of the accidental explosion of a munitions ship in Halifax Harbour. The training I had given my nurses who were still running the Military hospital in Nova Scotia was invaluable, as the injuries were most certainly as bad as any in wartime. I could not have known that staying in Halifax at the beginning of the war, despite my frustration, I would furnish such assistance at one of the worst accidents ever to happen in Canada. God does work in amazing ways.

*So you finally got to Flanders?*

I did, but let me tell you something, young man: have you read the poem by the Canadian doctor about Flanders fields and poppies? I see you nodding. McCrae makes it sound quite pretty doesn't he, even though we know it's a graveyard? The poppies swaying in the warm summer breeze, neat white crosses over the burial places of Canada's and England's hopes for the future. But the lark soaring in the sky probably either starved to death or was shot and eaten. There *were* no poppies. There *were* no fields. There was not a thing of beauty in the entire landscape. Just ruins of houses, churches, countryside, and dreams. And everywhere, everywhere … mud, filth and terror.

A description written by Colonel Adami MD from our Medical Corps says it better than anything I could tell you. Wait, let me find it …. Here it is.

*"Never was it fair to look upon, this land of dykes and ditches, of mud and water, of miserable farms and miserable people, of flat acres bordered by straight trees, of dreary villages and squalid towns. Today it is as if the curse of God had fallen there. To desolation is added the stench of death. If this held true in 1915 when I first saw it, in 1917 the Ypres salient is more appalling, more hideously naked than ever. Under the incessant shelling of all these months no scrap of cover is left; everything is churned up until the roads are indistinguishable from the surrounding fields. Autumn days, perfect in themselves, yet of treacherous if presaging clearness, have alternated with spells of chill and heavy driving rain. The sodden ground has not been given time to dry, nor the floods to drain from the low-lying ground. There is mud unutterable everywhere – mud in which a man may sink, not merely to his knees, but to his shoulders; mud in which the badly wounded sink helplessly and add to the roll of "Missing"; mud that makes movement so slow and difficult as – with six men to each stretcher carrying one wounded man – to demand six hours for the one journey from the front to the nearest collecting post and back, and shell holes filled with water so abundant as to preclude movement in the dark."*

The Battle of Passchendaele had just finished with 320,000 murdered British boys, and 260,000 Germans. The soldiers were not the murderers you understand, but the politicians and generals – like Haig – who were seldom at risk themselves. Half a million young men in one battle, plus the wounded. *In one battle*, do you understand?

*Miss Pope was talking with great determination in a firm voice, but her body was shaking. No – more like shivering. Her face was almost mask-like, as if she had denied herself the luxury of showing emotions. I wondered if that was a trait that came with nurse's training or whether, if she let go she would not be able to control herself.*

*I offered to give her a rest, but with one eyebrow raised, she straightened her back as she must have done many times when confronted with horrific eviscerations or amputations. And we "got on with it".*

The bombardment was so intense that the stretcher-bearers in fact *had* to work in the dark. No white flags or red crosses would stop the enemy shooting in daytime. These brave young men would go stumbling across no man's land, not able to see the wounded they were supposed to pick up. They could not use any form of light.

Everyone knows about the trenches and the mud, but what many people forget is that there, under the slimy water, were bodies rotting, limbs suppurating and garbage with huge glossy rats grazing on discarded food and human bodies. Often the six stretcher-bearers came back minus one or two of the party. Can you imagine the horror of losing footing at the edge of one of these cesspits, knowing that you were going to drown in a soup of decomposing companions? Once in, there was no way to climb up the viscous, slithering side of this cloaca of death.

The stretcher-bearers were the first in line in the conveyor belt that passed the human destruction to our aid at the hospital. They had they most dangerous job of all. This was not a coincidence. Many of the English bearers were despised conscientious objectors who had refused to fight. I suppose those poor lads felt it was preferable to being ridiculed, taunted, labelled as a coward and, in the UK, being imprisoned and often losing your right to vote for five years.

We were in a bricks and mortar hospital, which you would think might have been an advantage. In fact it made us a fixed target. The Red Cross label made not one whit of difference. Throughout the day, even when there had been no special activity in the trenches in the matter of shelling, the German shells roared over the hospital with the sound of a passing train. The men spoke of them as the "Wyper's Express". Unfortunately on several occasions we received direct hits and not only had to cope with the battlefield injured, but those injured on site.

Nothing ... nothing in my experience of the Boer War prepared me for the sights of Flanders, for being bombarded and for the new and "improved" weapons. The Germans, used a terrible green gas – a mixture probably of chlorine and bromine. The survivors were haggard and in agony. They would stagger in, weak and semi-stuporous, with bloodshot eyes and hacking coughs. Some had attacks of vomiting; all had an intense shortness of breath; rapid heart-beat, and the severer cases a ghastly ashy colour of the skin. The acrid odour given off from their clothes was so powerful that it affected the officers and orderlies who attempted to alleviate their distress, bringing smarting tears to the eyes. The gunshot wounds were not comparable to those I'd dealt with in Africa. The bullets were now larger and ripped their way through all tissues, shattering bone on the way. At times I felt helpless. Legs, feet, hands missing; bleeding stumps controlled by rough field tourniquets; large portions of the abdominal walls shot away; faces horribly mutilated; bones shattered to pieces; holes that you could put your clenched fist into, filled with dirt, mud, bits of equipment and clothing, until it all became a hideous nightmare – as if we were living in the seventh level of the inferno.

The horrendous Passchendaele offensive ended after the troops had fought each other to a standstill. There was a pause in the hostilities, as both sides needed to regroup during the winter. Even so, the number of injured we were managing was at least 50,000 per month. We had a death every second night and by the early spring, when the battles started up again, we feared being overrun by the Germans. Their camp was fifteen miles from the hospital.

We were working day and night. One is in a stupor and working like an automatic machine. There were times when I could not remember walking back to my quarters, was too tired to eat and, strangely, too tired to sleep. The hallucinations kept one awake. I was not alone in this experience.

The night duty seemed to be the worst. The ward would be dark, apart from a small light on Sister's table at the end of the ward. A little pool of safety. We would walk around the beds that, even in this chaos, were arranged with military precision, with mitred sheet corners and all the openings on the pillowcases turned away from the door.

This order did not extend to the patients themselves. Often one would hear a gurgling or shallow irregular breathing and find a soldier drowning in his own blood. He had a chest wound that, despite the surgeon's skill the day before, "decided" that three in the morning was a good time to hemorrhage. The flickering shadows, so dark between the beds made one feel superstitious that a dark entity was waiting. Waiting patiently to claim the young life for himself. Often we lost, and Charon received another passenger for his boat. We did our best, but trying to find a bag of the correct blood and getting the extra intravenous up and running in the gloom of a flashlight was difficult, as you can imagine. Discovering a "good" vein that hadn't been damaged previously, putting hot cloth on it to try and raise it, just a little. This, in an exsanguinating patient with no blood pressure, can be hard even in daylight. To do this with delirious patients on the ward shouting, trying to get out of bed and pulling their hard-fought-for intravenous lines out, was extremely stressful and may have contributed to my subsequent illness.

Late at night, alone on the ward with sixty critically ill patients, German planes flying overhead, no sleep or food for two days, I would occasionally get a panicky feeling and a tightness in my chest. I was getting frequent headaches with dizziness during the day and, with the ongoing stress, would find myself crying for the patients while I was doing their dressings. It was difficult to see an eighteen-year-old with a bad compound fracture of the tibia, whose toes were already going black, a sharp demarcation line half way up his calf below which I knew he had gangrene, his wound oozing green, foul-smelling pus. Do you tell him, when he asks if he'll be alright, "We will have to take the leg off because it's badly infected and you have no circulation going to your foot"? Well, do you?

I think one of my last stressors, the straw that broke the camel's back, was this. Early in the morning a little Ford car was returning from a dressing station with two slightly wounded officers, when outside Ypres a shell fell immediately behind it. The car was riddled by fragments, and the driver badly wounded in the head. Another driver was later sent to retrieve the car and, finding that it could still be run, he brought the battered car to a standstill in the hospital courtyard. The force of the explosion had exerted itself just over the top of the car. There sat the two officers, rigid, each in a perfectly natural position, but headless, or – what was yet more awful – the one completely headless, the other with his face blown off, the back of the head flapping to and fro with each jolt of the car.

By April, 1918, I had been diagnosed with hardening of the arteries. At times I would start to shake uncontrollably when I heard a plane or a sudden loud noise; plus I still had the panicky feelings with all the other symptoms that just wouldn't go away. I could only sleep three hours a night, and in August I collapsed. I was invalided home with arteriosclerosis and neurasthenia. I was fifty-six years old. I was given a military pension so that I could retire and return here to my family home in Prince Edward Island. I never nursed again.

*Georgina Pope, having escaped from society's constraints with her strong spirit, had survived two wars. She had so many "firsts" in an era when most women stayed at home, made a good marriage and had babies. She trained as a nurse when nursing was not a respectable profession, made her brother pressure the army to let her go to the Boer War as a military nurse and then, after gaining first-hand experience in South Africa, was the first matron of the new Canadian Army Medical Corps nursing school in Halifax, setting training standards for generations of young women who came after her. She was the pioneer of Canadian Military nursing.*

*Post scriptum: Miss Pope died about a month after this interview and lay in state in Government House prior to a full military funeral. She was seventy-six. Before her coffin was finally closed, a veteran of the Halifax Garrison asked if he could leave a keepsake with her. Permission granted, he placed one of his own medals beside her. "She was the Island's Florence Nightingale," he said.*

# A Painted War

## *Al Straitton*

Raising one's head above the parapet is never a good idea. Hun snipers are accurate from ranges of two to three hundred yards and a moment of careless curiosity has cost many a life. With this in mind, I was happy to look through the lens of a simple trench periscope affording me safety, if somewhat limited sightlines. Fifty yards directly ahead, a belt of barbed wire had captured an attacking German soldier leaving his lifeless body upright, arms and legs askew as if frozen in a macabre last dance. The landscape beyond was pock marked with water-filled shell holes; the remaining trees had been shattered, leaving branchless black poles of varying heights; and the uneven shapes of fallen soldiers from both sides littered the ground. Death and destruction dominated the front lines just as they had when I was last in Ypres a little over a year ago.

I had spent a full day observing in the trenches near Passchendaele, a sketchbook in hand instead of a rifle. I was no longer Private A.Y. Jackson of the Canadian 60th Infantry Battalion. Wounds to the hip and shoulder suffered on June 11th, 1916, had sent me to England to convalesce. While there, I was interviewed by Lord Beaverbrook and shortly afterwards given the honorary commission of Lieutenant as the first Canadian artist recruited for the War Memorials Fund. Although some of my prewar works were still on display in the Art Gallery of Toronto, I hadn't painted anything since enlisting and my art experience serving in the 60th had consisted of drawing a few diagrams and enlargements from maps. Now I was tasked with painting a war full of horrific images that were completely alien to the Canadian landscapes that had inspired me in peacetime.

Returning to my billet, a derelict old monastery some distance from the front lines, I counted my blessings. Years of neglect had caused much of the roof to collapse, leaving a few areas open to the sky and the rest loosely covered with thatch. This afforded some protection from the elements and was a far better option than sleeping in a rat-infested, muddy trench. In fact, there were many nooks and crannies where beds made of wood, wire and canvas allowed for cozy little sleeping compartments. A spacious communal room with tables, chairs and a heavy-duty cook stove served as a kitchen and general gathering place. I was seated at one of the larger tables with the day's rough sketches spread before me, making notes on tone and color, when a fellow commissioned war artist from Scotland, David Young Cameron, arrived. He had been observing on the lines at Merckem.

"Hullo, Alex. I hope your day was nothing like mine."

"Well," I said, "I can't believe it would be any better. There's not much difference from one part of the line to the next."

He placed his rucksack on the table, sighed deeply and said, "So many terrible sights ... mutilated bodies ... bits of horses lying around ... fields torn up and twisted beyond belief. It was absolutely mind-boggling."

"No matter how many times I've been up here, I still find it shocking. And the front was calm today. Wait 'til all hell breaks loose!"

He pulled a backless chair from the far corner to the table, sat down heavily and taking a crumpled packet from his breast pocket, offered me a cigarette.

"Something's terribly wrong when civilized nations come together ... and the result is such a nightmare."

We lit up, inhaling deeply, enjoying the warmth of the smoke entering our lungs.

"I lived with this madness in the trenches for two years. My fondest wish is to have politicians from both sides spend time at the front. Most have no idea what it's like. And here we are, after everything we've seen, trying to paint it in some sort of presentable way."

"Aye, it's certainly a far cry from the lovely braes I was painting at Ben Lomond last summer. But I suppose for the record it's our duty to show the bravery of the lads fighting for King and country."

I began gathering my sketches into a pile and said, "Quite honestly, I don't consider all the heroics, death and glory stuff to be an option anymore. In a war like this there's no 'Thin Red Line', or 'Scotland For Ever' crap. We need to portray the hellishness of it so people will understand what's happening in this godforsaken place."

After peering intently at the sketch on top, he looked up and said, "These mangled bodies lying across the battlefield appear to do that rather effectively."

"I don't think so," I replied. "Photographs show war's brutal reality better than any painting. I think we have to create images that are more than just visual impressions. There's no place for art that ..."

The roar of a low flying airplane interrupted our conversation. We pushed back our chairs trying to look up through the opening at the far end of the room, when a frantic shout of "Take cover!" had us diving headlong underneath the thick oak table. Within seconds, an ear-piercing explosion violently shook the building, causing large patches of thatch to tumble down around us. Three more distant explosions followed and although windows rattled from the concussions, little damage was done. We later learned that German bombers had been targeting a nearby railway station and one of the pilots had prematurely dropped a bomb, which landed just outside the monastery gates.

Rising from the other side of the table, dusting off his trousers, David was wide-eyed. His normally ruddy complexion had paled considerably. "That was just a wee bit too close for comfort."

I picked up my sketches shaking strands of thatch from them and said, "I've thanked Lady Luck many times for near misses when I was at the front. Always happy to be spared, and hoping to be in the right place next time."

"So, it's all up to Dame Fortune, is it?"

"In the trenches, men pray for luck, hoping their number doesn't come up. Fortunately, our odds are much better. Compared to them, we've got it easy."

"And, thoroughly grateful, I am. I've seen too many familiar names on the lists of killed or missing in the Glasgow papers. But no matter, we still have a job to do and it'll be an early rise in the morning … so, I'm away to get cleaned up before dinner, and then I'd like your opinion on the sketches I've done today."

"And I yours. Let's hope tomorrow is another quiet one. We don't want to be wandering around with sketchpads when trench mortars are being lobbed in our direction."

We dined that night on decent rations of pea soup, stale bread with cheese, and a bit of chocolate, all washed down with some lovely hot tea. Not exactly the Ritz, but better than the bully beef and hard biscuits which had been a staple in the trenches. Afterwards we enjoyed a generous tot of rum while reviewing our day's work. David, mentioning Aristotle's idea that the purpose of art is to purge the emotions through pity and terror, sparked a lively debate between us about how this might apply to our jobs as war artists. Eventually the combined effects of rum, heat from the stove and a long day caused us to become drowsy, and we headed off to the separate alcoves housing our beds.

Sleep did not come easy. My restless mind kept going over the sketches David and I had completed. Both of us had either focused on realistic portrayals of grisly battlefield scenes, or had looked away from the gore, desperately trying to find some picturesque landscapes that we'd observed on our way to no man's land. None of it was inherently satisfying. I lay awake for hours, struggling to discover a direction that would illustrate this tragic war in an acceptable way.

I woke in the morning to the full-throated rumblings of several motor vehicles accompanied by the shouts of men trying to be heard above the noise. A group of English camouflage artists who had been billeted in an outbuilding of the monastery were assembling in the courtyard to load their gear onto cattle trucks. They were on their way to an artillery unit to mark out and paint all of the big guns in readiness for a proposed new push against the enemy. They were "artists" as well, but their mission was quite simple – to apply colour or materials to military equipment in order to hide it, or make it look

50

like something else. Back at their Special Works Headquarters, they painted huge spreads of canvas to cover gun emplacements from aerial observation, or mock scenery as a façade to hide big guns. They also painted sniper suits, and observation towers that were to look like the partially demolished tree trunks left standing in no man's land. The quality of their work would be proved by how well they deceived the opposing forces. While most of their work was done far from danger, occasionally they would be brought up to either supervise an installation, or actually paint on the spot, as was the case today.

Obviously their work was of great value and, with its life-saving possibilities, earned a good deal of admiration from men at the front. On the other hand, what I did was seen as unnecessary, and I didn't receive any sort of a welcome until the men discovered that I'd been wounded serving in the infantry. Then they couldn't do enough for me and were eager to see the results of my work, but all I could show them were rough sketches. The paintings themselves would be done later at our studio in London. I'm certain the lads were disappointed in what they saw, because I had no interest in depicting the exploits of heroic warriors on the battlefield. Yes, we had been commissioned to paint pictures for a Canadian public eager to see positive results of the war effort, but I believed people back home needed to realize that all romantic notions of war had been shattered by "the war to end all wars".

With a quick "Haste ye back!" as a farewell, David joined the camouflage crew transport which was heading to a section near Langemark where he was to report for the day. I had asked and been granted permission to spend the day in a shell of a town known to the British Tommy as "Wipers". This once magnificent old town was now mostly reduced to rubble with only a handful of buildings still standing. Captured briefly by the German army at the beginning of the war, Ypres had been retaken and staunchly defended by the allies against several subsequent attacks. Since it was still within range of the Boche artillery, the town appeared empty during daylight hours, but came alive at night with thousands of troops tasked with relieving front line soldiers, or bringing forward supplies and ammunition. I felt a mysterious attraction to this lifeless daytime landscape with its ruined

51

buildings, and wanted to spend time exploring the peaceful streets.

The November morning was raw with a biting east wind and the wintry sky had ominous dark clouds scudding across it. Streaks of blue showed through, but the overall look was foreboding rather than promising. When my adjutant and I set out along La Rue Carton, there was no specific goal in mind. Indeed, he questioned why we weren't going to see the action up front. But I was in search of inspiration and had a gut feeling that this was the place to find it. The deserted streets ahead were dominated by the ruins of the Cloth Hall and St. Martin's Cathedral. Once described as medieval gems, these buildings had been reduced to hollow shells with battered bell tower and spires still standing defiantly above the town. There was a beauty in these massive ruined structures that easily caught the eye and several artists, myself included, had sketched them with plans of painting some sort of grand canvas exhibiting the grace that still existed in spite of the destruction. But was this enough?

We had long since passed the market square, and were walking north along a silent unknown street, when I heard the clip clopping of horses' hooves behind me. I turned to see a row of war-blasted ordinary homes. In the middle of these stood the skeleton of a peak-roofed house providing a frame through which you could see the ruins of the rest of the town. Moving from right to left, four mounted officers, dwarfed by the devastation around them, rode past the opening. I immediately called for my tools. No pencil sketch here! I wanted to sketch with oils on wood, eager to capture my vision using the colors of the scene in front of me.

I perched on a canvas stool, opened my paint-box, inserted a new birch panel and squeezed the different paints onto the palette following my usual pattern of cerulean blue in the lower left corner and ending with viridian green at the top right. I began mixing paint as I examined what I saw before me. Somber browns of the mangled wooden structures contrasted with a lighter sky, which showed fragments of blue through ragged white and grey clouds. What once had been flat ground in front of the houses was now a series of undulating mounds and hollows. Artillery shells had churned the earth in such a way that it was a chaotic mix of colors ranging from vivid ochre to dull khaki brown. But most striking was the vibrant green interior wall of a house to the left. A Flemish family had painted the walls of their home in an uplifting shade of green associated with hope and peace. Enjoying the rhythms of everyday life and celebrating important family moments, they would have had no idea of the cataclysmic forces destined to overtake them. Now all that was left were these exposed walls and questions about the fate of the people who had lived within them. With these thoughts, I confidently set brush to board, the strokes becoming ever more forceful as the painting leapt to life.

Finally I had found a way to convey the truth of this so-called "Great War" to the people back home. It wasn't enough to simply show dead bodies on the battlefield. The war had wreaked havoc on this town and its inhabitants. The blighted landscape, the ruined homes, the absence of the family who had painted those cheerful green walls, all contributed to an overwhelming sense of loss. I wanted my paintings to reveal how this part of the world, with its rich history and culture, once full of passionate living beings, had been turned into a wasteland. Here was my mission ... and unfortunately, beginning with these houses in Ypres, I knew, there would be no shortage of subject matter.

*Author's Notes:*

The painting produced that day is titled "Houses of Ypres". It, along with subsequent paintings A.Y. Jackson produced as a war artist, ably depicted a war without glory where the devastation wrought by this modern war had such a tragic effect on the humans caught up in it, as well as on the territory over which it was fought. Returning to Canada after the war Jackson and another official war artist, Frederick Varley, were founding members of The Group of Seven. Their experiences as war artists had a huge impact on them and their subsequent paintings of the rugged Canadian landscape owed much to a style they had begun to develop while serving overseas.

Jackson's autobiography, *A Painter's Country* gave me the expressions "Thin Red Line" and "Scotland For Ever", used in Jackson's dialogue with fellow artist D.Y. Cameron.

The following quotes illustrate how important the war experience was in the development of Canada's most famous 20th century art movement.

Historian Maria Tippett in her book, *Art at the Service of War: Canada, Art and the Great War,* states: "Nothing came to symbolize the war for the artist and the combatants as much as the land upon which it was fought ... Pock marked with gaping water-filled craters, strewn with bones, metal and the refuse of modern warfare, the topography of the front line offered few familiar associations ... the machine had superseded God's handiwork; his landscape was being reshaped by man's instruments."

Jackson himself knew he needed to change his style and was quoted as follows: "the impressionist technique I had adopted in painting was now ineffective, visual impressions were not enough."

And Tippett writes, "After the war, Jackson and his fellow artists deliberately sought to paint 'swampy, rocky, wolf-ridden, burnt and scuttled country with rivers and lakes scattered through it.' The Group of Seven's concern to demonstrate ... the spirit of painting in Canada, was thus associated with a sense that this could be best done by employing methods and techniques they and their colleagues had either seen used, or themselves employed to paint the war-torn landscape of the Old World."

Colleen Sharpe wrote in *Art at the Service of War: The Emergent Group of Seven*, "Artists and Soldiers": "The low-keyed colours of no man's land and the trenches – muddy brown, yellow ochre, and cool grey – came to permeate the post-war canvases of Varley, Jackson and others who had lived and painted at the front."

# The Deconstruction of
# Edouard Quirion

*Lise Lévesque*

*November 1968*

Yvette Petit, my mother, stood by the electric stove in her Montreal abode. Armed with a spatula, she seemed eager to show me how to cook a meal that three generations of women had prepared before I would. After warming up a Teflon skillet to *sauter* chunks of salted lard until they sizzled, she stirred in diced boiled potatoes and filets of fresh cod before turning down the heat for the concoction to simmer. Then, she poured small rations of rum into small tumblers so that she and I could toast the Veterans of World War One on the fiftieth anniversary of the Armistice.

Since mother and I were not in the habit of consuming alcohol when I paid her a visit, the ritual puzzled me until the liquor took effect and she voiced the question that had been in her mind for a long time.

"Lise," she let out tentatively, "how much do you know about your grandfather?"

Unaware that a family secret was about to be revealed, I began to scan through my childhood memories before I realized that the question was rhetorical. My mother had already launched into a discourse that, while we savoured the traditional family dish, offered a rum-fueled account of Edouard Quirion's life.

The previous summer, stirred by her curiosity about her ancestry and an undying affection for the sea, she had driven herself to the Gaspé Peninsula. After, a stop in Rimouski to consult the military archives, she had pushed on to Percé where, between long walks on the shores, she had visited the old parish, the cemetery and the municipal archives. Very few traces of the Quirions could be found. Yet, proudly displayed on the heritage site of the Rocher, she had found a plaque with the following inscription:

"To commemorate the valour of officers and men of Percé who fought in the Great War with his Majesty's forces for honour and freedom."

After the names of men lost in combat had been cited, another inscription said: "And in honour also of those who served between 1917-18."

More than thirty combatants were listed on the plaque and among them appeared the name of her father, Edouard Quirion. What follows are the depictions, stored in my memory, of my mother's discourse about the man's life and his contribution to World War One.

*August 1917*

Henriette Quirion stood by the wood stove in the cottage that her husband had built in Percé. Distracted by the scene beyond the kitchen window, she kept an unfocussed eye on a cast iron frying pan. Despite the height of the midday sun, gloom overshadowed the seascape. A warship was progressing toward the harbour with the bearing of a hungry whale, eager to consume the latest serving of local boys and regurgitate them onto English shores. Among them, her son Edouard.

The scene conjured up a military convoy that, three years earlier, had stopped in the Percé Basin in order to avail itself of regional volunteers before crossing the Atlantic. Composed of large vessels with escorting ships, it carried the troops that the Canadian army had hastily formed in Valcartier. The fleet aimed to transport these men to a training camp in England and, later on, to France where World War One already raged on several fronts.

Gaspé, by then, had become an important commercial fishing center. Accustomed as the locals were to the sight of foreign ships moored on their shores, an armada idling in the foreground of the Forillon Peninsula felt to them like an invasion.

When Henriette heard the sizzling sound of salted lard, her attention returned to the stove. She stirred in diced boiled potatoes and filets of fresh cod before moving the pan to the back of the stove and allowing the mixture to simmer. The aroma of this tasty dish usually called her family to the table. That day, however, everyone appeared eager to avoid one another. As soon as Charles, her husband, had noticed her stuffing the stove, he had invoked pressing chores beckoning him to the barn. She knew he would not be back. And *who could blame him?* She thought. *What kind of man would have an appetite on the day that his son is boarding a war-bound ship?*

And precious cargo he was, this son of theirs. With six feet of might hung on a flexible spine, he had become indispensable at handling fishnets through the cod-trawling season. *From now on,* she pondered, *we will be on our own, the husband and I …. Only the two of us to spread hay beds in the stalls, harness the horses and deliver the daily catch to the market.*

Filled with anxiety but refusing to dwell on crueller outcomes, Henriette relinquished the family meal to a serving dish on the sideboard and made herself a cup of tea. There seemed to be no point in trying to rally her men. She knew how they handled dark moments and she yielded to their need for privacy. *If only Lucie was home,* she pondered. *Women are better at reassuring each other.* But, her cherished daughter had relocated to Sorel after marrying Télesphore Petit, a brakeman from the railway company. Henriette's mournful eyes glanced in the direction of the mail box, her closest link to the absentee, and she took a deep breath.

"Lord, grant us courage!" She exclaimed out loud, as she picked up her rosary beads and surrendered her tired body to the rocking chair.

* * *

In the village, Flore Roy, Edouard's sweetheart, equally mystified by the activity in the Basin, struggled with his imminent departure. On the weekend, a Mass had been held at Saint Michael's church. The attendants had prayed for the soldiers already on the frontlines, and for the ones about to join them. Afterwards, she and Henriette had had a quiet talk while father and son stood by the church steps, smoking industriously to avoid serious topics.

The previous night, the parish had yielded the hall to the youth so they could have a dance and an opportunity to say their goodbyes. Despite the musicians' efforts to remain upbeat, the dancers could only move to the rhythm of their hearts. When the pace got too slow, the priest sent everybody home, recommending that they avoid hapless detours. But, from the exhausted expressions of his young parishioners, the next morning, he sensed that few of them had heeded his advice.

Edouard's girlfriend, for one, vacillated between sadness and anger. She felt abandoned. *How could so many strong and healthy young men surrender to the call of the army?* she wondered. Yet, her feminine intuition suggested that peer pressure was the culprit of her own fellow's decision – that, and his desire for adventure.

People knew that, so far, the war had not been kind to the Canadian Divisions. In fact, the army had confirmed leaving more than half of their men in Flanders fields. As a French-Canadian, Edouard's allegiance fell to Quebec rather than Britain, but patriotism held little room in his psyche. He belonged to the sea, any sea, but the one close to home fed his loved ones. So, it was with mixed emotions that he was leaving its shores to join the army.

Of late, though, there had been much talk about conscription in political circles. The Military Service Act seemed to be in the cards. *It is only a matter of time before enlisting becomes compulsory,* he had told himself to justify his decision. Yet, he was aware that the *S.S. Cassandra* had not returned the men it had borrowed from the Gaspé fisheries two years before, and that nothing guaranteed his own safe return.

Hence, the morning of his departure, to hide this ambivalence from Flore and his family, he kept to his room and killed time by trying on odd pieces of military garb and repacking his satchel.

\* \* \*

Regardless of personal concerns, with the exodus of the warship from Gaspé, the history of World War One continued to write itself like a giant spider expanding its web over the fate of North Americans and Europeans. Once on board, Edouard's vivacious individuality quickly faded within the throngs of uniforms. His sun-fed complexion became pallid and, while training in the wet and muddy conditions of Plymouth, his affable disposition soured. Since he had already acquired muscle strength from the hauling of fishing nets, he was assigned to artillery duty. The sought-after adventure had been demystified. From thereon, he would be feeding cannons and machine guns rather than his people. So, armed with newly acquired skills, he and his peers boarded a transport ship to France where they got initiated to trench duty and nature's own war on the combatants in the form of winter.

The overall choreography of World War One consisted of a series of battles that either kept the Germans from advancing further into France or forced them out of occupied territory. One of these engagements was unfolding in Arras where the British, after launching a large offensive, had parcelled out part of their campaign to the Canadian Corps. Their directives were to regain the control of an escarpment at the northern most end of the city. For that purpose, the new recruits were sent as reinforcements to the Second Division which, in coordination with the other three, began a systematic reacquisition of the Vimy Ridge. As expected, a large plan was already in place when the fresh troops joined the Second Division's members in the war zone. Only slight variations were introduced as the days produced gains or losses of manpower, equipment and terrain.

The Battle of Vimy Ridge was fought in less than a week. It was the first time that all four Canadian Divisions were participating in a battle together. What seems notable is that they had received three times the artillery usually allotted to such operations, with orders to set up heavy guns twenty yards apart and a field gun every ten feet. To orchestrate the maximum effectiveness of this weaponry, an enormous communication system had been established by laying more than a thousand kilometres of telegraph and phone cabling. Since the region favoured tunneling because of the chalk contained in its soil, an impressive underground network had been created. It enclosed more than a kilometer of ten meter deep subways which allowed more troops to move hastily and surreptitiously to the front. It also housed light train tracks, casualty clearing stations, command and communication posts, water tanks and ammunition stores.

On the battleground, four to six people were required in order to man an Artillery's machine gun. Each one had the fire-power of one hundred guns. But these raging dragons did not only deliver death, they evoked responses from the enemy lines. Soon, the area surrounding Edouard's position became carpeted with inert bodies. Regardless, the large weapon operators were instructed to continue pounding the enemy until their own unit ran out of ammunition. At that point, tanks and infantrymen were ordered to leapfrog over the artillery in order to recover a larger portion of the escarpment.

Since leaders were not immune to becoming casualties, the army had trained foot soldiers and artillerymen to take over posts above their status. On one occasion, when a tank was advancing towards the ridge, Edouard witnessed an officer being hit. Without a moment of hesitation, he surrendered his own post to a fellow gunman and took control of the tank's cannon and machine guns. This monster sported a revolving turret and travelled at the speed of four miles per hour. As it moved on the rugged terrain, it could not always avoid the bodies strewn in its path. Although Edouard tried to avert his eyes from the spilled brains and guts on the field, he could not shield himself from the stench of blood, the fumes of recently exploded chemicals and the relentless noise. Finally, shaken to the core, his body came to a standstill, shell-shocked.

In Canada, Edouard's sweetheart had been in touch with Henriette who relayed the news to Lucie. Flore was with child, a fact at once exhilarating and deplorable. He, of course, was unaware of the situation and both families resolved to keep the matter private until his return. Under the guise of furthering her education, the young woman was sent to Lucie's home in Sorel until the baby was born. At that point, no-one knew that the child's father had been taken to an underground medical station where he had been assessed, taken on foot to a French hospital and given electro shock treatments.

* * *

In Arras, once three of the Canadian Divisions had reported reaching their objectives, the soldiers were allowed to pause, regroup and establish their positions. That done, the order came to fire every piece of weaponry on the terrain simultaneously, and to detonate all the mines that had been strategically laid under German trenches. Afterwards, the Second Division reported capturing Les Tilleuls and later, the town of Thélus. Thus, in very few days, the Canadian Corps had regained control of the Vimy Ridge, but at the cost of more than ten thousand casualties. One third of its men had been killed and two-thirds of those who survived were wounded.

At the onset of the war, shell-shocked victims had been greatly mismanaged. The British had even executed hundreds of their own soldiers for failing to obey orders. No consideration had been given to the side effects of chemicals on the brain of combatants who stood in the proximity of exploded ammunitions. These men were simply deemed to be defiant or non-compliant cowards. In Edouard's days on the battlefields, however, the medics had become cognizant of these symptoms. Since his initial state of inertia had occurred as the result of an enemy attack, he was diagnosed as wounded and sported the letter W on his uniform when he arrived at the hospital. His life had been spared; however, the shock treatments that he received only served to induce a more significant amnesic condition.

Although the Treaty of Versailles was not signed until the next year, the fighting of World War One ceased in November of 1918. Afterward, the logistics of repatriating more than two hundred and sixty-eight thousand men with close to fifty-four thousand dependants became an enormous task. People had to wait long and boring periods of time before the transportation problems were remedied and they could go home. Families had been able to correspond with their loved ones during the war. When a man had suffered a mental trauma, though, the news from Europe became sparse. Military headquarters and hospital staff relayed only short and vague messages. By the time Edouard arrived in Gaspé, his parents had realised that all would not be well with their son, but they were not prepared for his degree of unresponsiveness.

After a short stay in the family home, he was briefed about his having fathered a baby girl and taken to visit the mother of his child. Yvette, who was approaching her first birthday, had remained in Sorel in the care of Lucie. Neither the nearness of his once-treasured lady friend, nor the photo of the bright-eyed child, managed to stir sentiments in the man that would motivate him to stay put. Edouard had become a body in a perpetual state of alertness with hardly a word to convey. The only thing that betrayed his feelings was an occasional flicker of fear in his otherwise cloudy, dark eyes. The slightest noise could provoke him to run or hide, and often signalled his departure from places deemed safe by anyone else.

*May 1919*

Lucie Petit stood by the gas stove in her Sorel home to warm up an aluminum frying pan. She had just picked up her brother Edouard at the train station. Still in shock from his appearance and demeanor, she had chosen to delay introducing him to his daughter. Not only did he look gaunt and ashen, but he seemed distant and jittery. To make him feel at home, she was preparing his favorite dish of cod filets and home-fried potatoes sautéed in salted lard. As well, to anchor him in the kitchen, while Yvette remained upstairs in the care of her husband, she had poured him a shot of rum and set the bottle on the table within his reach. The alcohol did stir the man's interest, but he remained mum to her inquiry about his stay in Gaspé and seemed oblivious to the existence of his daughter. In fact, his discourse, when he did speak, sounded incongruous with the situation at hand. *Too much pressure,* she fathomed, referring to his need to make decisions about supporting himself and his new found family. The rum aiding, Edouard ate his meal and allowed his sister to set him up on the parlor's sofa bed. Later, Lucie and Télesphore had a long talk about the man's condition and decided to offer him a shelter in Sorel for as long as rest would be in order. Unbeknownst to them, at the first unfamiliar sound that their hyper-vigilant guest had heard, he had grabbed his belongings and slipped quietly into the night, hugging the half-empty bottle of rum as if it was a teddy bear.

Despite a meticulous search for the war veteran in the city of Sorel, no one knew what had happened to him. Months passed before the Montreal police contacted the family. Edouard had been arrested for vagrancy and sent to a psychiatric hospital. The Canadian specialists referred to his condition as Battle Fatigue. From then on, Lucie, as his next of kin, saw to it that whatever could be attempted to ensure his recovery would be put into motion. Regardless, his mental health continued to deteriorate. When he began to struggle with frequent bouts of hallucination, it became obvious to everyone that this war veteran needed to remain institutionalised.

In order to earn a living as a teacher, Yvette's mother needed assistance with the child's care. Her own parents were too old for the task. Being childless, Lucie and her husband offered to adopt their niece. Yet, Flore could not bring herself to let go of her daughter entirely. Henriette suggested a compromise. So, it came to pass that Yvette legally took the name of Petit – Lucie's married name – with the proviso that she would live in Sorel during the school year and spend her summers close to her birth mother at the Rocher de Percé.

In his youth, Edouard had been a loving son, brother and suitor. At this phase of his life and despite his confused state of mind, everyone gladly took turns visiting him. From time to time, Yvette was taken to see her father at the St. Jean de Dieu Hospital and she continued to call on him after her own marriage and my birth. We referred to him as Uncle Edouard. When Lucie Petit – my grandmother by adoption – and Flore Roy died, my mother took over the full custody of his care. I was twelve, then and was deemed old enough to visit a mental institution. The man I met appeared to have no connection with the eager-looking soldier standing proudly for a picture that my mother had framed and set on the upright piano. In the fifties, the post-war Edouard Quirion, looked gaunt and grey before his time and sat in a perpetual slump, whether he was in a chair or on the edge of his hospital bed.

Through most of our visits, he remained mute, staring at his feet and seemingly unaware of the conversations taking place around him. When he did speak, his discourse sounded at odds with the questions that we had asked him. One day, however, he told me a long story about a little statue of the Virgin Mary. He was all smiles and kept pointing at it, as if it stood on a table behind my chair. I had no idea how to behave and, somewhat scared to curb his enthusiasm, acknowledged the object that only existed in his imagination. He had bought it in Europe, he said, and would be glad to see me take it home. No one knew if he understood that Yvette, my mother, was his daughter and I, by osmosis, his granddaughter. On an emotional level, though, he appeared to know that we were all connected. The man had little to give, yet he was offering me something that had been precious to him in one of the few happy moments of his life. With tears welling in my eyes, I accepted the gift and, to this day, it stands proudly in my mind's eye.

Though the Second Division of the Canadian Military, where my grandfather had served, received a degree of recognition for participating in the Battle of Vimy Ridge, no other distinction was ever attributed to the soldier himself. Only the mention of his name on a plaque in his hometown – the name of a man who had entered into a nightmare while fighting for his country – a nightmare from which he could not escape until he died.

# The Original Peruvian Doughnuts

*Todd McKinstry*

It's so strange now as you take the train along the north shore of Lake Ontario into Toronto. You see the brand new Union Station ahead of you, but at the last moment the train veers away and pulls into the old train station instead. I must have a strange look on my face for the woman across from me explains that the new station is fully built, except for the train tracks. She says the politicians have been arguing about it for months. I nod to her and I can see's looking at my uniform in particular.

"You must be happy to be home," she says with an easy smile.

I have no smile for her. "I'm happy to be gone from there."

Toronto has grown since I was here last. It has been a little over two years but it has, of course, been a lifetime. It is still Toronto the Good with all of its churches, all those gothic spires that dot the horizon. Sadly, unlike Europe, there are no bars here. One cannot simply go out and buy oneself a drink. You'd think a war might erupt if that were to happen.

As I walk along the winter streets people seem drawn to me, compelled to explain the changes.

"King and Yonge is where all those skyscrapers have sprouted up," an old man offers. "Those damn wind tunnels will pick a man up whole and send him to God knows where."

I think it must be the uniform that draws them out, their need to connect with returning soldiers. It's strange they are drawn to me, for there is nothing in my countenance that can possibly evince any sense of wanting to talk with anybody about anything, let alone the just-ended war.

I get myself a room on King Street West and pay a week's rent up front.

"We're all proud of you," the man at the front desk says.

I stare at him for a time, turn and trudge up the stairs. I find my room, go in, throw my duffel bag on the bed and take a shot of rum. There is a cafe just down the street across from *The Toronto Star* building. I go down and find a table in the corner, order a cup of coffee and add some rum from my flask. You can tell this is where all the people come who work across the street. It is all shop talk, the headlines of the day and who is winning the circulation war with *The Telegram*.

There is one young man dressed in the cap, cape and boots of an Italian military officer. He is so young he barely looks the part and seems more likely dressed for a high school play. He is tall and slim with a round face, flushed cheeks and tousled black hair. He is right into it telling his war stories, how he fought with the Arditi regiment, a vagabond group of criminals who'd been released to fight for their country. It is the usual stuff, dodging mortars and machine gun fire, dragging men to safety. You get used to it now and you can tell just by looking at them just who is who. Those who've seen true, hard things don't talk about them very much and when they do it is never about bragging. This fellow can't stop himself.

It isn't long before he has his medal out and I can see by the look of those around him it is genuine. He's won the *Medaglio d'Oro per valore*, the highest Italian award. I follow the conversation from where I sit and can tell it has been engraved. He's done something, I gather.

I pour a little more rum in my coffee and sit and watch as the group of them file out one after the other. The young man stays on and comes over.

"Do you think you might spot me a little of what's in the flask?" he asks.

I nod and he holds out his coffee cup and I pour him a little.

"Thanks," he says. "It's bloody awful in this city with its temperance laws."

"You've got that right."

"I'm used to having a damn drink whenever I want and here it's a damn chore, I'll tell you."

"Toronto the Good," I say and we toast.

"Ernest Hemingway," he says introducing himself and offering a hand.

"Robert Smith." We shake.

He puts a hand on the back of the chair opposite me. "Do you mind?"

"Be my guest."

He sits back in the chair, takes another sip and a smile comes to his lips and he flashes his eyebrows a little. "That's what I've been waiting for all day."

I smile.

"You been back long?" he asks.

"I arrived in Toronto today. I shipped into New York last week."

"New York?"

"I fought with the British. I had to make my own arrangements."

"The British," he repeats, nodding agreeably. "I fought with the Italians."

"I heard."

He looks at me and I can see the wheels turning. "It's the plague of all fishermen," he begins. "You learn to embellish stories at a very young age."

"Of course."

"I've been back a year. From that moment on everybody's tried to make a hero out of me." He sips on his coffee and rum and stares out the front window. The snow is coming up, twisting its way through the streets. "I don't have to tell you that all the real heroes are dead. If I'd been a really game guy, I would have gotten myself killed off."

I smile a little and hold out the flask and he is happy to accept.

"What did you do in the war?" I ask.

He begins to laugh. "I drove a Red Cross ambulance for the Italians. Pretty routine stuff except the Austrians decided to drop an arsenal on me. I got hit with a load of shrapnel. I thought I might even lose a leg for a while."

"You won a medal."

He nods. "I dragged a wounded fellow back to safety, which is something I guess, but the truth of it is the Italians wanted the support of the Americans in the war so much they were dying to hand out any medal they could to any American fighting alongside them."

We sit silently for a time sipping on our drinks.

"You work across the street?"

"I'm a reporter," he says. "Well, sort of. I'm still waiting for my own by-line but it's good training for a writer. At this point, for me, it's the original Peruvian Doughnuts."

I smile at the expression. "Good for you," I say. I hold the flask up and give it a shake. "I'd offer you more but I'm empty."

"No matter," he says and stands up. "Come by tomorrow about this time and we'll share war stories." He has a big jaunty grin on his face and I watch as he limps away, leaning heavily on his cane.

I pick up a plate of food and take it back to the room, eat a little, then lie down on the bed and stare at the ceiling and get what sleep I can. Whatever sounds drift up from the street transform into shattering crashes that make the earth tremble. I wake as if somebody has slammed me in the face, the sweat rolling down my brow as I dart up in the dark. At one point there is knocking at the door and a neighbour asks if I am alright. I say that I am and know I must have screamed out loud.

The next day I wander around the city for hours, find a pharmacy and stand in line until my turn comes up. I feign some mysterious illness until the pharmacist makes a face and goes for a bottle of liquor to ease my malady. This is how it is done now that the temperance laws have been relaxed.

Ernest is in fine form when I go into the café and find my table. He is instructing his group on fishing, telling how difficult it is to catch grasshoppers as bait. He says the key is to get them early in the morning beneath logs on the grass before the sun has dried the dew, when they are still stiff and cold and unable to hop very well.

He winks at me as I come in and when he is through with his lecture he comes right over. "I hope you've reloaded since I saw you yesterday."

"Of course," I say and hold up the flask. He holds out his cup and I give him a good pour.

"You're a good chap, Robert."

I smile and he sits down.

"You owe me a war story," he says. "And a real one too, not like one of my fishing tales."

I refill my own cup and sit back and take my time. "We'd been there a year and it was back and forth between the two trenches the whole time. They'd shoot at us and we'd shoot back and men would die and nothing ever changed, day after day. Then one day they gave us the order to climb out into no-man's land, cut the wire and attack the Germans right there in their own trench. No prisoners at all, no matter what, the officers told us. Well, we crept out in the early morning and shimmied along the ground, cut through the wire and crept up towards the other trench. The whole year we'd never even really seen the enemy. When we got there they were all just waking up, just a bunch of kids, maybe a half dozen of them. When they saw us they didn't even go for their guns, they just started pleading for mercy. I can't speak a word of German but you could tell exactly what they were saying and all you could do was put them out of their misery."

Ernest just listens and nods and we sit for a long time silently and then I refill our coffee cups and we drink for a time and we talk of other things until the flask is empty.

"Well, I guess that's it," I say.

"Nonsense," he says and stands up. "You're coming with me. It's my treat now. I know the best bar in town."

"There are no bars in town."

"You'll see," he says with a big smile.

Ernest tells me he's been hired to be a baby sitter of sorts to a young man in his teens with some physical ailments whose parents thought he was in need of a role model. The Connable home is a palatial residence on the top of a hill overlooking a ravine on the northwest perimeter of the city. They are away in Florida at the moment and he has the run of the house, which means we have a fine pool table and a fully stocked liquor cabinet. He is quick with the drinks and after a few rounds of pool we sit down and take a break with an excellent rye whisky.

"How long were you there?" he asks

"Two years."

"How did you end up fighting with the British?"

"I enlisted with my friend. His family were English and that's what he wanted to do. I didn't even want to go but he talked me into it, said it was our duty and we'd have a grand old time. We weren't even seventeen. We both lied to get in."

"And where's your friend now?"

I shake my head from side to side. I hold onto my glass, take a long drink and it seems to steady me.

"Sorry to bring it up," he says.

"It's okay. It never goes away. Bringing it up doesn't make it any worse than at any other time of the day."

He nods. Ernest is silent but goes for the bottle of rye and fills our glasses and then sits back in his chair. He has these black eyes that pore over you and draw things out.

I take a deep breath. "He didn't die in combat. He was shot on the orders of the British High Command." I've told the story before and seen the same look. "They call it shell-shock now, I think. Fellows who got stuck in the middle of the battles, the bombardments where the noise was bloody awful and a lot of the guys would come out of it in a daze. But with some of them it didn't end. They were like that for weeks. They couldn't function and the officers would just scream and yell at them like they weren't doing their job. 'Malingering' was the word they used."

I take a long sip of the rye and feel it warm me a little, feel the inviting numbness that is a mask over everything that is true.

"He was ordered to deliver a message but he got lost ... didn't know where he was or what he was doing. He was gone a day before we found him, propped up against a tree not very far from our trench. I can remember the look on his face when we found him. He looked at me and smiled and said, 'You found me, Robbie. Thank God. I didn't know where I was and the noise, the noise was so bad.' He was crying."

Ernest leans back in his chair and I see him breathing heavily, sipping on his rye.

"They court-martialled him. It didn't even take a day. It was for desertion and cowardice. The last time I saw him he was so confused and he asked me, 'Robbie, where are they taking me. Are they sending me home?' I couldn't even answer as the soldiers took him and he looked around one last time and stared at me and he had no idea at all."

"I *had* no idea," Ernest says

"Three-hundred or so men like that shot on orders of some General. Half of them were probably underage like us for God's sake. Just kids. All he wanted to do was make his father and mother proud. 'C'mon Robbie,' he said. 'We've got to do our duty.'"

Ernest offers to get me a car but I want to walk back to my room downtown. The snow is coming down but it isn't very cold. I have a week to go in Toronto before I'm supposed to head north. A week to try and find a way to tell his parents what happened. Perhaps the best I can do is write it down. Maybe Ernest can help me to get it right. Once the letter is done and posted I know the only thing I want to do in that room is to sleep a proper sleep, the one that will release me from those terrible dreams, to a dream where I might see a smile on my friend's face again.

# Growing Canada

*Frances Hern*

In 1914, with the uncertainty of war looming, British authorities feared that food prices would increase. They were correct. People began to hoard dried and canned goods, along with staples such as sugar, flour, and tea. Prices continued to rise until August 11th, seven days after war was declared, when the government set official retail prices. Reassured that prices would not continue to climb, the British people stopped panic-buying, for the time being at least.

As a dominion of the British Empire, Canada was automatically involved in the conflict and the mother country turned to Canada, asking her to send both soldiers and food. Canada was already exporting items such as cheese, fish, beef, and especially wheat, to Britain. Now the port of Montreal became busier than it had ever been. During the third week of August, 1914, fifty-six ships came in, creating a new record. By the end of the month, fifty-six million bushels of wheat had arrived, fifty-one million of which were sent across the Atlantic.

Farmers were pressured to produce larger crops, while profiteers seized opportunities to make money. In the fall of 1914 a smooth-tongued individual tried to talk Canadian farmers into buying world-famed, seven-headed Egyptian wheat which, he claimed, would yield 230 bushels per acre. With the high price of cereal, such a productive wheat could make the grower fabulously rich in the course of a few crops and, to make the deal even sweeter, the salesman was offering this highly desirable wheat at the reduced price of $10/bushel to introduce the grain to Alberta farmers. The Department of Agriculture advised farmers to beware and not buy, but some went ahead anyway. Not surprisingly, it was found to be an indifferent variety. It did not yield as much flour or meal as other kinds of wheat and the flour was scarcely superior to that obtained from the finest of barley.

While the transatlantic journey from North America to Britain was shorter than that from elsewhere in the world, the ocean was the Achilles Heel of the delivery system. By 1917, German submarines were sinking any merchant vessels that came within range suspected of trading with the Allies. Between April and June of 1917, over two million tons of Allied shipping sank to the bottom of the sea. The British attempted to increase their own food production but also pressed Canada to send more food, as well as soldiers.

In Canada, the government asked citizens to voluntarily reduce consumption of scarce commodities and not hoard essential items, however prices rose faster than wages. In the summer of 1917, Ottawa appointed food and fuel controllers to encourage production, avoid waste, and manage shortages.

Wanting to help with the war effort, and believing that it would be over by Christmas, Canadians were initially enthusiastic about signing up for the armed forces. However this posed difficulties for farmers who couldn't increase food production if their labourers were leaving to join the army. They needed more workers, not fewer.

As the war dragged on, soldiers and politicians came to realize it was not going to end quickly. When people learned of the awful conditions in the trenches and the enormous casualties, men stopped volunteering. Canadian casualties on the Western Front began to exceed the number of new Canadian recruits. There were over 300,000 recruits by 1916 but Prime Minister Sir Robert Borden had promised 500,000 by the end of that year, despite the fact that Canada's population was only 8 million at the time. Canadian farmers were urged to increase wheat production at any price to feed Britain, making them indispensible in the fields, while military recruiters covered the length and breadth of the countryside trying to sign up more men.

In order to maintain Canadian forces, Borden decided to bring in conscription. Farmers were among Borden's fiercest opponents. He went ahead with his Military Service Act anyway, which came into effect on 29 August 1917. In an attempt to appease opponents, the act allowed two-person tribunals to grant exemptions to anyone necessary to vital industries, those whose absence would pose serious hardships for themselves or their families, and genuine conscientious objectors. In April 1918, however, these exemptions were lifted and farmers were among the young men shipped over to Britain. Farmers claimed the labour shortage would cause Canadian food production to drop by at least 25 percent. The Canadian Food Board issued a national appeal, asking boys aged 15 to 19 to spend their summers as "Soldiers of the Soil" (SOS) on farms desperately short of labour.

The SOS received food, board, and spending money in exchange for their labour. Upon completion of their term they received an SOS badge acknowledging their service. High school students also received exemption from classes and final exams. Over 22,000 boys responded and farmers continued to increase the amount of cultivated land, but despite these efforts the wheat harvest of 1918 was disappointingly low.

Girls and women, known in Ontario as Farmerettes, were also recruited to help with the agricultural labour shortage and they soldiered on with back-breaking work in the absence of male relatives and labourers.

By May of 1917 food and fuel shortages for the coming winter loomed. The Canadian Food Board licensed and monitored food sales in public establishments and encouraged food or ingredient substitutes for high-demand items. Posters urged "fuel-less Sundays", "meatless Fridays", and the elimination of wasteful shopping and cooking practices. Newspapers published special "war menus". Provinces and municipalities managed local hydro and power shortages, sometimes by short-term closures in schools and factories.

In the United States, Charles Lathrop Pack proposed the concept of War Gardens and these "Victory Gardens" – considered to be a morale-booster because gardeners could feel proud of their contribution to the war effort – soon became popular in Canada, Britain, and Australia as well. Some home gardeners also raised chickens to provide fresh eggs.

Booklets were published by the Ministry of Agriculture with step-by-step instructions on the care and cultivation of gardens. They also told how increased food production would help reduce the price of produce required by the military, leaving more money to purchase equipment, uniforms and weapons.

Men, women and children worked together to use every available space to grow vegetables. In High River, Alberta, the council prepared vacant lots and urged citizens to provide the manpower for planting and growing. It was estimated that between 1917 and 1919 over five million Victory Gardens were planted in North America. Other initiatives to provide food included stocking rivers with spawn supplied by the Fisheries Department. The Highwood River, Flat and Cataract Creeks were among the best fishing streams in Alberta, and were visited annually by thousands of Albertans hoping to supplement their available provisions.

In Britain, waste ground, golf courses, and lawns were requisitioned for farming or growing vegetables. Some sports fields were grazed by sheep instead of being mowed.

In April 1918, horse rancher George Hoadley suggested that scrub horses in the western provinces be purchased for victory bonds to provide 60 million pounds of palatable meat, similar to moose meat, not for the British armies but for the French and Belgians who were accustomed to eating horse meat. However horsemeat may well have made its way into British soldiers rations. At the beginning of the war they were allowed ten ounces of meat and eight ounces of vegetables per day. By 1916, the meat ration had been reduced to six ounces a day and, later, only once every few days. Dried, ground turnips replaced flour, which was in short supply. This "turnip" flour produced unappetising, diarrhea-inducing bread. A staple food became pea soup with chunks of canned corned beef known as "bully beef", or meat of a more questionable origin. Weeds and nettles replaced vegetables in stews. Everything began to taste the same and was often cold by the time it reached the men in the front lines. Not wanting to appear weak, army officials tried to hide the desperate food situation from the enemy.

By 1918, the impact of the German U-boat campaign, along with panic buying, had created serious food shortages in Britain. It became a criminal offence to throw rice at weddings, and to adopt or feed a stray dog. Bakers were allowed only to bake government-regulation bread. Malnutrition became a problem in poor communities and so, ten months before the war ended, the government finally introduced rationing. At first, sugar was rationed, and by the end of April, meat, butter, cheese and margarine were added to the list of rationed foods. Everyone was issued a ration card and had to register with a butcher and a grocer. While this was inconvenient, to say the least, it more evenly distributed the available food and helped to resolve the malnutrition problem.

By the fall of 1913, Canada had been in the grips of the worst depression in two decades. The war brought an end to this by boosting economic activity and reducing unemployment. It also strained the country's fragile, resource-based economy. Between 1913 and 1918 the national debt rose from approximately $450 million to $2 billion, owed not only to other countries, but also to Canadians who had supported the war effort by buying victory bonds. Many government controls ended during the months following Armistice Day, but in some areas – such as taxation, social welfare, and the responsibility for veterans – the state assumed powers it would never again relinquish.

However, the Great War helped Canadians develop a sense of national pride. Canadian soldiers had fought bravely and distinguished themselves at Ypres, Vimy Ridge and Passchendaele, while Canadians at home worked to provide necessities such as food and ammunition, as well as much-needed capital to keep the country running. Canada went into the war as a colony of Britain. By the time it was over, Prime Minister Borden was able to demand a seat at the 1919 Paris Peace Conference, where Canada independently signed the Treaty of Versailles that formally ended the war. This was in acknowledgement of Canada's significant contribution to the Allied victory. Canada was also given a seat in the new League of Nations, and was on the long road to independence.

# Seeking Alice in Flanders Fields

*Alexander Binning*

The inner history of war is written
from the recorded impressions of men
who have endured it.

*– Sir Andrew Mcphail (1919)*

*January, 1972. In the Study of Cyril Allinson. Guelph, Ontario.*

"Well, there it is, then. Almost finished, thank God. I've done my best for the old boy. Long overdue. It's very messy and over 200 pages. Somebody else will have to set it properly if anybody is to read it at all."

"I'm very glad, dear. I am sure they will. Come out and have some tea before bed." Cynthia Allinson retired to the kitchen, leaving her husband to ponder his seemingly unending dutiful project.

Cyril continued shuffling through the typed sheets and then paused at page 90. Wonder if I should say more here about the start of the whole mess? So much written about it since. Favourite subject in university history departments now. Whole courses given on "The Origins of the First World War". But we knew well enough why we were there in Ypres. It was made very clear to us. He read over the passage again:

> *Because Belgium, France, and Great Britain, all held large colonial areas in Africa and in Asia, Wilhelm's overall strategy was to over-run Belgium, then France, then insulate Great Britain, and get naval superiority in the North Sea, the*

79

*English Channel, and the Bay of Biscay; at the same time the
eastern end of the Mediterranean, and the Suez Canal, would be
blocked by Turkey (which held Palestine until 1918).*

Yes, I think that says it shortly and crisply. "War to end all wars" indeed!
Poppycock! I remember John telling me he had nightmares about it all.
He didn't know the half of it, poor man. I still have nightmares fifty years
later. But all of those things will be remembered now, including his old
family house here in town. The poem was magnificent of course, but
how valuable those diary letters to his mother. Good job by Mcphail
back when, to have put them all together.

   Cyril Allinson closed the folder and then reached again for the copy
of Ruskin's *Proserpina* which a friend had recently sent him with a
note attached, advising him to look at what the grand old Victorian
had said about poppies.

> All silk and flame, a scarlet cup, perfectly
> edged all around, seen among the wild grass
> far away, like a burning coal fallen from
> Heaven's altars.

*March 8, 1890. Burns Presbyterian Cemetery, Erin, Ontario.*

William McRae put a hand on John McCrae's shoulder. "It means much
to us that you were here with us today, John. It cannot have been any
easier for you than for us. Alice would have wanted you here. I know that.
We all think that. She was always smiling when she spoke of you."

   "I've been distraught for the last few days. I was very anxious to be
one of the pall-bearers so I am grateful your family approved. Alice
and I ... we always laughed together ... and so it was important to me
to walk with her one more time ... give her courage ... be among those
to let her go. Yes. We did laugh ... from the first day you introduced us.
We accused each other of spelling our family names incorrectly and it
just went on from there. How very sad I am today. And so sad for all
of you."

"I'm glad you're staying with us tonight. We think of you as family, even if you *do* spell your name wrong. We can all take a walk in the hills tomorrow, drab though they are at this time of year."

"I think you call these the Caledon Hills?"

"Yes. Some of our good Scottish predecessors here named them after Caledonia."

"That's good. She will be among her own then."

*March 15, 1890, University College. Toronto.*
*John McCrae to Janet McCrae.*

> *Perhaps it is because I was brought into nearer connection with*
> *a death than I have ever been before, that I think so much about it.*

*Oct. 24, 1894. The McCrae Home, Guelph, Ontario.*

Janet McCrae was putting away dishes when David McCrae came in with a fistful of mail. "Well Mrs. McCrae, I see there is one here for me from your youngest son."

"Oh, do read that right off. He had such a good time down in Massachusetts at Woods Hole this summer, sailing, swimming – even studying marine biology." Janet looked slyly at her husband.

"I see that smile you are holding in. Conniving woman!"

· "I'm so glad you found the money to send him."

"Yes, yes. *Studying* – I hope!"

"But he's anxious about his studies I think. Perhaps he's made up his mind."

Her husband worked the envelope with an ivory opener. "It's usually money well-spent on those lads, of course. What's this? Wonderful! A photo of him at Kingston a year ago, all uniformed up, just after being made Second Lieutenant in Artillery." He handed the photo to Janet.

"Oh, that is lovely. We will have to frame it."

"Now *there* was money well spent, sending him to Royal Military. He's best in the outdoors you know. No time that way for moping around and writing that oppressive poetry of his. He still has his mind on that poor girl. Keeps mourning for her in the *Varsity Magazine*."

"It's just his way my dear. He'll come to terms in time. But the letter, the letter!" David fumbled for his glasses and then leaned up against the stove near the window and read it studiously for a few moments.

"Seems that Dr. McCallum wants him to study medicine first and *then* pursue biology if he wants to later. And Jack wants to do it in Toronto, rather than Baltimore at Hopkins."

"Well that is very good I think. The boys can live together and keep an eye out."

"Yes. A lot cheaper, too. Here's what Jack says. 'If science does not turn out as I expect or if anything untoward turns up, I could fall back on practice.' Good, good I think. Practical all around. Done."

*Dec. 22, 1899. The Common Room. McGill College Medical School. Montreal.*

Professor John Adami passed the newspaper over to John McCrae. "You've no doubt heard about this already?"

"Indeed, I have. And I'm glad to hear about the plans for us here in Canada. Everyone is now calling the recent debacles in the Orange River country 'black week'. It makes sense to send more people over to get the job done. About time the ones in charge in England figured it out."

"I think I know why you asked me here for a drink and I don't think it's about the newest theories in pathology – *or* about the scholarship which we have all broken our backsides over to obtain for you. But I'm not sure I want to hear it."

"Guilty as charged, I'm afraid. I think you know how much I wanted to go over on the first round. But they closed it down so fast. Not much of a show if you ask me. 'South Africa be damned' seemed to be the message!"

"Adventure! You all want adventure! What a curious man you are, McCrae. Part poet, part artillery man, part doctor! Extraordinary really. Not sure what my old Cambridge crowd would make of you."

"You forgot *rugby player,* Professor."

"Just adds to the confusion."

"But what do you think, sir? If I went mainly in a medical capacity, would that be looked upon favourably? And would you be prepared to put off my scholarship for just a year?"

"*Just* a year! So you say. I know damn well that if I don't I will never hear the end of it. And your father, of course, would be on me, to boot!"

"He would indeed, sir."

"Yes. Osler has told me something of your father's preoccupation with artillery games." Adami paused, pulled out his waistcoat watch and stared at it for a number of seconds. "And so, if that is *really* what you want, the answer is yes. I will see what I can do with the College people. Just don't get yourself bloody killed. You're too valuable to lose over all this South African nonsense."

"Thank you, sir. I greatly appreciate it." McCrae rose from his easy chair and placed a small volume of verse on Adami's side table.

"What's this rubbish you're reading?"

"For you, sir. Some Kipling. I've been reading him for a few years. Solid fellow."

*February, 15, 1900. Cape Town, South Africa.*

After the military games had wound down, word quickly circulated among Canadian D Battery that Rudyard Kipling was about. John McCrae and two of his comrades were fast to set out on his track. At the Mount Nelson Hotel they encountered a young subaltern, Lord Woolverton, who offered to introduce them.

When the great man was eventually located, McCrae approached and told him of their regret at not meeting him at the games the day before. The author laughed and replied he was reluctant to interrupt, "for I could tell you were up to your eyes in work, licking things into shape to get to the front."

Before parting Kipling cautioned them to watch out for unboiled drinking water and to keep a firm hand on directives to the men: "The only way to do it is to fine them."

*April 24, 1915, Saturday. Ypres, Canal Side. The "Square Hole" Dressing Station.*

> *Fumes came down very heavily: Some blew down from the infantry trenches – some came from the shells. One's eyes smarted, and breathing very laboured.*

Lieutenant Colonel John McCrae put his pen and diary aside and walked over to one of the recent casualties who was suddenly stirring on his cot. He adjusted a light gauze mask over the man's nose and mouth. "Try and sleep. It's important." He returned to his makeshift desk.

> *The shelling was steady during the night, but not too much gas, thank God. The bloody fumes from the guns are bad enough.*

That would do for Mother at the moment.

He got up and walked over to the sandbag pillars which constituted the doorway of his so-called hospital. "The Hippocratic Oath" he whispered to himself, staring out towards the distant pattern of cesspools that defined the immediate battlegrounds of Flanders. "How does one say anything useful about this version of Hades?" Flashes broke over the horizon like sheet lightning. It was starting again. "The *hypocritic oath* would be more to the point!" he blurted out a little more loudly.

"What's that sir?" said a man behind him who was on crutches, unsteadily trying to get some exercise.

"Oh, nothing, friend. Just thinking out loud. How are you feeling? Good to see you on your feet. Anything I can get you?"

"Nothing you can get me *here*, sir. Thanks again for patching me up, sir. Not sure I'll be much bloody good anymore."

"No. I'm sorry. That leg is pretty bad. But you will live and you will keep it if we can just keep it clean enough and get you out of here, lice-free. Let me check those bandages."

McCrae went about his work keeping his thoughts to himself now. He should be at the front fighting beside the men. Not back here behind the lines looking after the wounded. Christ was right. Let the dead bury the dead! What was needed was to get the job done. Time enough later to pick up the pieces. I need to write that down somehow. Good God man, do you hear yourself? Think! Do you really believe that? At your age … not to even have it sorted. This man is going to live and he would not have, otherwise. No shame in that. He did his duty. The Oath, the damned Oath!

"There, I think that all looks good. Don't forget. Drink only boiled water."

"Yes, sir. Thank you, sir."

A matronly figure suddenly rose unannounced out of memory.

What was it auntie said? Yes – I "only wanted to know the why and wherefore of everything". Then she accused me of pulling all my toys apart to see what they were like inside. And so now here I am tearing apart the Hippocratic Oath. Surely a military doctor is as much a contradiction as a military chaplain. We come here to kill, not to pretend we're Christians. And medicine is for the living, not for those marching into hell. Damned Oath! I'm trapped. Alice, Alice, where are you? I need you here beside me to talk sense to me.

There were no stretchers approaching and all was quiet again. McCrae went back to the desk he had improvised from empty shell boxes, retrieved a small waterproof case and took out a reprint of one of his early poems. He walked outside and went up to the crest of the canal edge where he could better see the full extent of what used to be the productive fields of Flanders. He unfolded the copy of "The Hope of My Heart".

"Twenty years since I wrote this, and yet she is still with me. What a sentimental fool I am! I should have married."

I left to earth a little maiden fair,
With locks of gold, and eyes that shamed
The light;
I prayed that God might have her in His care
And sight …

God's kind words come –
"Her future is with Me, as was her past;
It shall be My good will
to bring her home
At last."

*May 2, 1915. Ypres, Canal Side. The "Square Hole" Dressing Station.*

"Not for nothing we call this the 'square hole' dressing station, eh, John?"

"Damned right."

"Pretty rough with the gas. Scared those North Africans out of their wits. So much for the rules of warfare. How are you holding up? You told me once you had to watch out for asthma."

"I think it started in my university days, in the early 1890s. There were earlier intimations, but nothing too worrisome."

Cyril Allinson closed McCrae's text on pathology he had been flipping through and placed it back on the crude desk. "Was your asthma what took you towards medicine, then?"

"Yes, I think so. In part. But it was also my contact with Wright – a very good teacher I had."

"Come again?"

"Robert Ramsay Wright. Brilliant lecturer in biology at the University of Toronto. Very much up on the new medicine. That is to say, microbes and wee beastie things. Studied with Pasteur in Paris. That's why I'm always going after the boys here about lice and water all the time. Can't pick too many lice to suit me."

"Seems you have to be careful yourself then. Asthma can be pretty serious, can't it?"

"It can kill you. It kills lots of people. Do you know the name Osler? Another brilliant man. Toronto man. Went to Johns Hopkins in

Baltimore in the early days of the school. I met him when I studied there for a while. He was very interested in asthma. I was lucky to work with him. Even luckier to know him still. The world needs more Oslers I tell you. Doing a marvellous job now for the war effort in England."

"I've been lucky. No serious afflictions. Certainly not asthma. If I may ask for an informal analysis, what's an attack of it like?"

"Frightening! Especially when you're very young. I was fortunate, if I may put it that way, not to have it come at me until later. Mainly brought on I think by all that putrescence in the air around Toronto. You have to really fight for air for a few moments. It brings all of your instincts for survival into play. And you have fleeting glimpses of what may be 'the end', if you know what I mean. You are, after all, thinking very acutely as you struggle for air. When you come out of it you're grateful and more philosophical for being suddenly acquainted with the fragility of your own life. That's why it's so disturbing to witness it in young children. They don't have any philosophical resources. However, there's some progress being made in treatments."

"Good to know."

"Odd, is it not, that you and I find ourselves in the killing business at this hour? But it needs to be done. Is that not the thing?"

"That's the thing."

"Lord, look at that swamp out there where poppies are supposed to grow. Not much like your Forest Hill back in London, is it Cyril?"

"I dare say not. Nor like your fine green fields about Guelph. But at least it's quiet right now. Cigarette?"

"Thanks, but I'll smoke one of my own. Special kind from India that I came across some years ago. Supposed to be good for asthmatics. Contains *cannabis* I'm told."

*May 15, 1915. Ypres, Canal Side.*

Cyril Allinson was delivering the mail, but stopped in his tracks when he saw McCrae sitting on the back of an ambulance, writing. He paused, waiting for a suitable moment to interrupt. Close by was Essex Farm Cemetery where their comrade, Alex Helmer, had so recently been laid to rest. The doctor raised his head now and then and stared out towards Helmer's grave. He eventually stopped writing and got up. Seeing Allinson he walked over and gave him the note pad in exchange for the mail, mumbling that he might send it in to *The Spectator*.*

*June 2, 1915. Ypres, Canal Side. Dressing Station.*

"Damn it Cyril, I don't want to leave the front now. All the goddam doctors in the world will not win this bloody war. What we need are more and more fighting men." McCrae glared at the dispatch in his hand ordering him to report to the new Canadian Hospital 3 at Dannes-Camiers.

Allinson did his best to soothe his friend after this rather unmilitary outburst, assuring him that the men understood. He would do a vast amount of good in supervising the new hospital on the coast. There would perhaps be a chance to see Osler and visit Oxford and catch up on new medical developments.

The logic was undeniable. Everybody knew it. McCrae knew it. Here at the front he had been sleeping in a tent, as did the soldiers, even though there were wood huts for commanding officers. Nobody thought that McCrae should be doing this. His solidarity with the soldiers was not in question and, to a man, they would have said they needed him as healthy as possible. Everybody could see what Allinson had noticed. Dr. McCrae was tired.

---

* The poem "In Flanders Fields" was eventually published in *Punch Magazine* on December, 8, 1915.

*July 1915. Oxford. The Osler Residence, Norman Gardens.*

"Jack, you look terrible. First we have some tea and then you are going to get twelve hours sleep."

"People tell me I look hopeless. I find it hard to stop my work when for so many it's their last day on the job."

"Now Jack, you must not ... there, there now, you are not to think of all that when you're here. The men are right, you know. You are tired and you can't do them much good if you are not right yourself. Are you listening?"

"Yes, yes. I always listen to you, *Lady* Grace, and to *Sir* Willie. You are right of course."

"Oh, you! How you love to tease us about that knighthood business! I see that wicked grin on your face."

"What with you being related to Paul Revere!"

"In Baltimore they haven't stopped chuckling over it." Grace laughed and then poured some tea for John. "Now that's better! We need the joking Jack back with us. Of course I'm right. So there's an end to it. You will get in some riding and fishing while you are here and you will eat properly."

*September 10, 1915. Dannes-Camiers, near Boulogne-sur-Mer,*
*Northern France. Canadian Hospital No. 3.*

"The McGill people have done a splendid job in helping set this place up, don't you think, Jack? Quite a change for you isn't it? From looking at you, I would say you needed this appointment. You look better than when you visited us in July. And I'm a doctor you know! Pine forests, sand dunes, the sea ... You'll do more good here – trust me. Come, let's take a walk and forget all this for an hour."

William Osler and John McCrae headed out from the hospital, through the open woods, towards the bay, quickly losing themselves in memories of Baltimore and Montreal. They returned to dinner at seventeen hundred hours, following which they made an inspection of all the patients before retiring to the mess.

"Sir William, I really *am* very glad you were able to get over here. I needed to see you and get your advice."

"And I to see you. But before I go back I want you to give me a bit of a tour of the front areas. I need to know what the hell is going on. It's not just the wounds, as you know. It's what sets into them afterwards that's taking such a toll. I have to convince the people back in London of that. I've heard tales of how you brow-beat the troops about lice."

"What about your friend Paul Ehrlich? Nice to know we have one German friend at least."

"*Had* a German friend. He had a heart attack just this summer and has left us. A brilliant man gone. Regrettably his Salvarsan drug has not worked very well. *Streptococcus* is not responding to it with any consistency. I had great hopes for it, especially with respect to pneumonia. We need to find something else."

"I'm sorry to hear it. I know he was your friend, as well as a good scientist." The men fell silent and looked for a long moment out toward the sea. Osler eventually reached inside his coat, withdrew a report and shoved it into McCrae's hand.

"Read this when you can. Something I wrote lately on recent treatments, including the problem with Salvarsan. It might help you out a bit."

"Thanks. I'll read it carefully. Tomorrow we can start on a tour. We'll keep well back from the contact zone but you will see a mobile laboratory and some of our dressing stations, pathetic though they are."

"Good. I told the other BMA* men that I would try and get a first-hand look. See what the medical staff are really up against, day to day. If I had my way, the whole lot of them would be over here with me."

---

* With the outbreak of war, Dr. William Osler had joined the War Committee of the British Medical Association.

*January 25, 1917. Dannes-Camiers. Canadian Hospital No. 3.*
**Diary of John McCrae:**

> *The cruel cold is still holding. Everyone is suffering and the men
> in the wards in bed cannot keep warm.*

The year of trial for Canadian troops had not begun well. Better news
came in April with the announcement that America was joining the
war effort, and with the victory at Vimy Ridge. But there was still no
end in sight on the northern front. With revolution and the collapse
of Russia's eastern front by August, the German Army took new heart.
The third battle of Ypres seemed to go nowhere. The push towards
Passchendaele ended in the bloodiest of victories on November 6th.
The horror of the cost flowed steadily into Canadian Hospital No.
3. Over eight hundred wounded were admitted on one day. McCrae,
with all the others, was exhausted. To complicate things, in August
he had experienced what he considered an absurd attack of his old
nemesis, asthma. But at November's end there seemed at least *some*
reason to try and celebrate Christmas at Dannes-Camiers with a bit
of gusto. There was talk of a much-deserved promotion for McCrae to
the directorship of Canadian Hospital No.1. Then on January 5, 1918,
the promotion was increased to that of Consulting Physician to the
British Troops in the Field.

McCrae was pleased but he carried on at Hospital No. 3 for the
early weeks of January. During the afternoon of January 23, Colonel
Elder came across McCrae asleep at his desk. He was ailing and was
sent to bed. McCrae suspected pneumonia but tests over the next two
days did not seem to confirm that condition. He was then taken to
British General Hospital No. 14 at nearby Wimereux and given the
best care available.

*January 27, 1918. Wimereux, France. British General Hospital No. 14.*

McCrae had slept fitfully and now, in the early morning hours, recognized the time for its import, for he had rehearsed it many times in the
past. He called it "the soldier's hour". It might be a split second at the

end of a shell or it might be a long drawn out period of agony. Dying, like living, required discipline, training, practice, revision. His lungs were failing. He knew his own diagnosis better than the doctors and nurses around him.

"How right you were, William. Pneumonia *is* an 'old man's gift.' My own 'hour' will be shorter, rather than longer. Time enough to review the good and the not-so-good. No time for the shameful – that is just a waste of emotion. I've atoned for the shameful already. No need for a Presbyterian lad to have a bloody priest! Knox was always my man."

The golden moments now rose in memory. There were the sweet moments with Alice, picnics, days in the library, hours on the playing field. There was the great adventure north with Governor-General Grey's party: Red River, Lake Winnipeg, Norway House, the Heyes River and York Factory, Churchill and the stunning *aurora borealis* in its late August splendour. There were the canoe-paddling, Methodist hymn-singing, tobacco-chewing Indian guides and their easy philosophy of the stars.

"What had they called those northern lights? The dancing souls of the departed? I shall dance with you soon, Alice. How I admired those Indians with their own kind of discipline, fasting for days in search of a vision of 'destiny'. Yes, that was very good on their part. And they have been good soldiers here with us. How magnificent they were back then, shooting the rapids on that journey. And that night about the fire at York Factory when I compared notes with John Mooneas about the respective merits of our religious beliefs – and how we laughed when we realized we were both heretics, each in our own way."

And the sad moments. The lost hours with Alice all these years. Surely he had kept faith with her, she who died so young. Would they not finally be reunited? He could see her now, all in white, walking towards him through Flanders Fields, she carrying a canteen, giving water to the soldiers she passed still struggling for breath in the mire. Alice reached out towards him and smiled, just as the darkness closed in and the coma, mercifully brief, descended upon him.

Every attentive school boy and school girl in Canada knows "In Flanders Fields", but probably, as with most of us, not a great deal about the man and his life. In reviewing the main studies and biographies which have come out since 1919, (along with the important unpublished manuscript on McCrae by C.L.C. Allinson, in the McCrae House Museum, Guelph) I quickly became intrigued by how preoccupied McCrae was with death, owing, it seems, to the passing in 1889 of young Alice McRae (no relation) by typhoid. She and John had become very close when he was at school in Toronto.

# Billy's Story

*Pauline Hewak*

Everybody was surprised how things ended up for me, but there wasn't anything I could do about it. That's just how things were – nobody could do much about anything then, not in my hometown of Hamilton, or anywhere else.

But everyone tried real hard. Except for me ... what's a ten-year old kid supposed to do in war-time, and with everybody dropping like flies from influenza? I was scared, all the kids were, not for ourselves because most of the kids didn't get sick, and the old people neither, but we were afraid for our parents and older brothers and sisters and aunts and uncles.

Nobody knew whose cow kicked which lantern, you might say, and some people thought that the soldiers brought the germs back with them but nobody is sure even now. In Hamilton, one of the men at the Armament School of the Royal Air Service in the west end of the city got sick and died in September, 1918, and that was the start of it for us.

When my mother's kid brother, Fred, came home from the war after going over with the Rileys – wounded but walking with a cane – he felt good when he landed in Halifax, he wrote, although a couple of his buddies died of the 'flu on the ship on the way over. But, he took sick and died on the train coming west. It was rotten luck that he survived Vimy and then died anyway. When he finally came home he was in a pine box, and that was that. His letter arrived after he did.

My mother cried in the bedroom for one whole day and when she came out, she took off her apron and put on her hat, and went and joined the Sisters of Service volunteers. They were angels, those ladies, and the nurses too, and everybody knew it.

Nobody could keep up with caring for all the sick. Doctors stopped having office hours so that they could help in Hamilton City Hospital and St. Joe's. The city took over the Jockey Club Hotel to make it into a hospital, and that big house on James St. South, Ballinahinch, became an isolation hospital, too. But there weren't enough places for people to go, and most people just stayed home. The grim truth of it is that they didn't last long anyway .... Most were dead in two days. If a face looked kind of purple, you knew.

So much for scientific medicine.

But for us kids, that autumn of 1918 was good and bad. They cancelled school, which was good, so we just hung out in the playground and wandered around the stores until they kicked us out. Stores hours were cut to keep people from spreading germs, and the owners didn't like it much. But people were scared and scared people buy stuff – warm coats, liver pills, influenza masks – all you had to do was mention influenza and you had a sale. People tried all kinds of things, like sniffing concoctions of borax and carbolic, eating yeast cakes and even drinking a quart of booze a day. My mother put on a clean apron every day and ironed everything to kill germs. We kept our feet dry and sipped cold water. If there was no proof that it didn't work, we assumed it did and it wasn't a time for taking chances anyways.

Everybody was worried, and because they were worried they were mad most of the time, from the milkman to the mayor. It was better for us kids to lie low, if you get what I mean. The streets were pretty quiet. They made rules. Only five people could stand in a streetcar, and only five people could ride an elevator. Church services and meetings were cancelled, except for the volunteers' meetings because they needed them. A priest got fined for holding a service at the Polish church on Barton St., but he fought it and won. The pool halls and bowling alleys closed, and the movie theatres, too, though at first they conned us into going in by advertising that the air inside was healthy. Public funerals were banned and parades. We all went to the Victory Loan parade in November, but then lots of people got sick again. You would've thought we'd danced around the golden calf or something, the way everyone went on about it afterwards.

Like I said, things for me weren't too bad, but I did kind of run away from home when they put my best friend Tommy in St. Mary's orphanage.

His mother was a SOS volunteer and she must have breathed in germs when she was caring for a sick nurse, because the nurse died, and then she did, too. Tommy's father had to take care of the four kids. The diet kitchens sent food over, which helped a lot, but when his father got sick himself and died, Tommy and the little ones were sent to the orphanage. I walked there from my house on Catherine St. and we both cried a little when we saw each other through the fence. I knew that everyone would be worried, so I decided not to run away after all, but that was the last time I saw Tommy.

Everybody was surprised when I got sick. My mother put me to bed with warm socks and the window open. When my sister Frances came home after work at the foundries, she told me stories about the liquid steel that ran like lava that she saw there, and I thought that I might like that kind of job when I grew up. But I mostly looked out the window at the snowflakes and tried to remember the faces of people I knew who had died that autumn. One night I had a good dream about my father who died at the factory when I was seven, but I couldn't remember it when I woke up.

So that's basically my story. There is a small, grey stone in the Hamilton Cemetery with the name of William Foster on it, and that's me. Billy. Like I said, children didn't usually get sick with influenza, but it was a bad time and a lot of bad things happened to a lot of people, not just me.

But that's where I am, if you ever want to pay a visit.

# The Bullock Cart

*Cara Loverock*

The elderly woman carrying the potatoes and scraps walked with a limp. She was short and stout with frizzled greying hair and one leg appeared shorter. In her left hand the pail containing the rotten food swung back and forth. She hobbled her way into the compound. The starving men were huddling to keep warm. It was a matter of seconds before they descended on her like a pack of wolves. They knocked the woman over, desperate to get something in their stomachs.

The pail flew onto the ground. The starving soldiers clamoured to get the scraps they would have turned their noses up at and tossed into the garbage back home. No one showed any concern for the old woman, who writhed on the ground as she attempted to get up. Eventually she used her girth to help her onto her side and hauled herself up from there. By the time she was standing the scraps were gone – every last bit consumed by the prisoners.

It was February, 1916. Allied troops – French, British and Serbian – wasted away at the internment camp at Alexandrovno, Bulgaria. They had been taken prisoner at Salonika, on the Macedonian front. William Gould, the lone Canadian among them, was just seventeen at the time.

William's mother would not have recognized her son, and she didn't when he eventually made his way home years later. His face was no longer chubby, his cheeks sunken. His usually pink skin was pale. His teeth were stained and ached constantly. His eyes bulged out of his head. He had been interned for a three-month eternity.

William had enlisted in the Canadian military on August 8, 1914. He made it through basic training at Valcartier, Quebec and then boarded a ship for London, England where it was discovered he had lied about his age. He was discharged. Instead of heading home to Canada, the British-born William joined the King's Own Royal Lancaster Regiment.

Early in his internment William was sent to work at Sela-Bela, on the Serbian boarder. He worked with fifty other men to build a railway. At night they slept in huts, without beds and with only each other for warmth.

"You don't work, you don't eat!" William was reminded daily.

The most difficult part of prison life was the hunger. Starvation was a daily reality for William and the other prisoners. He soon came to learn the Bulgarian word for bread was "leba." It was the only food he was given.

William was lucky enough to become ill during a march to Alexandrovno. He was ordered to the hospital at Vidin, a port town in northwestern Bulgaria, close to the borders of Serbia and Romania. It would take five hours by bullock cart to reach the hospital. Bulgaria in January was a miserable place to be – frigid, with little sunlight.

William was being transported with two other soldiers. Pillar, sick with jaundice, and a man named Harper who was severely ill. It was not clear what exactly was wrong with him.

The nameless man driving the cart was also acting as a guard. He had a rifle across his lap. The smell of his cigarette wafted back. William inhaled; it reminded him of the life he'd left in Toronto. He often worked in his father's cigar shop on Yonge Street. He knew most of the customers by name, often chatting to them as they purchased cigarettes and newspapers.

Blizzard winds stung William's face, bringing him back to reality. The three men sat uncomfortably in the rickety cart, uncovered. The changing landscape that was barely visible through the blowing snow looked bland and grey. William, with only rags for boots, tried to shove his feet deep into the straw beneath him. He lay crosswise at the feet of the other two, covered in lice.

"What happened to your boots?" Pillar asked, sitting up. He could feel William's feet shoved into his back searching for warmth.

"They were taken by peasants. Our camp was raided when the Bulgars were marching us across the mountains."

"You'll be lucky to avoid getting frostbite. I know a man who lost both feet."

William nodded in agreement.

Pillar lay back down. William shoved his rag-covered feet deeper beneath the straw.

Harper was delirious. He shouted and rustled about for hours as the cart lurched along.

Night fell before they reached the hospital. The darkness swallowed the trees and scattered buildings that had been somewhat visible in the daylight. As night grew darker it seemed as though they were travelling into an abyss. William wondered how the driver knew what direction to go in. He felt pain in his ears and fingers. Fearing frostbite, he tried to pull his shirt up over his head.

Harper suddenly fell silent.

"Thank God he's quieted down," said William.

Pillar did not reply, only scratched furiously at his head and neck. William pushed himself up from the straw he had sunken into. Peering closely at Harper he could see faintly in the dark that his mouth was turning blue. His eyes looked glassy, unblinking.

"Harper?"

William shook him gently. No response. He reached under his chin in search of a pulse.

"He's dead," William said. "Did you know his name?"

Pillar turned his head to look at the dead man. "Harper."

"What was his first name?"

Pillar shrugged.

The cart rumbled on for two more hours as William sat beside the dead man known only as Harper. They finally arrived at Vidin.

At the hospital the pair was shaved, bathed and fumigated. Pillar was infested with lice so badly he was fumigated a second time. William was grateful to be cleaned up, but the standards at the hospital were far from what he was used to in Canada.

"Things here are so primitive. So little thought is given to hygiene," he said to Pillar as they waited for discharge.

They watched as a doctor aided a man with an open wound on his hand. The doctor took a swab, rubbed some ointment into the wound, then used the same swab on another patient's throat.

"Do you know what happened to Harper?" Pillar asked.

William shook his head. They had left his body in the bullock cart as ordered by the guard who had escorted them to the hospital. It was hard to say what would be done with him.

After he was discharged William was given back the same filthy clothing and frayed rags for his feet. He was marched back to Alexandrovno.

It was March 22, 1918, William's eighteenth birthday.

*Author's Note*

"The Bullock Cart" is based on the journal of my great-grandfather, William Gould. He was a British-born Canadian soldier. William was the only Canadian known to have been held as a prisoner of war by the Bulgarians. His journal was discovered in my grandmother's basement a few years ago. The journal details his entire three years of internment, but I write here only about the early part of his life as a prisoner.

# Tom's Tale

*John Dickenson*

I was baptised Thomas Abrahams, after my father, though I never
knew him. He died at Christmas 1894, before I was born, and my twin
brother George died within the year.

Me Mam was over forty when we were born, and she always seemed
old to me. She was pale, thin and poorly dressed. One of my sisters told
me Mam had had other children, besides us eight, but they'd died
young, like my little twin. Dad and George and perhaps some of the
others were buried in Toxteth Park Cemetery. Mam took me there
once, but there was nothing to see, because she was too poor to afford
gravestones. I remember a great big grim grey building on one side.
Mam told me it was Toxteth Workhouse, and that if things didn't get
better, we'd both end up there.

I was too young to know what went on after Dad died. It was pretty
complicated, so I don't know if Mam decided it all, or whether somebody else gave her advice about what to do with us. Isabella, who was
the oldest, was courting, and early in 1896 she married Philip Nelson,
a docker. Fred, who was born in 1883, was sent to join an old Navy
sailing ship moored in the Mersey, which was used to train sailors'
orphans for careers at sea. Sam, who was nine, went to the Bluecoat
School down in the town. It had been set up by a wealthy shipowner
for orphans and other poor children, to give them a basic education.
Elizabeth – who we all called Bessie – was eight, Percy six and Amy
four, and they were sent to Mrs. Louisa Birt's Liverpool Sheltering
Home. It was a place which took orphans and children like us to be

prepared to be sent to Canada for adoption or to work as farm labourers or domestic servants. As the youngest, I got to stay with Mam.

When I was six or seven, Mam took me down to the Pier Head, and pointed to several old-fashioned sailing ships moored in the River Mersey.

"That one's the *Indefatigable*," she said. "That's the one Fred was on."

He was a proper sailor by then, but he came home sometimes on leave, with tales of strange places he'd been to, and the tattoos to prove it. On the way back, Mam led me to a nice little square off the main street, with lots of smart gentlemen and ladies strolling about. Behind it was a very handsome old building.

"That's the Bluecoat, where our Sam was at school."

After he left there, Sam went away to Preston to join the South Lancashire Regiment as a boy soldier, and was sent to India.

For a while we lived in a court dwelling. It was horrible – a lot of cramped but tall houses round a courtyard with a narrow tunnel entrance. There wasn't much daylight, and there was a dirty gutter down the middle, and a water pump. At one end there were privies, which everybody used. They were supposed to be kept clean, but they made the whole courtyard stink. Mam took in a lodger for a bit of extra money. He was supposed to work at the docks, but he was around a lot, and I didn't like him. Mam had another baby, who she called Daisy. I didn't like her much either, because she cried all the time, which was awful in our tiny rooms.

We got a few letters from Percy or the girls, so we knew how they were getting on. Mam didn't read very well, so she had to get Isabella to help her. One day, when there seemed to be even less cash, and not much to eat, Mam said, "I think you'd better go to Mrs. Birt's."

At least I knew what she meant, and because the others had gone there, and then to Canada, I wasn't too scared.

So a few days later I was cleaned up and put in my best clothes, which had belonged to one of the others, and walked down there. I was still a bit nervous though, standing outside that large, ugly red-brick building, with its big gold-painted letters: **The Sheltering Home for Destitute Children. 1888.**

Eventually Mam pushed me in to where Mrs. Birt was waiting.

"Hallo, Thomas," she said.

She had a funny accent – I found out later she was Scottish – and she was wearing an elegant long dress and a small bonnet.

"Say goodbye to your mother, then I'll show you round."

Mam hugged me briefly against her thin, rough skirt, then left. Mrs. Birt took my hand to lead me to the dining room, the schoolrooms and the playground, and then up to the boys' dormitory. She pointed to a bed in the corner.

"If I remember rightly, that's where Percy slept. Perhaps you'd like to have the same bed."

I thought that was really nice.

I soon settled to the Home's routine. Mrs. Birt and her daughters and the other staff were strict, but not unkind. We had to be clean and punctual and polite. We had lessons in reading and writing and arithmetic, and about Canada. The boys had handicraft lessons, and the girls did cooking and stuff like that. A few times a man brought a horse into the yard, or a cow from one of the town dairies, and talked about looking after them. The food was good, or at least there was lots of it. Children came in at different times. Some were orphans or had lost one of their parents, like me, and were often sad and weepy. Some had been living rough and were brought in by the police or street missionaries. Others came from towns outside Liverpool, and a few had been in workhouses. Their stories made those places sound just as nasty as what Mam had said about the Toxteth Workhouse. A few didn't stay very long, because Mrs. Birt didn't think they were suitable to be sent to Canada. A lot were quite scared, because they were lonely and didn't know what was going to happen to them, so I was able to tell them what I knew about my brother and sisters. By the middle of June 1904 there were about sixty of us in the Home, more girls than boys, and one morning Mrs. Birt announced we would soon be sailing.

We were each given a green trunk with new clothes and a Bible, and few days later we marched down to the Pier Head. We were sailing in the *Ionian*, and once aboard, we shared six berth cabins, which was great fun. As we sailed, Mrs. Birt talked to each of us about what it would be like in Canada. She asked some of the others about their families, but she already knew a lot about mine. She told me that Bessie was a "domestic servant" at a place near the St. Lawrence with a funny French name – Chato-something, and that Amy was near to Knowlton, which is where we were going, so I hoped I would get to see her. She was a domestic servant too, but getting on with the family, so she was starting to use their surname. Percy was a bit farther away, at a place called Compton. He was supposed to have been adopted, but that didn't seem to have worked out.

After about ten days, we landed at Quebec, where we were inspected. The food at the Home and on the ship had filled me out, and the sea air had put some colour in my cheeks, so I was passed. Lots of the people around us spoke a strange language, but eventually a tall man with a moustache found us. He was Mr. Drummond, a teacher at Mrs. Birt's Distributing Home at Knowlton in the Eastern Townships.

We all got on a train. I had never been on one before, and it was noisy and bumpy, and smelled of smoke. I hadn't really seen country-side either, so I just stared through the window at the fields and small towns as we travelled through Quebec to Knowlton. The Home was a rambling old place on the edge of town, but it had a nice view of the lake. It had originally been given to Mrs. Birt's sister, Miss Annie Macpherson, who was one of the first people to send children like me to Canada. Some local politicians and businessmen thought it would be a good idea to bring in us youngsters to keep up the English population in French Quebec – and to provide cheap labour for the farmers and their wives! It seems to have been a success, because there were always more people wanting children than arrived in a party. Mostly we were spoken for before we arrived, so we were only in the home a few days.

My first placing didn't last very long. Despite what I had been taught at the Sheltering Home, I was nervous around the animals, and a bit clumsy. The farmer was impatient and couldn't understand my accent. I suppose I was a bit lippy, and he called me a "Liverpool loudmouth" and sent me back to the Home. My next place was a bit better, but it was a long way from Knowlton, so I couldn't get to see the others. Creenmore was across the St. Lawrence and up the Ottawa Valley. It was pretty rugged and rough up there, and the farming was hard. I did get moved around a bit, but I got pretty strong, and learned how to do my chores properly. Sometimes Mr. Drummond or one of the other staff would come on visits to check if I was properly looked after. I always said yes when they asked me.

It was alright. There was fresh air, not the stinking court; sometimes I even had my own room, even if it was a freezing cold attic. I got three square meals a day, and mostly I went to school, unless the farms were extra busy, with ploughing or the harvest.

Finally, I finished my years of service and was free to leave. There was a bit of a problem because, as well as providing my bed and board, the farmers were supposed to pay a sum of money each year for when I finished my indenture. It was supposed to be $24 the first year, $36 the second, and so on, to give me a nest egg to start my free life. There was some confusion because I had worked for several men, but eventually it was settled, and I got just over a hundred dollars.

Some Home Boys stayed locally, even with the farmers they had been placed with; others went to try their luck out west; some just wanted to get to the big city. I wanted something a bit different, so I went to work for a Mr. Anderson at Bristol Ridge, down in the valley. The land was better there, but though the Andersons had eight children, it was still hard work for us to raise the crops and look after the stock. The family were kind to me, and I was pleased when Mr. Anderson said to me one day, "You can't just be plain Thomas Abrahams. We'll add my name and call you Thomas William."

Eventually though, I decided to move on, so I went to Rockcliffe, just outside Ottawa. Despite my early problems with animals, I had got to like working with horses. I had made a little money, and with my nest egg, I set up as a teamster, hiring myself and my wagon to farmers and merchants to move crops, groceries and stuff between Gloucester County and Ottawa.

When the war broke out, I was over eighteen, so I could have gone off to enlist straight away, but I didn't. I was interested in a girl, though she wasn't too keen on me. She knew I was a Home Boy, and I guess sometimes I smelled a bit too much of horses. One day she said to me, "Why don't you go off and fight?"

I didn't think it would really make any difference to what she thought about me, but anyway, on September 23rd, 1915, I went off to the recruiting office in Rockcliffe and signed up. I was a bit unsure about my birth date, but my Apparent Age was recorded as 19 years, 8 months, and my height 5 foot 5, so I was fit to enlist. I was a bit stumped when they asked about next-of-kin, and in the end I gave Mr. Anderson as "friend", which he was, and because he was nearest.

I don't know if it was because I looked rugged, or because I knew about horses and wagons, but I was put into the 4th Draft Canadian Engineers. This meant we had to do all the basic training of marching and drill, then learn all the fighting stuff with rifles and bayonets like the infantry, and after all that we had to do all the engineering training about digging trenches and latrines, building roads and bridges and railways, and laying water supplies and drainage. At least a lot of the slog in that was like farm work. Then we got shipped to England, though not through Liverpool, and there was more drilling, and rifle practice, and more digging dugouts, trenches and latrines, and building roads and tramways. Eventually, we got sent to France, and through 1916 we got moved around a lot, sometimes to quiet areas to repair trenches and roads, but if something big was on, like Mount Sorrel or the Canadian part in the Somme, we would be making roads and railways, digging trench systems and emplacements for the big guns, and providing the basics for the infantry. In September and October we were around Pozières. My brother Fred got his Blighty wound there. He had migrated to Canada on his own and joined up a few months before me. Courcelette and Regina Trench was non-stop bloody hard work, and towards the end the weather made it even worse.

After that I got into trouble for the first time, for going Absent Without Leave for a few hours. I got seven days Field Punishment Number 1, which was pretty unpleasant. For two hours each day I was tied to a wagon wheel, whatever the weather. It depended who tied me up; some NCOs were pretty good and didn't do the ropes too tight, but some bastards really lashed me up, so I could hardly move, and some so-called friends would come and joke. I didn't think it was very bloody funny.

I don't know if it was because of that, but in January 1917, I got transferred out of the Engineers to the 13th Battalion, who were billeted near Bethune. I became a Poor Bloody Infantryman, but, as the Royal Highlanders of Canada, the 13th wore kilts! Kilts? What sort of idiots wore kilts in the trenches? However, I wasn't with them long, because early in February we got called on parade, and the sergeant said, "Right, you men, General Haig wants some husky Canadians to help his men dig holes in the ground so we can blow up the Hun. I need a hundred volunteers."

Nobody moved.

"Right," said the sergeant, "First four ranks, two paces forward."

Bugger! We gathered our kit, and got on lorries to Ypres, and then marched three miles to near Saint Eloi to join the 1st Canadian Tunnelling Company.

I HATED being a tunneller. From the first morning, when we tumbled down the ladders into the ill-lit, cramped space at the bottom, and were led to the workface down a gallery so low I couldn't stand up straight, I loathed it all. I didn't mind the work – long hours and hard physical labour were no problem, but I had done that in the fresh air and open fields of my farm placements. I hated being under the ground, the narrow tunnels, the near-darkness, the foul air, the dripping walls, the trickles of loose earth, the sound of shells exploding nearby. And I was afraid. Afraid of roof falls, flooding water, gas, German counter-mines, of breaking into their tunnels and having to fight them in such alien places. Not long after I arrived the Huns blew a counter-mine, which damaged our galleries, and another on April 7th killed four men, and let in a lot of gas. We hated the monoxide gas most of all. You couldn't see it, or smell it, or taste it, but it could do nasty things to you, and kill you very quickly. I think I got some then, and there were other gas incidents. Anyway, soon after that I started to get headaches and stomach pains, and I would wake up cold, wet and twitching. I also had spells of feeling very sorry for myself. But a lot of us were like that, so we just carried on.

Eventually, on June 7th, the mines were blown, which sure made a mess of the Hun trenches, and allowed our boys to capture Messines. That fighting didn't involve us, and we were put on surface work, building roads, trenches, dugouts and the like in the Wipers area. In October I was transferred out of the Tunnelling Company, and almost immediately I began to get into trouble again. My nerves were shot, and from early December I was almost constantly AWOL, in confinement, or receiving field punishment. I just wanted to get away from the noises, the smells, the trenches and the ruined brown landscapes. These weren't planned escapes; they were spontaneous. I simply wanted open air and green fields. I don't think I ever planned to go very far, and always intended to go back. Of course, I had little money and no kit, and once I got into the fields and villages a few miles behind the lines, I was very conspicuous, and got stopped by officers or picked up by the Military Police, and returned to the battalion.

After each of my offences I would be paraded before the C.O., and each time he would ask me why I had done it. I would say, "Don't know, sir."

I didn't. I couldn't explain it. I couldn't say I was sometimes confused. I wasn't afraid to fight. I wasn't a coward, but something from those months underground bothered me, so I just wanted space and freedom. Then, to everyone's astonishment, including mine and the sergeant's, in February I got a Blighty leave! It was a time to forget, in a dream world of fresh air, relative quiet, no lice, clean clothes, proper beds, going to pubs, dance halls or the theatre. It goes without saying that the temptation was too great. When my leave ended on March 3rd, I didn't go back. I stayed another ten days, but eventually, even in a city thronged with soldiers from Britain, Australia, South Africa, New Zealand and India, the Military Police managed to pick out one solitary Canadian who had overstayed his time. Being absent so long after a leave was a serious offence, and I got a proper Field General Court Martial, with senior officers and even a defence lawyer – not that he was really interested or helpful – so I got eleven days loss of pay and sixty days Field Punishment.

I had already been in confinement for several weeks, and this was a very long sentence, and I found being locked up and tied up day after day unbearable, so in the middle of May I took a chance to escape from the detention hut. I was on the run for eleven days, but eventually I turned myself in back at the battalion. When he saw me, the sergeant poured out a torrent of abuse.

"Abrahams, I didn't think even you were that fucking stupid! Escaping from court martial! With a record like yours, they'll be delighted to put you up against the bloody wall. There's a big push coming up, and bloody Field Marshal Haig gets very trigger-happy before an attack. He likes to make sure everybody's up for the fight. Pour encoorargez lez ootrez! They've shot twenty-one good Canadian boys for desertion or cowardice already, and they did for a Van Doo only a couple of weeks ago. The brass are going to just love a record like yours."

Hearing those words, even in my addled state, I realised how bloody stupid I had been. With my previous offences, going AWOL on leave, and escaping from imprisonment while under a court martial sentence was certain to get me in big trouble! They had me up on two different charges. I don't remember much about the trial, though I had a different lawyer, and I don't know if the C.O. or the M.O. said anything about my problems. Anyway, they didn't waste much time, and when the presiding officer said, "Guilty" I was sure what was coming next – the sudden end of Thomas Abrahams. To my amazement however, he said, "Fifty-six days Field Punishment #1 and stoppages."

When I went on the run I always left most of my kit behind. The other times it was there when I got back, but this time it had got lost (or nicked) so I had to pay the army £7/17/8d for a new rifle and bayonet, pack, bits of uniform, and mess tins! Because of my record the NCOs gave me a really hard time with the field punishment, but this time I stuck it out, and eventually I got sent back to the battalion, near Arras. This was a good spell, because they were mostly out of the line, and we spent our time training, in sport, and having entertainments.

At the beginning of August we set off south, by bus, train and long marches, to near Amiens. On the 8th we were at Hangard Wood, as part of a major attack and we made a very successful advance. I discovered later that my brother Percy had been in the battalion next to us. He died gallantly that day. Over the next ten days we kept pushing the Huns back, and advanced about twelve miles. Then we were pulled back, and transported north to the outskirts of Arras. This was to prepare for another big push, but I didn't get to see any of it. At the end of August we were in rough ground, mainly sheltering in shell holes, with no hot food, and subject to gas attacks and heavy shelling. We had got used to the sound of our guns and the German retaliation, but on the 31st there was an almighty bang near me and I felt excruciating pain in my legs. I had been hit by a bit of shrapnel, which smashed both bones in my lower right leg.

I must have passed out. I don't remember much of the next few days, but I suppose I was picked up by the stretcher-bearers and taken to a field ambulance. I remember being bumped around on a train, and then the smell of the seaside at Boulogne. What happened next was very confused, but I remember being peered at by doctors and nurses, drugged, and waking to even worse pain. Eventually they told me that they had taken off part of my leg.

After about two weeks I was shipped to England, still in great pain, despite the drugs they gave me. There were more peering doctors, and eventually they told me that the surgery hadn't worked, and they needed to take some more off! Bugger! So more drugs, surgery and pain. I spent the next four months in hospitals and convalescent homes in the south, being treated, getting used to hopping with a crutch, and being fitted for a false leg.

In January 1919 I was sent up north to Buxton. Though my stump ached all the time, and using the crutches was knackering, I went AWOL three times, for over a month altogether. They scarcely got me back before I was off again, but they could hardly string a one-legged man up on field punishments, so I got stopped thirty-five days' pay. When I was in France I could never explain why I went AWOL, but now I was back in England I wanted constantly to be free and away from the military. Perhaps, after whatever had disturbed me from the tunnel work, things got worse with the shock of being wounded, the agony of the train journey across France, the terrible pain of my lost leg, and then the horror of being told it needed to be done again.

In March I got sent to the Canadian Hospital at Kirkdale in north Liverpool, so I could visit me Mam. I also went back to the Sheltering Home a few times. Old Mrs. Birt had died during the war, but her daughter, Miss Lilian, remembered me. They had stopped sending children in 1915, and the house had been used as a military hospital, but she said they hoped to start again next year. She told me that they thought over seventy of our boys had died in the war, two of them from my ship. Willie Brereton made sergeant and was killed at the Somme when I was there. The other one, Henry Calverly or something like that, was invalided back and died of the 'flu out west.

Finally, they decided to send me back to Canada, and I sailed off down the Mersey again. Three days out, we were summoned to parade on deck. When I hopped to the front, the sergeant said, "Where do you want to be discharged to?"

"What do you mean, Sarge?"

"Because of your long and distinguished service, His Majesty is kindly pleased to pay to deposit you wherever you wish to go." He looked at my crutch and stump, and said with a hint of kindness, "For you, my lad, I suggest somewhere near a decent hospital."

I thought quickly. I no longer knew anyone in the Townships, and Bristol was a bit remote. I had heard that both Bessie and Amy were having marriage difficulties, so I didn't want to burden them with a one-legged brother as well. Besides, where they were living, in Belleville and Brome, were probably not the best places for amputees with nerve problems.

"I guess it had better be Toronto."

He raised an eyebrow.

"Got family there?"

"No, but they probably have the best hospitals for one-legged nutcases."

We were landed in Portland Maine, but when I got back to Canada, I spent a lot more time in hospitals. Eventually, in December 1919 I had a medical, where the medics reviewed the treatments I had for my leg – but not my mind. They decided that I had "a good stump" with "a suitable artificial leg", and discharged me with a "War Service Gratuity - No Dependents"! I got a place in Toronto on Dupont. It wasn't much, but money was tight. I couldn't work with horses again, or go back to farming, and there wasn't much call for one-legged hole-diggers! Things didn't get any easier in Toronto in the twenties, especially for a crippled vet, so I came out west. It wasn't much better, but at least I got married. It didn't last, though. I suppose it was pretty hard on a woman, being married to a cripple on a measly war pension. I couldn't get much of a job, and couldn't hold one for long, what with my nightmares and the bad times. We had a boy. We called him Fred Percy, after the brothers. He went off to the second war and got captured at Hong Kong. He spent most of the war in a bloody POW camp in Japan. When I got to see him after, he never talked about it much.

I read in the papers that some people were saying nasty things about Home Children. They said we were 'bad stock' and genetically inferior – whatever that means! They said we were polluting the purity of the Canadian Race. Some doctor in Toronto claimed we were British riffraff and that Home Girls became tarts, and a Miss Whitton reckoned us immigrant children were feeble-minded, diseased criminals! Anyway, by the mid-twenties the two governments had decided to stop migrating children.

I know I was having some problems, but I got them fighting in their bloody war! Christ! I gave them two chunks of my bloody leg. What more did they want? We all did our bit. Percy gave them his life, and he got a medal for his gallantry. He's buried in the communal cemetery in a little village in France, and there's a memorial to him in the local *mairie,* so at least the military and the Froggies thought he was pretty good. Sam and Fred weren't Home Boys, but they were ready to fight too! Sam was ex-regular, so the British called him up as soon as the war started. He was one of them "Old Contemptibles", and got killed early on. He had a wife and I think there were kiddies, too. He doesn't even have a grave, so he's listed on the Menin Gate in Wipers. There's lots of good Canadians on there, too. Fred got knocked about a bit, but at least he got back. He went off to sea again, and finished up living in

B.C., near Isabella and her family. Genetically inferior? Bollocks! Not the Abrahams! We did more than our bit for King and Empire – and for Canada.

*Author's Note*

I am deeply grateful to Mary Monks Hatch of British Columbia, whose extensive family history research includes five generations of the Abrahams family. The surname is variously given as Abram, Abrams, Abraham and Abrahams in British and Canadian records, with Abrahams seemingly the most common usage.

6441 Pte. Samuel Abrahams. Second Battalion, South Lancashire Regiment. Killed in Action 13 November 1914. Known unto God. Listed on the Ypres ( Menin Gate) Memorial.

77972 Sgt. Frederick Abrahams. 16th Battalion, CEF. Wounded Mouquet Farm, 5 September 1916. Died 19 August 1959, Victoria, B.C.

748749 Pte. Percival Abraham, MM. 16th Battalion, CEF. Killed in Action 8 August 1918. Buried Hangard Communal Cemetery Extension.

500495 Pte. Thomas William Abraham. 13th Battalion, CEF. Wounded near the Drocourt-Queant Line 31 August 1918. Died 9 December 1957, Winnipeg, Manitoba.

# The Ross Rifle

*Vicki Delany*

The Canadian-made Ross Rifle was a great weapon for hunting deer, but they were not hunting deer out here. They needed a weapon that would kill men.

Not only did the magazine on the Ross hold only one clip of cartridges, whereas the British Lee-Enfields took two, but the bolt was notorious for jamming in the ever-present dirt of trench warfare, and the safety catch cut more than one man's thumb. Worst of all, it was too long and too heavy for fighting in close confinement.

The soldiers hated it.

But Sir Charles Ross was a friend of Sam Hughes who was the man in charge of procurement for the army. That his rifle wasn't up to doing the job didn't seem to matter to the politicians back in Ottawa.

*April 1915. Belgium. The Ypres Salient. The Second Battle of Ypres.*

Private Henry Hall of the Winnipeg Light Infantry had survived the five hellish days of that battle, but he figured that if he was to get through any more he had to find himself a better weapon, one way or the other. The British troops were armed with Lee-Enfields, which were far superior to the Canadian weapon, as far as the soldiers were concerned.

Hall had turned twenty-one the previous Valentine's Day, but was so short and slight he had once been accused by an officer of being the regiment's mascot. In later years, he found it difficult to remember the days and nights of the Second Battle of Ypres. The chaos and confusion, the noise of shells constantly roaring overhead or exploding nearby, of men screaming in pain, in fear, or in an attempt to bolster their courage. The horrendous casualties as men fell around him. All of this on a diet of nothing but canned bully beef and very hard biscuits with only water to drink and very little sleep, made it impossible, even at the time, for him to fully grasp what was going on. Over those five days, all of their officers except for two had been killed, and Hall and the remnants of his 1st Division were ordered behind the lines to be reorganized.

The end of the battle came as a welcome relief for the survivors. They eyed each other warily, checking out who was no longer with them, hefted their rifles and kits, and climbed, gratefully, out of the trenches. The trenches were filthy, noisy, crowded, often full of water, but this early in the war at least they weren't full of rats. The rats came later when piles of rotting bodies were available to feast upon.

The men weren't able to find a farmhouse or village with spare billets, so Hall and his platoon wound up sleeping out in the open. They simply threw their exhausted bodies down on the grass of a farmer's meadow. But they were dry, if not exactly warm, and safe. For awhile. To everyone's intense relief, that most valuable member of any troop – the cook – found them and they were able to enjoy their first hot cooked meal in a long time. They even had tea, although there was no milk or sugar to accompany it. To have something warm inside was a joy indeed.

His father had died when Henry was twelve, and he quit school in order to find work to help support the family, but all his life he had a voracious appetite for reading, for politics and world affairs, and an intense interest in everyone and everything around him.

It was no different that day in April, during a break from battle and trench warfare. In the meadow near them, resting as they were, Hall spotted a group of dark-skinned men wearing turbans. Ghurka. Indian Army soldiers.

"Let's pay those chaps a visit."

"Why?" replied Hector McIvor, a large tough Scotsman. McIvor had been in Canada for all of three months when war broke out in

Europe. He'd enlisted immediately. McIvor and a fellow Scot by the name of Duncan Cross were Hall's two best friends, and they'd stayed close since leaving Winnipeg.

"Because they're interesting." Hall stood up. "I bet they have stories to tell. Do you have something better to do, then?"

"No." McIvor and Cross exchanged glances. Nothing better than to rest and get some sleep. But they pushed themselves to their feet, and the three young men crossed the field. Hall shouted and waved in greeting as they approached.

The Ghurka were tall, heavily-bearded men, with dark faces and black eyes. Foreign and somewhat frightening looking in their turbans, although their uniforms were British. They were delighted to have visitors and made the Canadians welcome. They even shared their food – a small round pancake cooked over an open fire.

"This is good," Hall said truthfully. McIvor and Cross nibbled at the food cautiously before wolfing it down. The Indians beamed.

"Where are you chaps from?" Hall asked. He couldn't help but notice that they were equipped with Lee-Enfield rifles.

The men, most of whom spoke English, named places Hall had never heard of. Towns and cities with exotic names, full of the flavor of spices, colourfully dressed women, and steaming tropical sunshine.

"This place," the largest of the Ghurka said, shaking his head so hard his beard shook, "is cold. So cold."

Everyone nodded silently. The Lahore Regiment fought only one battle in Europe. They simply couldn't bear the weather – and were not equipped for it in any event – and soon shipped off to the Middle East.

The men – the Canadian with the boyish build, the giant Scots, the burley, battle-hardened Indians – shared their food and talked about home and better times, about families and warmth and comfort.

At last Hall stood up. Duncan and Hector followed. The men all shook hands. They did not exchange words of luck or wishes for survival. Words were of no help out there.

\* \* \*

Hall woke after a rough night on bare ground. Fortunately it hadn't rained, and no one was shooting at him. He knew to be grateful for small luxuries. Duncan and Hector were still asleep, snoring loudly. Hall eyed his rifle. That hated Ross. Canadian casualties at Ypres had been enormous, and Hall knew that he and his friends were lucky to still be in one piece. But a man needed more than luck.

He needed a better rifle.

He swallowed a quick breakfast of hard, flavourless dried biscuits washed down with a mouthful of tepid water and set out at a gentle pace between the ranks of sleeping and stretching men.

The best place to find a rifle, he figured, would be at the casualty station. Plenty of soldiers there who wouldn't need their weapons any more. Some of the walking wounded might have brought their rifles with them and left them unguarded while they were being treated.

The advanced dressing station at Essex Farm was little more than a few rough rooms cut into the banks of the canal. Small, crowded, ill-lit, low-roofed, and dirty, this was the place where it is believed John McCrae wrote "In Flanders Fields". But Hall wasn't thinking of poppies row on row as he made his solitary way several kilometers across formerly lush farmers' fields and roads that were now little more than muddy tracks. Clouds were heavy overhead, but the rain didn't fall. He closed his eyes for a few seconds and tried to imagine that he was back home in Winnipeg. Walking with his mother in a leafy city park maybe, or taking a stroll outside of town with a young lady. Not that he had a young lady, not yet. It had always seemed as though there would be plenty of time. He pushed the thought away.

Three of his mother's four sons were in the army. Fred was also in the Winnipeg Light Infantry, although in another regiment. Fred, too, was somewhere in Belgium. Ted was with the Scottish Rifles. When last heard from he'd been heading for the Mediterranean. Fred's Regiment, the 8th, Henry knew, had seen some heavy fighting at Ypres. Word had spread fast through the army that the Germans were using a dreadful new weapon. A yellow-green gas that moved like a blanket across the open fields and mud of no-mans-land, rolling over entire armies and drifting silently into trenches. Men either died where they sought shelter, or fled, eyes and throats feeling as though they were on fire.

Fortunately, Hall and his division had not been exposed to the gas. Rumour said the French had got the worst of it. He hoped Fred had been well clear.

As he approached the dressing station, he felt a grin spread across his face. He was in luck. A Ghurka, not one of the men he'd met the previous night, was coming from the opposite direction. The Indian walked slowly, his arm cradled in a filthy sling. Deep lines of pain were written on his dark face. He carried a Lee-Enfield in his good arm.

While Hall watched, the Ghurka propped his rifle and bayonet on the wall outside a medical hut, and ducked through its low doorway. The dressing station was a sea of barely-organized confusion. The walking wounded staggered in for help; others were carried on stretchers by their fellows. Doctors, nurses and orderlies hurried about their business, and ambulances were being loaded to take men in need of further medical care behind the lines. In all the activity and disorder, Henry Hall was just one amongst so many; no one paid any attention to the small Canadian soldier. He quickly took his bayonet and scabbard off the Ross, put them and the useless Canadian rifle up against the wall, grabbed the Lee-Enfield, along with its bayonet and scabbard, and ran for it.

No one stopped him.

"What the hell have you got there, Henry?" Duncan called to him as he reappeared in their patch of meadow.

Hall grinned and held up his prize. "See for yourself."

"How'd you manage that?" Hector asked.

Hall shrugged modestly, and explained.

For the next couple of days, Canadian soldiers hung around the dressing station. A major attack by British territorial forces had resulted in enormous casualties and the dressing station was overwhelmed. Ross rifles were surreptitiously exchanged, mostly not for Lee-Enfields, but Lee-Metfords – not quite as desirable, but better than the hated

Canadian Ross. For the rest of his time on the Western Front Henry Hall's platoon fought with three different rifles. Fortunately, they all used the same ammunition.

All too soon the rest period was over, new officers arrived, the division was reorganized, and Hall, Cross, and McIvor were returned to the front lines.

The next time they were withdrawn, they were billeted in a barn near the Belgian village of Abele. The farm was small, and looked to have been – even before the war – not at all prosperous. The barn was old, ill-maintained and drafty, but it was better than an open meadow. And infinitely better than a slot in a trench. The Canadians were delighted to find that the farmhouse had been turned into an *estaminet* – a small cafe.

The men had been paid the day before. Hall had never been a drinker, and he wasn't about to start now, but more than a few of his companions immediately spent most of their pay on drink. And more than a few of them couldn't handle it too well, not after weeks of sobriety. Fights broke out, between soldiers, between soldiers and military police, and between soldiers and the townsmen and farmers.

The afternoon following their arrival, Hall slipped into the estaminet in search of a break from milk-less tea and army rations. The daughter of the house, young and pretty but with wary eyes, was serving, along with the wine and brandy, watery coffee and fresh bread. Her English appeared to be good and, interested in people as always, Hall started up a conversation when she dropped his food onto the scarred wooden table in front of him. The bread was excellent, crusty on the outside, soft and white on the inside. The best thing he'd had to eat in weeks.

"Heard you had some Germans in the district before our lot," he said, simply because he was curious.

"Yes."

"Did you meet any of them?"

"A cavalry regiment camped out in our field for a few nights."

"What were they like?"

She tossed her long dark hair and gave him a look that would have curdled the milk in his coffee. If they'd had any milk. "Better behaved than you." She turned at a shout and walked away without another word.

Hall finished his snack and left, making no more attempts at conversation.

Back at the barn, Hector McIvor was propped up on his bed in the straw chewing on the end of his pencil as he struggled to write a letter. He looked up when Hall entered, stamping farm muck off his boots. "Got some news for you, Henry."

"What?"

"One of our chaps ran into a couple of fellows from the 8th earlier, in town. I knew you'd want to know."

Hall ran out of the barn. Like every other place in Europe he'd been in, Abele was a churning mass of soldiers and horses, numerous languages, equipment, fleeing women, children and old men. But common soldiers are good at keeping track of each other and he was soon directed to the 8th Battalion's billets.

He didn't have to go far before he recognized a man up ahead. It was a sergeant, a friend of Fred's he'd met before leaving England. Hall broke into a run, shouting at the sergeant to hold up. The man turned. He recognized Hall immediately, and his face fell. Hall stopped running. He didn't have to be told the news.

The sergeant touched his arm.

"He's dead?"

"Yeah. Morning of the 24th. Fred was killed out in no-man's land. Got a bullet to the head. We had to leave him there. Leave him for the Germans to bury. I'm sorry, Henry."

Hall nodded.

"Your brother was a good man. And a brave one. He saved a couple of men, wounded men who couldn't get back to our trench. The last one he went out for died with him, though." The sergeant spat into the dirt. "Everything okay with you and your lot?"

"Yeah."

"Got yourself a good rifle, I see. That'll see you through."

* * *

From Abele, the Winnipeg Light Infantry was sent south, into France.

Henry Hall's war ended a few weeks later. In May of 1915, he was wounded at the Battle of Festubert. He spent several months in a convalescent hospital in Glasgow before being returned to Winnipeg. It was in that Scottish hospital where he learned that his brother, Company Sergeant Major Frederick William Hall, had been awarded the Victoria Cross for his actions under enemy fire on April 24th, 1915.

Hector McIvor and Duncan Cross were both killed in action in 1917. Henry Hall died in 1985 at the age of 92.

Henry Hall was my grandfather. And I wonder, sometimes, if I'd be here today if he hadn't found that Lee-Enfield resting against a wall at a casualty dressing station at Ypres. I wonder, also, about that Ghurka. Did he go back for his rifle, only to find that it had been swapped for an inferior one? Or was he lucky enough – or unlucky enough – to never need his rifle again?

# Honouring an Unsung Hero:
## George Hilton Soles

*Frances Hern*

The Great War was nicknamed by some The Chemists' War. The chemical revolution of the previous century that helped reduce infant mortality and increase average life expectancy also paved the way for the most destructive war in history. The First World War was fought with hardened steel, high explosives, flame-throwers and poison gas. Roughly 400,000 Canadians went overseas between 1914 and 1918. Of these, 60,000 never returned. Many of those who did return had dreadfully disfiguring scars, missing limbs, lungs drowning in their own fluids, or were mentally broken. War was a nightmare but it also gave some, often unassuming and seemingly ordinary individuals, a chance to show what they were made of. George Soles was one of them.

George Hilton Soles was born on April 7th, 1894, to Wesleyan parents Richard Hilton Soles and Elizabeth Margaret Storie, in Boulter, in Carlow Township, Hastings County, Ontario. George was the middle child, with three older brothers and three younger sisters. The Soles family were loggers who made railroad ties. They might well have stayed in Ontario if tragedy had not struck the extended family two years after George was born.

His Uncle Andrew was cleaning a gun when it accidentally went off and killed one of his uncle's younger sisters. That same year the uncle lost his infant daughter. Overcome with grief, he could no longer stay in his family home. He made his way west, worked on the Crowsnest Pass railway, then travelled on to Golden. When Andrew found work there, he sent for his wife and children. His brother Richard, along with Richard's wife, son George and his siblings, followed him to British Columbia a couple of years later and settled in Castledale, just south of present day Parson near Golden. Like many others in the Columbia Valley, the Soles family were also farmers and, when George left school, farming became his full-time occupation.

Along with his older brother Bill and cousins Jack and Ed, George Soles enlisted in the Canadian army in March 1915, just before his 21st birthday. He stood 5' 8" tall with brown hair and grey eyes. Initially he was assigned to the 48th Canadian Infantry Battalion and sailed for England July 1st where they resumed training. In January 1916 the 48th was re-designated 3rd Canadian Pioneer Battalion.

The Pioneer Battalions worked in conjunction with the engineers in the forward area where they consolidated positions captured by the infantry. They tunnelled, mined, and wired. They dug trenches and kept them in repair.

In March 1916 the 3rd Pioneers sailed for France and the following spring Lt.-General Sir Julian Byng and Major-General Arthur Currie sent all four divisions of the Canadian Corps to capture Vimy Ridge in Northern France. The ridge, approximately seven kilometres in length, was held by the Germans and gave them an uninterrupted sight line of all enemy advances across the surrounding Douai Plain. The Allies could only see beyond the crest and into enemy territory from the air, where they were exposed to enemy guns. British and French forces had already attempted to take Vimy Ridge and suffered horrendous casualties. However Currie and Byng had experienced previous massacres and, determined not to repeat them, had devised a different approach. At the end of four days, the Canadians had taken Vimy Ridge but this formidable task took weeks of planning and training and it was in the days leading up to the attack that George Soles earned his Distinguished Conduct Medal (D.C.M.) for marked courage and good leadership during operations near Cambrai.

The article that appeared in *The London Gazette* on March 28, 1918, reported that on September 29th, when the left flank was held up during a manoevre, Soles led his men to the right until he was close enough to take out a German machine gun, kill eight of the enemy, and take another eighteen prisoner. Soles told it somewhat differently:

*I had been wounded in the head and figured the best I could do was to make for a dressing station. I started back, threw away all my equipment and was well into the village trench when I suddenly saw a German sentry. He was standing guard at the entrance of a deep dug-out. I had to pass him, but I didn't have a rifle. I scouted back a few yards, found an abandoned German rifle, and sneaked back, put it against the German's back, and said "Hands up". He couldn't understand English, but he knew the feel of cold steel. He dropped his rifle.*

*There was a pile of hand grenades near the sentry and I could see the entrance to the dug-out. "How many?" I signalled, holding up my hand, fingers spread, and pointing to the dug-out with the rifle. Fritzie wasn't dull. He put up eight fingers and two thumbs, four times, closed both hands, and then held up two fingers. Forty-three, including the sentries. I thought I might as well take them along, because if I don't Fritzie will get me after I pass. So I pointed to a box of hand grenades standing near the sentry, and then motioned for him to tell his comrades to come up, or else. And he understood. He yelled something in German. I guess it meant come up and give up. Anyway, up came forty-two Germans, unarmed and with their hands reaching. I took them along and later was awarded the D.C.M.*

These two accounts hardly sound as though they detail the same event. Perhaps Soles was being modest, however he was commended for conspicuous gallantry and devotion to duty.

The 72nd Battalion, a light infantry regiment known as The Seaforth Highlanders of Canada, was left with only eleven officers and sixty-two men after Vimy Ridge. George Soles was one of the Canadians seconded to this regiment. His regimental dress became the kilt and Glengarry cap.

Soles' new battalion took part in the Hundred Days Offensive, and during one particular attack a British tank fell behind the advancing infantry. In the confusion created by mist and smoke, the tank began to fire on the Canadians in front of it, mistaking them for the enemy. Soles took off his helmet, balanced it on top of his bayonet and ran through a storm of bullets to grab the attention of the tank's operators at which point they realized their mistake and redirected their fire onto the enemy. For his actions, Soles was awarded a bar to his D.C.M.

Acting Sergeant-Major Soles of "A" Company was awarded a second bar to his D.C.M. for his actions on September 29th. He rushed an enemy strong point single-handedly and captured three machine guns. He later worked his way along a railway cutting and shot eight of the enemy. Following this, Soles positioned one hundred and twenty men to block an enemy counter-attack. The counter-attack was successfully repelled although Soles was one of only eighteen men to survive. Against the odds, his brother Bill and two cousins also survived to return home.

After the war ended, the 72nd Battalion returned to Canada and, in 1919, was demobilized. On August 20th of that year Soles married Eleanor Victoria Brett, a twenty-two year old British Columbia woman, and their son Frederick, the first of four children, was born the following year. However, the postwar years in Canada were not easy. When the soldiers returned home from Europe, they unwittingly brought the Spanish influenza with them, and over a two-year period 50,000 Canadians died of it. Added to the 60,000 war dead, this left many families without a primary wage-earner and thousands of children orphaned. On top of this, booming factories that had churned out bullets, shells, ships and aircraft ran out of work and had to close. Unemployment went up, while wages went down. With a young family to support, Soles found a steady job with the British Columbia Provincial Police (BCPP), where he stayed for twenty years.

Soles' final career was cut short when he suffered a heart attack after chasing a suspected criminal over miles of rough country. As he was not yet fifty, perhaps his injury and years in the trenches were finally taking their toll, or perhaps his heart had never been that strong to begin with. Either way, he decided he was no longer up to the task, and retired in 1943. He passed away on July 26, 1945 and was buried at Mountain View Cemetery in British Columbia.

Six years before this, however, in 1939, King George VI, accompanied by Queen Elizabeth, the queen mother, made the first visit to Canada by a reigning monarch and Soles was asked to be a security guard. He had to travel to Ottawa, and was expected to wear his medals, so he dug them out and polished them. Eleanor, his wife, had never seen nor heard about them them before. She had no idea that her husband was a well-decorated hero.

The D.C.M. was awarded to Warrant Officers, non-commissioned officers, and men serving in any of the English sovereign's military forces, for distinguished conduct in the field. It was the second highest award for gallantry in action, after the Victoria Cross, for all military ranks below commissioned officers. A silver bar with laurels on it was awarded for a subsequent act or acts of distinguished conduct in the field. Between the Crimean War (1853-1856) and 1993, 2,132 awards of the D.C.M. were made to Canadian Army and RCAF personnel, along with 38 first bars. George Hilton Soles is the only Canadian to have been awarded a second bar.

Names of Canadian heroes such as General Arthur Currie, field surgeon John McCrae, and flying ace Wilfrid 'Wop' May, live on in our culture and in our history books. Many of those who died during the Great War are remembered on cenotaphs around the country. Other heroes are remembered only by their families. George Hilton Soles will be remembered forever in Golden, British Columbia.

By the end of the Great War, the revulsion against chemical weapons ran so deep that organizations have been working to ban and eliminate them worldwide ever since. Sadly, the Great War was not "the war to end all wars" and when global conflict broke out again in 1939, the Great War was renamed World War One.

*Author's Note*

Besides printed resources, I am indebted to the Soles family members (Dan Soles, Jean Dakin, and Darcy Soles) and to Colleen Palumbo, curator of the Golden and District Museum, for support in the writing of this essay.

# Broken Bird

*Jean Ryan*

"You're going home."

"You're the lucky one."

"Wish I was goin' with you Maude."

I heard those comments as though I had cotton wool in my ears. I was boarding the ship for the final trip back to Canada and all I could think of was getting to a bunk and sleeping until we docked. I felt neither lucky nor joyful. I felt instead as if anything I may have done had made no difference at all and that the horrors continued even as our ship went underway.

Almost four years had passed since I completed the process of recruitment into the Regular Army. I remember it so clearly now, that day in August, the day we heard that England had declared war.

All the boys I knew growing up had rushed to enlist, and most of the able-bodied men too. It seemed that everyone was doing something. Then I learned that they were asking for nurses.

My mother was surprised when I came through the door of our house. I wasn't emotional by nature. I had always been the calm, practical, reliable one, even as a child I had never acted in haste. "Mamma, Mamma. I'm signing up!" I called out.

"Signing up? What're you talking about Maudie?"

"They need nurses in the war and I want to go. If they accept my application, I'll have to undergo a physical examination and then training."

"I suggest you think this over very carefully, my girl. You're doing good work here, Maudie. I don't know if going overseas is a good idea. Where would you be going? Not near the battlefields?!"

"Mamma, I am almost forty years old. I've never been farther than Toronto. I've had a good life, but an ordinary one. This is an opportunity to do something for the Dominion, to support our troops in the fight against tyranny. Besides, now that Great Britain is in the war, it'll be over in a few months. I want to do my part."

"You're not going over there to make a spectacle of yourself like those women in England I hope."

"No Mamma. I'm not going to starve myself or parade in the streets. All I want to do is what I'm trained for and have been doing for all these years. I expect they'll want nurses with good experience, and I have that.

"Look at me Mamma I am unfashionably tall and thin and truth be told, I'm set in my ways. I'm a spinster with no prospects. If I do this I will feel that I've accomplished something meaningful in my life."

And so it was that on September 24th, 1914, I found myself on a train to Quebec. Other than noting that I was taller than most, narrow in the chest and had scars from kidney surgery years ago, they had little to say during the physical examination. I heard references to my eyes being blue (they all agreed on that), but my hair presented a challenge. The descriptions varied from fair, to brown to dark brown. I suppose mouse brown was not among the choices.

Those of us who were declared to be in good physical condition were directed to go for training. In my ignorance I wondered what they could possibly teach me that I hadn't learned early on and through experience. The training turned out to be military training: a new set of terminology, forms of address, the ranking system, and the behavioural expectations of a nursing sister. We were informed that we were Lieutenants in the Canadian Army Medical Corps and given uniforms of pale blue with white aprons and sheer white veils.

I wrote home with some regularity during that time and I'm sure that Mamma prayed that orders to depart would never come, that I would stay here and care for the soldiers that were sent home.

In the evenings, the nurses often talked about sailing to Britain. My only experience on the water was as a girl in small boats on the Grand River. I'd never expected to see England and now it seemed likely that I would see France as well. Of course we wouldn't be going on the Grand Tour like some of the prominent families in Toronto, but I would be travelling more than anyone I knew back home.

The other topic of discussion centred on what awaited us on a more personal basis. I laughed with the younger women who shared their dreams of caring for a brave soldier, falling in love and going home as a bride. Their heroes of course all looked like Douglas Fairbanks or even Max Linder in the uniform of the Canadian Expeditionary Forces. I had no such illusions; I just wanted to help the soldiers as best I could.

The day finally came and we began our voyage. It took about ten days and with each passing evening, the tension grew. We landed near Liverpool and were then transported across the country. England was a blur of moving scenes through clouded windows.

The next step was being sent to the theatre of war in France, where we were first assigned to hospitals. Those in charge took little time to realize that the number of casualties far exceeded expectations and additional facilities were required. Casualty Clearing Stations were established to accept those whose injuries were too severe or complex to be treated at the Front.

As one of the most experienced sisters, I was sent to a Clearing Station in October of 1915. Nothing could have prepared us for what we were to experience over the next months and years. The stations were set up in canvas tents with wooden flooring to keep us out of the mud. We sisters had to constantly be on guard for fleas and lice which were transferred from the men's uniforms. We laid white cloths on the ground and brushed toxic powders into our clothes. The sheets allowed us to see what had migrated onto us, causing rashes and bites. We also regularly used fine toothed combs, slowly drawing them through our long hair to dislodge unwanted guests. It was disgusting initially, but over time we didn't notice the smell of the powders and the rest was integrated into our routine. There were rats too, constantly scavenging and carrying more fleas with them.

Despite all my years of nursing, I was surprised to find that I had the most difficult time working with our patients. The station was overcrowded and understaffed. There were shortages of medications. Too many times, I found myself offering solace and a cool cloth to a young man who had no chance of survival, staying with him through the night so he would not die alone. When we had a lull, many of us asked the boys if they'd like us to write letters home, to their mothers, wives or sweethearts. How many of those letters contained the last words of a boy who had lied about his age in order to have a grand adventure. It was many months later that we learned the men had taken to calling us the Blue Birds because of our uniforms and the comfort they said we provided.

We were up at 5 o'clock and the days lasted as long as there were patients to be treated. It wasn't uncommon to work for thirty-six hours or more with only short breaks for tea and calls of nature.

Sleep was like unto being dead. We dropped to our cots and lost consciousness, but we did not have restful sleep. There were the sounds of distant gunfire, the chance of shelling, and the wails and whimpers of the wounded.

I began to have occasional bouts of what I now consider waking dreams, unsure whether I had dozed off, had been working by rote, or if what I thought I had just done was something that happened yesterday or the day before. Everything was in a haze. Meals were all too often skipped because an ambulance arrived with more wounded men, screaming in pain or worse yet, still and silent. The doctors made immediate judgements about those who could be saved and those too badly wounded or injured in such a way that there was no hope.

Infections raged, and many soldiers died following what would have been a fairly routine procedure at home. Without clean floors and walls, with little equipment and medication, with exhaustion the usual state, I felt that all my years of experience were of nothing.

After weeks and months that ran together, one night I had a strange dream. In it I was once again a little girl in our house in Paris, Ontario. I was sitting on the carpet in the parlour, making paper dolls, cutting out pictures of ladies in the Eaton's catalogue, and using paste to affix them onto cardboard. I'd then snip out pictures of clothes and place them carefully on to my dolls. In the dream I accidentally cut a leg off one of the dolls. Try as I might, I wasn't able to re-attach it. I woke up in the pre-dawn light with tears running down my face, whimpering because I couldn't save the leg.

I began to have more frequent nightmares, gastric upsets as well as rheumatic pains in my joints from the cold and damp. In 1916 I was granted two and half months leave with permission to return to Canada. The medical officer determined that an ocean voyage would be beneficial and so I returned home. Four of my family members had died while I'd been overseas, and concerns about personal matters added to my distress. In the end my leave was extended for a further three months before I returned to duty in France.

Although I fell quickly back into the dreadful routine of the station, my symptoms increased. I developed insomnia and even on those occasions when I was able to sleep, my concentration flagged and I was easily fatigued. My appetite was gone, in part because there was so little time for meals, in part because of my increasing gastric distress and for the most part because I was no longer able to tolerate the working conditions and the hopelessness of it all.

On March 7th, 1917 I found myself classified as a patient, and was sent to No. 3 General Hospital in Le Treport. Discharged the following day, I was transferred to the Sisters Convalescent Home at Hardelot. Princess Louise, the Duchess of Argyle, had offered her villa for the use of nursing sisters who required some time away from their duties. It was indeed a respite, but I was apprehensive about returning to the station twelve days later.

Upon my return I was re-assigned to care for influenza patients. My nightmares continued and I developed palpitations of the heart. I'd begun having severe headaches, mostly in the frontal area. I also felt I was being treated differently by the other sisters, Matron and the officers. Over the six months with that duty, my symptoms continued to worsen and included intermittent vomiting. I had lost more than thirty pounds and the strength I prided myself on at one time had deserted me.

It is now April of 1918 and I'm on a ship returning to Canada for the last time. As I review all that has occurred in the last years, I am most astonished by how naïve we were. The confident assurances, that once the Dominion was involved the war would end by Christmas, were made of smoke.

The vivid images of France that had danced through my girlhood daydreams have been replaced by the drab reality. I can recall only passing through empty towns and villages which seemed to be watchful. Doors were closed and windows were shuttered. Fields had been destroyed by both sides. The only crop was stubble. There were no strolling couples, no old men smoking cigarettes, no laughing children. Few animals roamed, although I saw two thin cows near a field hospital once. The other memories are of mud and ice, sleet and rain. The smells weren't of flowers, but of Lysol and iodine, gas gangrene and infection. There's nothing to keep in an album to recapture happy times.

The deaths and massive injuries sustained by eager lads were in numbers I'm even now unable to calculate. Then there are those who suffered severe physical wounds, but were rendered more cruelly damaged by the mental scars that we were unable to treat. I've heard that there were places in England where many of those men were sent. They're unable to return to the society they had known, unable to engage in employment of any sort. They live in a place between what was and what might have been, reliving horrific events both day and night.

I'm being transferred to St. Andrews Hospital in Toronto for what is to be a six month period. I am to rest and engage in out of door exercise and will be given tonics to re-build my weight and strength. There is no mention of how to eradicate my nightmares, waking dreams, and excessive reactions to loud noises and sudden bright lights.

There are rumours of a German named Freud who is interested in the value of talking therapy. Some of the doctors believe that it may help the men who have been traumatized. I overheard one doctor suggesting that some of the nursing sisters might be suffering similarly and that he felt this new method might be of great value. I'd hoped they would allow me to try that, but the senior medical officers would not authorize it.

Any shreds of confidence and optimism I had latched onto scattered to the winds, when on February 1, 1919 I was officially "Struck off the Strength" as being medically unfit.

*Author's Note*

I wanted to write about a woman, since the voices of women are rare in stories of the Great War. This piece was inspired by a Heritage Day presentation at the Burlington Public Library. The more I learned, the more I began to consider the current day topic of post-traumatic stress syndrome. It has been 100 years since the War to End All Wars, and it seems humanity has failed to apply what we have learned.

# A Marriage and a War

*Susan Evans Shaw*

Whenever I think back to the years in Miniota, Manitoba, I remember a happy, carefree time before the Great War came along to destroy so many lives.

I was born Edith Eleanor Price in Flintshire, North Wales on October 3, 1880. With my five sisters and two brothers, I grew up at The Cross, Mold where my father was an ironmonger.

My future husband, James Lloyd Evans, always known as Jim, was born March 17, 1879 in nearby Flint. We knew each other from childhood.

In those days, our schooling ended at age fourteen. Jim apprenticed in my father's ironmongery for three years. Then, unwilling to settle to business, he joined the Denbighshire Hussars. In 1900 the Hussars were incorporated into the Imperial Yeomanry and sent to South Africa to fight the Boers. After several months garrisoning in Cape Town, Jim's unit deployed to the front at Pretoria, but by then Jim had fallen ill with enteric fever. Instead of joining the battle, he remained behind in the infirmary. Jim recovered but never got to Pretoria. Instead he was invalided home; the rest of his unit remained until the end of the war.

While Jim served his apprenticeship in the ironmongery, I trained as a pupil-teacher. Mother had been passionately fond of music and arranged that each of her children learn an instrument. I had chosen piano and organ, and took lessons from Mr. Jones at the Pendref Welsh Chapel. My playing became good enough that eventually I took on duties as chapel organist. By the time Jim returned to Mold, I had a position teaching at Ivy House Primary School and on Sundays played the chapel organ for all three services.

Now that he was back in Mold, Jim came courting. How my sisters teased! When he proposed, I happily accepted and Father gave his blessing. Jim brought a selection of rings from the jeweler. Unable to make up my mind I asked my sisters to help. They picked out a beautiful, and expensive, solitaire emerald.

Jim took an honourable discharge from the militia, leaving with the rank of sergeant. Lead and coal mining formed the backbone industry of North Wales. When the price of lead fell, the mines began to shut down. The local economy suffered and so did the job market. From the Canadian soldiers he met in South Africa, Jim learned about Canada's coast-to-coast railroad, which had made land available for homesteading. Jim had no interest in farming but felt surely there would be a need for ironmongers. With a promise to send for me as soon as he was settled, Jim took ship for Canada in the spring of 1903 – his destination, Winnipeg.

He soon found a job with the Manitoba Hardware and Lumber Company. They assigned him to their newest store in a place called Miniota, two hundred miles west of Winnipeg. He loved the little town on the banks of the Assiniboine River. He wrote home about places with such strange names that I looked forward to experiencing them for myself.

His first Canadian winter came as a shock. Jim had never known such cold or seen so much snow. In his letters he wrote about the warm and welcoming townspeople. Many had come from the Old Country themselves and understood his discomfort.

Once established in Miniota, Jim wrote to ask me to join him. We could be married in Winnipeg and he would find us a house to rent. I relished a new adventure, yet hesitated. To be married without my family present would be hard to bear. In the event, my father scuttled Jim's plan. "No daughter of mine will travel to a foreign country alone and unmarried. If he wants you, he will have to come and get you."

With good grace, Jim gave way. But that December our dear father passed away and wedding plans had to be postponed for the 135 mourning period. Even with Father gone, Jim abided by his promise and we planned the wedding for Mold in a year's time.

Jim took a leave from the MH&L and returned to Mold where we were married December 29, 1904 in the same Pendref Chapel where I was organist. Our families attended, as well as many friends and relations. My brother, Will, gave me away. My sisters, Susannah, affectionately known as Cis, and Gwladys were bridesmaids. Jim's cousin Edwin Lloyd stood best man.

Following a wedding breakfast at the St. James Hotel, Jim and I took the train to London for a brief honeymoon. We had booked passage for Canada, leaving January 12. I spent the last few days with my family, not knowing when, if ever, I would be back.

On the last evening, members of the Pendref Chapel auxiliary gave a little fête and presented me with a marble clock inscribed to commemorate my years as the chapel organist.

We sailed from Liverpool and landed at Halifax, which felt almost like home with its damp cold, and boarded the waiting train. It took a week to cross Canada, pausing at each city – Montreal, Toronto, Sudbury, Winnipeg, Brandon. At Virden Jim's friend, Jack Taylor, was waiting with a horse and sleigh. Wrapped in fur blankets we glided swiftly past banks of snow on the road to Miniota.

Oh, but it was cold! At the house, fires were burning in the grates and a meal was waiting. It was a wonderful, warm welcome to my new home. Jim had made so many friends in the town that invitations poured in and I soon got to know our neighbours.

After long discussions, I agreed that Jim use our savings to open his own hardware store. David Garrard was selling his business, which included a harness shop and an undertaking facility. I wondered if Jim was wise in this move, considering he would be competing with the much bigger MH&L, but he was determined to give it a try.

J.L. Evans & Co., Hardware Merchants opened its doors in the summer of 1905. The harness shop was an immediate success. Farmers like Jim's friend, Jack Taylor, took pride in adorning their animals with hand-made leather equipment. As well, Jim sold belts and canvas tarpaulins and he repaired shoes. Of course, undertaking always makes for steady business, so much so that Jim hired Sam Shier to assist. Our life in Miniota was unfolding more rosily than ever we could have wished.

Jim joined the Knights of Pythias, a branch of Masons. As they kept their rites secret, I knew little about their meetings. He also returned to his military roots and joined the A Squadron of the XII Manitoba Dragoons. Every few months he traveled the thirty-five miles to Virden for drills. When the Miniota Dragoons formed in 1907, Jim, as the only member with formal military experience, was promoted to Lieutenant and given command of the troop. About the same time, the Miniota Rifle Association formed as a local branch of the Dominion of Canada Rifle Association. Jim was Captain and Reverend Sidney Thomas, rector of Holy Trinity, was chief organizer. Periodically they held competitions and target records had to be sent to Winnipeg each month.

We attended many dances and several military balls. Jim helped organize Miniota's own military ball, a very grand affair with men in their blue dress uniforms and ladies in beautiful gowns. People came from miles around. A magnificent midnight supper was provided, the band played, and we danced until dawn.

Evenings of music, song and recitation were popular occasions. For a small village, there was plenty of talent. I was frequently called upon to act as piano accompanist. Miniota's little theatre company staged plays in which Jim and I often took parts – silly comedies mostly, but so much fun to perform. In those days we had only our own entertainments to pass long winter evenings.

When Dr. Chalmers confirmed my first pregnancy, I straightaway wrote home with the news and asked Cis if she would mind coming to be with me during my confinement. She arrived in the summer of 1906. Our son, dark-haired like his father, was born September 14. We named him Frank for Jim's little brother who had died of TB at age ten. Cis stayed with me for three months, returning to Mold in time for Christmas. My next sister, Gwladys, arrived on a visit in February.

While I was occupied with the new baby, I could pay less attention to Jim and the store, which now wasn't doing well. Jim made a critical error when he sold the harness business to Tom Conway.

He soon came to realize that without the harness shop he couldn't compete with the larger MH&L. In April, 1907, he sold the hardware stock and undertaking business to the MH&L and accepted a position as assistant manager of the Miniota store. It should have been a sad time, but Jim took the profits from the sale to buy two parcels of land on Louisa Avenue and began building us a house.

The Miniota Dragoons served to take his mind off the failure of his business. In June, under Jim's leadership, the Miniota Squadron joined the Virden Squadron for a field camp. They dressed in uniforms rather like what Jim had worn in South Africa – broad brimmed hats pinned up at one side, khaki blouses and breeches, polished leather riding boots, bandoliers of ammunition slung over their shoulders and each man carried a riding whip.

That first field camp became an annual event. For two weeks in June every year from 1908 to 1914 the whole regiment of Manitoba Dragoons would meet for drill and rifle practice. From 1909 these events took place at Camp Sewell (later renamed Camp Hughes) twenty-five miles east of Virden. A special train ran from the Miniota spur line. Horses were loaded into boxcars and the men in passenger cars, to join the rest of the regiment in Virden. Each year Allan Hodnett sent a report of the field camps to the *Miniota Herald*, always detailed and always amusing.

Our daughter, Gwladys Eleanor, was born in January 1909. I named her for my sister and my mother; Gwladys became her godmother. Having a son and now a daughter made me feel our little family was complete.

Just as we were planning to move into our house, Jim had a falling out with the general manager of the MH&L in Brandon. He had hoped to be appointed manager of the Miniota store, but instead they appointed Harvey Chappell. Jim resigned and accepted a position as manager of a hardware store in Saskatoon. I wasn't happy about uprooting and moving so far from my friends and family in Miniota, but, as breadwinner, Jim had the final say.

Our year in Saskatoon was highlighted by the marriage of my sister Gwladys to Jack Taylor. Jack never joined the Dragoons. His great black mustache and Irish blue eyes would have made him look handsome in uniform, but Jack's métier was farming. What a foil he made to tiny auburn-haired and bespectacled Gwladys! She caught his eye at a dance and from that moment he had no interest in anyone else. They married in December 1909 at St. John's church in Saskatoon and we hosted a small reception. Jack could be spared from the farm until spring so they used their honeymoon to travel to Mold where they remained until March. They returned to Miniota accompanied by our brother Llewelyn to help Jack on the farm.

To my delight, in March 1910 we returned to Miniota and at last moved into our new house. Harvey Chappell had not been a success at the Miniota store and the MH&L wanted Jim to take over.

In the coronation year, 1911, I took Frank and Gwladys on a visit to Mold. We stayed at The Cross with my sisters, Cis, Annie, Myfanwy and Blodwen. Will and his new wife, Eunice, lived near Hendre a few miles away. Will had inherited the ironmongery business when Father died but Eunice preferred to be mistress of her own household. Cis remained the chatelaine of our old home.

Mold celebrated the coronation of George V in good style. Banners were hung across High Street and flags festooned shops and businesses. From The Cross we watched the parade proceed along High Street to Bailey Hill where community celebrations are traditionally held. With the children I joined the throng. Choirs sang, the orchestra played and of course there were speeches. After the ceremony, tea, sandwiches and cake were served. To the delight of the children there was ice cream. Frank would talk of the day for months to come. In September, we returned to Canada and Jim met us in Brandon.

One by one, my sisters came to settle in Canada. In May 1912, Annie married her Mold sweetheart, David Jones, at Holy Trinity, Miniota, and the newlyweds moved to Vancouver. Cis decided to immigrate in 1912. Myfanwy and Blodwen followed in 1913. Blodwen set herself up in business as a milliner while Myfanwy registered for grade 12 at the Sarahville School. She needed Senior Matriculation in order to apply to Normal School to earn a Canadian teaching certificate.

In 1912 Frank started Grade One at the Sarahville School. He loved school and was consistently at the top of his class.

On May 25, 1914, Eric, our surprise baby, was born, a little redhead like my side of the family. Al Hodnett, ever the wag, soon took to calling him the leprechaun or the "Irishman".

A month later the "shot heard round the world" occurred when Archduke Franz Ferdinand was assassinated on June 28 in Sarajevo. In Miniota we heard nothing. We were fully occupied preparing for the Dominion Day celebrations of July 1st. Every business closed for the day; everyone gathered in the park to picnic and enjoy a sports day. It would be our last festive day in Miniota.

On August 3, 1914, Germany invaded neutral Belgium. Britain issued an ultimatum for Germany to withdraw. Receiving no reply, Great Britain declared war on Germany. With England at war, Canada, too, was at war. Men from our village soon began volunteering to serve.

Of course the Dragoons would go to the war and Jim wanted to go, too. I raised every objection I could. A married man of thirty-five with three children would be excused from overseas service. Let the younger men go. But Jim argued that he had been training all these years for just such an eventuality. He never made it to the front in South Africa and this war would be his last chance. In any case, it would all be over by Christmas. I would hardly have time to miss him.

Jim hoped to be in command of his troops from the Miniota Dragoons but new regulations were in place. The Dragoons were split up amongst different regiments. Even so, Jim remained determined to go overseas. I had to relent. At the beginning of November he left for Virden to join the 32nd Battalion.

He spent the first month at the barracks in Virden. Then just before Christmas his troop moved to Winnipeg. I travelled up once, leaving the children in the care of Cis. Jim did manage to get Christmas week off to come home for the holiday celebrations and had one more leave before they left for Halifax at the end of February. As he got ready for departure I saw he was in his element, so I could only find pleasure in his happiness.

They sailed for England at the end of February. From Shorncliffe, his new quarters at the military base, he wrote that he would not be going overseas, but to the School of Musketry at Hythe for training as a military instructor. Of course I was immensely pleased they were keeping him in England, but Jim remained eager to get to France. For the next several months our letters traveled back and forth. He spent his first leave visiting Mold and wrote a detailed account of home, family and friends.

You can imagine my delight when Jim's letter, written at the beginning of October, arrived reminding me of his suggestion we join him in England. I never received an earlier letter, which must have gone down with the *Hesperian* when she was torpedoed. Of course we would come. From England Jim made many of the arrangements but I still had to pack and organize. I found a tenant for our house and, as Jim suggested, arranged for the rent to go toward the mortgage.

Just before leaving I learned about the latest regulation requiring all overseas passengers to have a valid passport as a wartime measure. I had never needed a passport and had no time to apply for one. I consulted Gilbert Rowan, our town magistrate. He supplied a document certifying that I was a British subject and that Frank, Gwladys and Eric were my children. The document included a certified photograph of all of us.

Jack drove us to the station where we boarded a train and set off for New York. At the embarkation pier I presented my document. The official told me it was insufficient and I would have to get approval from the Consulate. Time was short and I became frantic, fearing we would miss the sailing. A kind woman, who was seeing her son off, noticed my predicament and offered to look after Eric. With Gwladys and Frank in tow, I went to the Consulate. To my dismay there was a long queue. I knew that by the time my turn came the ship would have sailed. In despair I returned to the pier, collected Eric, thanked the woman, and prepared to face down the immigration officer. There was no need; another officer had come on duty. He studied my document, paused a moment, then stamped the page. With Eric in my arms, and relief in my heart, I led Frank and Gwladys up the gangplank.

Our ship docked at Liverpool on December 16, 1915. Will was waiting at the port to drive us to Mold. We spent Christmas with Will and Eunice but Jim could not be released from his duties to join us.

However, he did find a suitable house to rent in Hythe. I sent our trunks ahead by rail and early on a January morning we boarded the train for the long slow trip to Folkestone. Jim met us at the station with a car and driver. The thrill of traveling in an automobile distracted the children, who by now were tired and very cranky.

Before leaving Mold I had hired a maid, twenty-three-year-old Prudence Roberts. I needed someone who would be willing to travel and live with us in Kent. She proved more than capable with the children on the tiring and lengthy journey to Folkestone.

Our rented home in Hythe, known as Haydn House, was spacious enough to accommodate our family of five plus Prudence, who would live in. The owner had been a musician and the children were fascinated to find the attic full of musical instruments. I had to warn them any number of times not to touch.

I settled in quickly. The first order of business was to arrange schools for Frank and Gwladys. Frank had been in Grade Four in Miniota and, at nine and a half, he was of an age for Preparatory School. Jim and I thought we would apply to Charterhouse School for September but for the first term in England, we decided a local school would accustom him to the different system. Gwladys had been in Grade Two in Miniota and we found a good Primary School within walking distance for her. Eric, at only eighteen months, would remain at home in the care of Prudence.

Now that we had a home in Hythe and so many boys from Miniota were passing through Shorncliffe, Jim and I decided to hold Open House every Sunday. I served tea, sandwiches and cakes. The boys could relax over newspapers, games of chess, draughts or cards. If anyone wanted a hot bath they were welcome. Haydn House faced onto the Hythe canal and on pleasant afternoons we made use of the rental rowboats. I have a lovely photo Jim took of me rowing the boat with Dick Waller in the bow. On one occasion, I dressed up in Jim's uniform for a photo. I barely came to Jim's shoulder; you can imagine the fit.

That summer Jim was promoted to Major. He was very chuffed. As well, the rise in pay meant a small but welcome infusion into our household budget.

In March 1917, Jim was transferred to Witley Camp at Bramshot. With great regret, because the children and I enjoyed Hythe so much, I prepared for a move to Godalming. Eric, Gwladys and I would board with Mrs. Gertrude Pettitt on Carlos Street. Frank boarded at Charterhouse School and Jim lived at Witley Camp, joining us whenever he got leave. To my great regret we could not accommodate Prudence and she returned to Mold.

From France, Al Hodnett sent me a newsy letter of thanks for the Sundays at our house at Hythe. I wept when news came in May that he had been killed at Fresnoy. How I would miss his cheerful and teasing ways! On his last visit Al had left his pocket knife behind and in his letter he suggested I give it to Frank. Frank treasures the knife as I hoped he would. But Al's death just added to Jim's discontent at being kept in England.

Jim managed to get leave at Christmas and we all traveled to Mold to spend the holiday with Will and Eunice at Gwernaffield where they had recently moved. Sarah, Jim's mother, joined us and was delighted to have time with her grandchildren. We returned to Godalming for New Year's Eve.

If only the war could have ended then. I felt quite content while we were together as a family, but Jim chafed at being kept in England. He fretted that he could not face his friends unless he had seen battle. Even though he had crossed to France the previous March he was not satisfied. His time there had been spent behind the lines updating troops and officers on the latest anti-gas procedures. Nevertheless, that trip was not without its perils. When he got home he showed me the small round pit in his breast-pocket notebook where it had stopped a bullet.

I pleaded with him to think of me and the children. What would we do if anything happened to him? He assured me that the war was changing. There would be little more fighting in the trenches and in the unlikely event anything happened, the army would look after us. He grew so unbearably depressed and irritable that I gave up and ceased my objections.

To go the front, Jim would have to revert to Captain. There were 143 already too many senior officers in France and the great need was for fighting men.

On our last evening together we were quietly reviewing domestic arrangements when there came a crash from the dining room. Mrs. Pettitt had set the table for the following morning's breakfast. Among the condiments was a pot of strawberry jam. Three-year-old Eric adored strawberry jam and had climbed onto the table to help himself to a spoonful. In the process he had knocked off a cup and saucer, which smashed on the tiled floor.

Jim scooped Eric from the table, spanked his bottom and I carried the howling child up to bed. When Eric was settled I returned to the sitting room where Jim was already regretting his moment of anger on his last night. Before dawn the next morning he left to join his company on their way to Folkestone.

Once again Gwladys would have to change schools. Jim and I had decided that I would be best in Mold near family. Eunice found us a furnished cottage, "The Rookeries" in Gwernaffield. It was three miles from Mold but within a stone's throw of the village church and a school for Gwladys. Frank would continue as a boarder at Charterhouse. Prudence was available and I was pleased to have her come as a daily.

Jim's letters home were certainly cheerful during the first weeks he was in France. Correspondence was censored but we had devised codes so he could keep me informed about where the 5th Battalion was based. A few Welsh words used here and there in the letter served to distract the censor from place names spelled backwards.

As time wore on he began to mention some of the discomforts of being in the front lines, like whole weeks of not being out of his clothes and boots. Scabies became a problem. I sent him parcels of food and clothing.

News of major battles began to appear in the papers in August as the Allies began their push in what was later called the Hundred Days. Jim wrote about soon returning home and began to plan for the future. He asked me to rent a bicycle for him so we could ride around and visit friends. My hopes rose. It looked like the war would soon be over.

On Friday September 13th, 1918, there came knock at the door. The boy from the post office handed me a telegram.

CAPTN JAMES LLOYD EVANS WESTERN ONTARIO REGT ATTACHED 5TH BN REPORTED KILLED IN ACTION 1ST SEPT.

I wanted to howl so loud they could hear me in Miniota, grief and anger mixed in equal measure. My legs gave way and I sank to the floor, weeping helplessly.

Frank ran to get Eunice who came immediately to take charge. The children were told the awful news. Eric began to cry without really understanding what had gone wrong. Cousin Charley Pownall arrived with his wife, Lizzie. She offered to take Eric for a few days. Frank and Gwladys, being old enough to be of help, would remain at home. Eunice made me a cup of tea to which she had added a generous dollop of brandy then sent me to lie down and rest – as if rest were possible. I wept and wept until, overcome by the brandy and exhaustion, I fell asleep.

On November 11, 1918 came the Armistice. War had ended, but for me and the children there was little to celebrate.

In February 1919, we boarded a ship for home. Just as he had all those years ago, Jack met us at the train station in Virden with his horse-drawn sleigh piled with fur blankets. Jim's absence felt more painful than ever, but the children delighted in their return. Eric thrilled to his first sight of snow.

As if Death hadn't been satisfied by the war, the Spanish flu followed to exact its toll. The course was swift. On Wednesday, my brother Llewelyn, was his usual robust self. On Thursday he fell ill. On Friday March 28, he died. He wasn't yet thirty.

Money was a worry. Jim's rank when he died had been Captain and the pension I would receive was that of a Captain's widow. I had three children and myself to support. Jim had had the rank of Major before he reverted to Captain. I wrote the Paymaster to ask for a correction and got a blunt refusal. I took the issue to a higher office and was again refused. I didn't give up. After I don't know how many letters and with the support of Colonel Clingan, our MLA and Jim's long time friend, I won my case and the army assigned me the pension of a Major's widow, but that was not until thirty years later.

I always dreaded Remembrance Day, but as Jim's widow I was expected to take part in ceremonies at the village cenotaph. I wasn't much of a one for crying, but on those occasions, to the dismay of the children, I always wept.

Gwladys seemed to recover from the loss of her father and Eric had been too young to remember much, but Frank took his father's death very hard and for a while his school grades suffered. Eventually he regained his former class standing and Miss Murphy, his teacher, suggested he apply for the IODE bursary reserved for the children of soldiers killed in the war. Frank won and in 1922 entered the University of Manitoba to study civil engineering. The bursary of $250 a year paid all his expenses. In 1927, Gwladys graduated high school with top honours. I decided that secretarial college would be more suitable than university for a pretty girl who would soon find a husband. Rather than pay her board in Winnipeg, it would be less expensive to have her live at home. Over heartbroken objections from both Gwladys and Eric, I sold the house on Louisa Avenue and prepared for the move to an apartment in Winnipeg.

Once more Jack Taylor took us to the train in Virden. This time there was no horse-drawn sleigh; we made the journey from Miniota to Virden in his Ford Model A motor car. As we turned from Louisa Avenue onto Main Street, I glanced toward the village Cenotaph just visible two blocks away. Jim's name is among the forty-one inscribed. How he had loved Miniota. He gave his heart to the community; now all that's left is his name on the Cenotaph.

The catalyst for my fascination with this era was the discovery of my grandfather's letters written home during World War I. The letters, supplemented by family stories, memories of my grandmother, Edith Price Evans, plus articles in the *Miniota Herald*, are the kernels from which "A Marriage and A War" grew.

# Who Would Be a Soldier?

*Linda Helson*

When I was a young woman I used to visit my grandmother in the nursing home. Although Nanny suffered from dementia, she still remembered me. Perhaps it was just family resemblance. People said I looked like her. I would hold her hand and think how similar my young hand was to her old one.

Like many victims of dementia she had a small treasury of stories that she told again and again. One of the most persistent of these was her recollection of walking into a room and seeing her mother seated at a table with her back to the door. Her head was bowed. She was weeping.

The year was 1918. My great-grandmother was trying to hide her grief. Her son had just been killed in France.

For more than sixty years – through marriage, births, deaths, divorce, remarriage, children, grandchildren, great-grandchildren – this scene remained prominent in my grandmother's memory and now she needed to tell it.

How does it feel, I wonder, to lose a son in war? To know that you will never see his grave? To wonder about his last agony? To remember his first cries, his childhood? My grandmother would have understood some of it. She lost two of her own sons when they were children – one to polio, one to an automobile accident. I can only speculate. Nanny never talked about these things.

My grandmother's family, the Nobles, had come to Canada at the beginning of the twentieth century. Her brother, Fred, twenty-three years old and single, had sailed out of Liverpool on September 5, 1907 on the *Corsican*, a ship of the Allan Line.

Had he been seduced by Clifford Sifton's campaign to lure immigrants to the Canadian West with promises of wide-open spaces and free land? Certainly Fred was not the stuff of rugged pioneers, nor did he have any experience of farming. In fact he only made it as far west as London, Ontario. Perhaps the name, "London", with its echo of the land he left behind was enough to draw him there. Perhaps there were friends.

Whatever rosy pictures of his new life Fred created in his letters home, they were enough that within two years the rest of the family joined him: his parents, John and Sarah, both fifty-one; and their other children: George, twenty-six; Albert, twenty-four and his wife, Alice; Lizzie, eighteen; Frank, thirteen and my grandmother, Lilian Christina, nine. Eight people bound for the new world and a new life.

They had left Rushden, a town of about 13,000 souls, in the East Midlands of England. There the men and Alice and Lizzie had been boot makers – not plying the ancient trade of cobbler, but workers performing again and again the assembly of one part of a shoe: treeing, lasting, welting, machining, finishing. In the nineteenth century Rushden had been home to more than one hundred boot and shoe factories and their associated trades. Sanders and Sanders, which makes boots for the British Army, as well as several other defence departments throughout the world, still operates in Rushden, but the rest of the boot factories are long gone.

If the Noble family had dreamt of fame and fortune in Canada their hopes were soon dashed. By 1913 Albert was forced to look for work in the United States, but he failed to find any. The jobs the family members had held in Rushden, with their very specific tasks, had not equipped them with skills that could be transferred to other employment. All they had was a willingness to work.

* * *

On June 28, 1914 Archduke Franz Ferdinand, heir to the Austro-Hungarian Empire, was assassinated by Gavrilo Princip in Sarajevo and the world was changed forever. By August Great Britain, and hence its colonies throughout the world, had declared war on Germany.

Suddenly men were needed – soldiers were needed.

Frank, the youngest son, was the first to enlist, on August 20, 1915. He was twenty, and as the cemeteries of northern France and Belgium attest, war is a young man's game – with many losers. But he already had two years militia experience with the Fusiliers, so perhaps he thought he knew what war was like.

He became a member of the Infantry in the First Battalion, First Brigade, First Division of the Canadian Expeditionary Force. The First Battalion had been recruited in Western Ontario beginning August 6, 1914.

Two months after Frank, on October 26, 1915, four days before his thirty-first birthday, Albert signed up. What possessed him? Back in England he had served three years in the Territorials militia. But he was a married man, although as yet there were no children. Was he swayed by war propaganda to do his bit to save his homeland and poor little Belgium? Did he feel shamed by his youngest brother? Or was he simply still out of work?

A month after that, on November 25, 1915, George enlisted. The eldest Noble son, he was now thirty-three and had been married for more than seven years to Mary Dix. He was the father of two children. He had varicose veins. What madness possessed men to think the Empire needed a man such as George to fight? As the oldest son, did he feel some impulse to protect his younger brothers? How could he know in Canada, and from his five years militia experience in the English Volunteers, the chaos and carnage that would reign in northern France and Belgium? He may never have seen his brothers again.

By 1916 the Canadian Expeditionary Force would be fighting in France at the Somme, at Vimy and in the mud at Passchendaele in

1917. As the cardboard soles of their shoddy boots melted in the ooze of the trenches, did the brothers have time to remember their hours on the line in Rushden? Had their experience of factory life prepared them in any way for the rigors of life on the Western Front?

And what of Fred, the fourth brother?

When I was a child I heard Fred referred to as 'Flat' or 'Flat Fred' and sometimes 'Lucky'. As he was a short round man with poor health and no fortune, these nicknames puzzled me. Later I found out that he, too, tried to enlist in 1915, but his flat feet made him ineligible for service. For all the years he lived after the War was over, he would be slightly out of step with the rest of his brothers. He could not understand them or how the war had scarred them and they would not, or could not, share their experiences in hell with him.

* * *

Frank's youthful enthusiasm for the War would soon be dampened by his first winter living in a tent on the Salisbury Plain. That winter of 1915-16 was particularly bitter and wet. By May 1916 Frank was down with pleurisy, then with pneumonia. He spent two weeks suffering in the hospital at Moore Barracks at Shorncliffe in Kent.

In June 1916 he was discharged to the Canadian Convalescent Hospital, but was soon back in the Moore Barracks hospital with bronchitis. After a week he was again transferred to the Canadian Convalescent Hospital at Bearwood.

Frank was obviously unhappy with his new lot in life as he went AWOL from September 4th to the 29th, 1916 and had to forfeit twenty-one days' pay. As this only amounted to $1.10 per day, much less than he would have earned as a manual labourer in Canada, perhaps he was not too concerned.

Unlike deserters in the movies, Frank was not shot for treason. Instead he was sentenced to forty-two days' detention, before being transferred to active service with the 21st Canadian Battalion. Perhaps his sense of humour saved him from the firing squad. His reputation in the family is one of a man who enjoyed a good laugh.

In March 1917, Frank was once again admitted to hospital, this time to the Canadian General Hospital at Le Treport in northwest France, with severe gun shot wounds to his back.

After his recovery he was sent back into service, but in November 1917 he was twice in the 26th Field Ambulance with myalgia in his legs. Myalgia is characterized by rheumatism and severe pain. It has several causes, but in World War I it was one of the aftereffects of trench fever, a moderately serious disease transmitted by body lice, which were rampant among the soldiers serving in the War.

Frank's myalgia persisted until he was finally released at the end of January, 1918. At this point Frank was transferred from active service to the Canadian labour pool. In mid-February he was granted fourteen days' leave, from which, once again, he returned late and had to forfeit two days' pay.

\* \* \*

Albert's military record describes him as being of very good character and conduct. He served in France and Belgium with the 58th Battalion. In 1916 he had three attacks of appendicitis between September and December, when his appendix was finally removed. Then he was sent into battle again.

In July 1917 Sir Arthur Currie, former real estate developer, now newly promoted to commander of the Canadian forces in France – the first Canadian to command Canadian troops – was ordered to take the town of Lens in Belgium. Lens was important to the Germans for its rail access, and the British coveted its coal for war manufacturing. Besides the British hoped the Canadian attack would distract the Germans from the real objective of the French and British attack in the Somme.

Currie refused to attack Lens as it was surrounded by high ground. He proposed, instead, to take Hill 70 just north of the town. Changing his orders did not make Currie popular with the British high command, but Field Marshall Douglas Haig allowed the attack, predicting that it would fail.

As they had at Vimy, the Canadians laid out an area behind the lines to simulate Hill 70 and units practiced their attack until every section knew exactly what it had to do. On the evening of August 14, 1917 the attack began with the bombardment of the hill. There were many casualties during the battle and Albert was one of them. However, the Canadians were successful and gained control of Hill 70 and hence Lens. Fifteen times the Germans tried to retake the Hill, but they were unsuccessful.

Mustard gas is an insidious weapon, creeping as it does close to the ground and sinking to the bottoms of the trenches. Fighting uphill, breathing hard, the Canadians were particularly vulnerable to the poison in this battle. The gas masks that had been issued made it difficult to see the target and aim precisely. In frustration soldiers sometimes removed their masks.

Albert was felled during this battle, but not solely by the gas. He was also shot in his right knee. While in hospital, he was diagnosed with palpitations of the heart, severe breathing difficulties, and pain in the scar of his appendix operation.

He was declared unfit for service and shipped home to Canada in April, 1918. While recovering he moved in to his parents' house on William Street in London where his wife, Alice, had been living while he was overseas. He and Alice never moved out. Eventually Albert found work at Labatt's Brewery.

\* \* \*

George soldiered on – never rising in the ranks, never winning medals for bravery or outstanding conduct – just keeping a low profile and doing what he was ordered to do.

George spent much of the war in the background posted to the 135th Battalion, a reserve unit, but in March 1918 he was sent to France to the First Battalion, Canadian Expeditionary Force. Less than a month later, on the 13th of April 1918 he was felled by a gunshot wound to his thigh. He was sent to recover, but four months later, on the 24th of August he was back with the First Battalion C.E.F. on the Western Front.

By October 1918 the German forces were in retreat in the West. The Hindenberg Line had been broken. Scouring the land of any food, cattle, sheep, or poultry the German soldiers made for home. When Canadian troops entered Pecquencourt, six miles east of Douai, they were greeted as heroes by 2,000 starving civilians. It was the first time the soldiers had ever felt like the heroes and saviours of democracy that they had signed up to be.

In the next few days the Canadians would reclaim more than forty communities in northern France, including the large industrial town of Denain, on the north bank of the Canal de l'Escaut. An advance of more than 12,000 yards was the greatest the Canadians made on any day during the War.

There were still places where the German troops resisted. On October 20, the First Division occupied Wallers, but encountered machine gun fire from the Germans. On the 21st George received gun shot wounds to his stomach and right forearm. Two days later – nineteen days before the Armistice – he died at the Second Canadian Field Hospital.

* * *

On November 11, 1918 the shooting was over, but the War was not. The War would only end when the Treaty of Versailles was signed on June 28, 1919 – symbolically five years to the day after the assassination of Archduke Franz Ferdinand in Sarajevo.

Until then, men in power were taking no chances. Until then, British and Colonial soldiers were sent to internment camps in Britain. After the Russian Revolution in 1917, there was a real fear of further Communist uprisings across Europe.

The excuse given the imprisoned soldiers was that it would not do to send them home in dribs and drabs. They must be sent home in sufficient numbers to create great military parades to impress the civilian population.

Imagine how this must have appealed to homesick soldiers.

Canadian soldiers were the victims of transportation logistics. The Canadian Pacific Railway had loaned all of their ships to the Canadian government for the duration of the War, but now the War was over. Now they wanted to get back to the business of making money. The British government offered some ships, but they were not enough.

It was estimated that it would take a year and a half to transport our soldiers home. Meanwhile they were interned in camps.

Some 15,000 Canadian soldiers were sent to Kinmel Park Camp in North Wales. In the camps rumours were rife. The expectation was that men first over, would be the first returned home. This did not happen. Americans, some of whom had not even seen a battlefield, as America had not entered the War until 1917, managed to commandeer the ships needed for transportation. As well, some transport ships were used to send food to Russia.

In the camps the soldiers did not know about mining strikes or strikes that held up fueling ships, or caused food shortages.

They did know they were put on half rations, and were not paid regularly. They could not even buy cigarettes. They did know there was no coal for the stoves in the cold grey huts they lived in as the wind blew in from the sea. They did know that forty-two men were forced to inhabit a hut built for thirty, so that they had to take turns sleeping on the floor, with one blanket apiece.

In such conditions they were ripe to be victimized by the Spanish Influenza that raged throughout Europe and North America after the War. Seventy-six Canadian soldiers died from the flu in Kinmel Park Camp along with one hundred and thirty-two others.

Their treatment and the conditions under which they were forced to live, led some of the Canadians to riot for two days on March 4th and 5th, 1919. The heartbreaking fact is that five men, identified as leaders of the riot, men who had volunteered to fight for their country and empire and only wanted to go home, were shot for treason. Four of them are buried in the cemetery of St. Margaret's Church, Bodelwyddan, North Wales, alongside those killed by the Spanish Flu. The body of one of the riot leaders, Gunner John Frederick Hickman, was eventually repatriated to New Brunswick.

We now know Kinmel Park was not the only camp to have riots. British and French troops rioted as well in their camps, but Kinmel Park was "Colonial", so the British military hierarchy was open to making this particular riot public.

Frank left Halifax in July 1916. Four years later, on July 21, 1920 he finally put his foot on Canadian soil again, at Quebec. Officially his war was finally over.

* * *

In 1936 Frank would go to France again to participate in the unveiling of the Vimy Memorial. On that trip he would also seek out and find George's final resting place in Auberchicourt British Cemetery near Douai in northern France. He had photos taken of George's gravestone and of himself standing beside it and brought them back to the family. I have my grandmother's copies sitting on my desk now.

Ten years later, Frank died at the age of fifty-one. He was not the best soldier Canada had ever fielded, but his early death was undoubtedly the result of his experiences and living conditions during World War I.

I look at my hands, so like my grandmother's, the greenish veins crabbing across their backs, and wonder what I will feel the need to tell the next generation about my life, when my mind has lost its way.

*Author's Note*

I am indebted to Robert Sharpe and to Susan Evans Shaw for directing me to websites with information about the soldiers of the Canadian Expeditionary Force in World War I. I thank Beryl Haslam for her recollection of the graves of Canadian soldiers in St. Mary's church-yard, Boddelwyddan, North Wales and David, always, for his abiding interest in all things military and for the stories he told me.

# We Gave Our Boys
# and We Gave Ourselves

*Timothy Christian*

When I was four years old my father was promoted to a foreman's job in Coalspur at the Canadian National Railway's roundhouse for the repair of locomotives. Dad left Mother in Edmonton – with me and my two-year-old brother – waiting for our home to be readied in Coalspur. We stayed for four months with Mom's mother and father in the house Grandpa had built by himself in the Highlands, next to the Exhibition grounds and zoo. My four-year-old's memory of that visit was my introduction to World War I.

There was a large sepia photo of Grandpa wearing his army uniform in an oval frame over the armchair in which he often sat. From his chair, Grandpa called me. When I ran to him, he picked me up and sat me on his knee.

"Don't drop the wee lad Alex," Grandma said. She was a war bride and had a soft Surrey accent. She smelled of lavender.

"Don't you worry Mum," Grandpa said. "I can manage this little man."

Owing to a bullet wound, Grandpa's left shoulder was always stiff and he had to bend at the waist and move his whole body to reach for me. Then he put me on his right knee, not his left, for there was still a piece of shrapnel in the joint of the left knee and every so often a grimace of pain spread over his face as the bullet fragment pricked him. There were still shards of shrapnel in his left thigh as well.

Sometimes Grandpa sat in his chair and pondered, clasping and releasing his fingers and staring off into the distance.

"Don't you be thinking those dark thoughts, Alex," Grandma would say, taking the brass key and opening the locked door of the walnut chest to offer us buttery shortbread biscuits and soft toffees. "You should count your blessings."

"You don't know, Pet. You just don't know," he'd reply, as he slowly came back to the light.

* * *

Sixty years later I decided to find out what happened to Grandpa. He died in 1952 and my mother is his only surviving child. There was no detailed family history and I began looking through military records. Once I started I broadened my search to find all of the men in my family who served in WWI. I found the stories of eight men in two branches of my family: the Welsh's on my mother's side and the Sheppard's on my father's. At first I had no idea who most of them were, but as I probed I began to feel closer to them and I saw that the war hurt my family in ways that reach through the years.

* * *

My maternal Great Grandfather Andrew Welsh was born in County Tyrone, Ireland, and his wife, Florence, was born on Colonsay, a small island in the Scottish Inner Hebrides.

They met in Canada and were married on September 6, 1878 at the home of the clergyman in Port Elgin, Ontario. Andrew was thirty and Florence nineteen. They took up farming in Grey County and their family grew to include three daughters and five sons.

In 1911 Andrew died of brain cancer and Florence moved to the town of Owen Sound. Their sons Stewart and Alexander (my Grandpa) moved out west to Edmonton to find work as carpenters. Three other sons, Angus, James and John, remained in Ontario and worked on farms. When the time came, four of the boys enlisted.

My paternal Great Grandfather Rice Sheppard was born in Lambourne, England and his fist wife Elizabeth was born in London. Rice became a successful baker, cook and confectioner, owning four shops in Clapham. When he was thirty-six his doctor told him he had six months to live unless he moved from the damp English climate.

Rice took immediate action and sold his business two weeks after receiving his doctor's advice.

Elizabeth fully supported the decision and told neighbours she did not fear the rough land or wild animals one bit and was concerned only with Rice's health. One week later the family left their home in "Chiselhurst the beautiful".

The family packed thirteen large trunks and two sacks of supplies and set off on their six thousand mile odyssey. They began with a sea voyage from Liverpool to Montreal aboard the *SS Tunisian* and continued on a C.P.R. train from Montreal to Calgary and two days later from Calgary to Edmonton and arrived in time for the celebration of Queen Victoria's Diamond Jubilee on June 23, 1897.

Luckily, the geographical cure worked and Rice lived another fifty years. He and Elizabeth had five more children, two of whom died in their first year. Of their five surviving sons, four enlisted.

Rice and Elizabeth took up homesteading in the wild, uncultivated land. Though Rice had never farmed before, he learned quickly, and began winning prizes at the Edmonton Exhibition for his vegetables, grain and flowers. Elizabeth won first prize for her butter. Rice and Elizabeth became successful and in 1908 Rice wrote an article for *Alberta Homestead* lauding the farming opportunities on the prairies for men willing to work hard. He and Elizabeth took part in government missions to England to recruit immigrants and were enthusiastic boosters for the young land.

After twelve years of hard work with his wife and children Rice fulfilled his promise to Elizabeth and built a great brick house, modelled on an English country manor, a mansion as my mother describes it, which featured a sprawling veranda and interior walls painted in country scenes by an Italian artist. The family took possession of the house located in what is now the district of Avonmore the year before the war broke out.

Rice felt first-hand the problems facing farmers when they tried to sell their products. The experience led him to support the cooperative movement and to press for political change. He helped found the United Farmers of Alberta, which was dedicated to forwarding "the interests of the producers of grain and livestock in every honourable and legitimate way." He served on its executive for twenty-one years. He later broke with the United Farmers of Alberta Government when he concluded that the party had abandoned its founding principles and he helped form the Social Credit Party. He was tirelessly active in politics and ran as a "People's Candidate" in a provincial by-election in 1937. He was an Edmonton alderman for twenty years, sitting as a member of the Labour Party and as an independent. He ran for mayor six times.

His politics changed over the years. Before the war he was a promoter of the new province as part of the empire, but as time went on he became a farmers' advocate, and then sought to bring labour and farmers together as a political force to defend their joint interests. As will be seen, the war changed him.

Soon after the outbreak of war Rice advocated recruiting a home guard for Alberta from members of the United Farmers of Alberta. Each man would provide his own horse and equipment and the mounted police would train them. This would free the regular soldiers to be sent to the front as needed. Rice argued his position in a letter published in the May 18, 1915 edition of the *Grain Grower's Guide*, together with a photo showing himself and two sons mounted on horses and carrying rifles. Standing next to them two more sons held semaphore flags. All the men wore militia uniforms and his daughter was dressed in a Red Cross uniform. He said: "This picture was taken in front of my house on the farm. One of my daughters is a member of the Red Cross Society, making six of one family ready to take the field if needed."

Later in the war Rice pushed for and helped organize the United Farmers of Alberta Mounted Infantry Corps (U.F.A.M.I.C.), a force of 800 men drawn from the members of the U.F.A. from farms and small towns around Edmonton. There is a family photograph entitled "On H.M.S. – Rice Sheppard and Sons" which shows: Rice Sr. in his Captain's uniform for the U.F.A.M.I.C.; Tim in the uniform of the Mounted Rifles; Sidney wearing the uniform of the Royal Navy; and

Bill and Jack wearing the uniforms of the Alberta Battalion. There was no question of Rice Sheppard's commitment to the war.

Some of my family members signed up out of patriotic enthusiasm, and some in response to the growing social pressure to join the war. I will share what I found when I searched the war service records of my Grandpa and great uncles in the order in which they enlisted.

* * *

Bill Sheppard was a twenty-one-year-old farmer when he signed up on November 16, 1914 with the 31st (Alberta) Battalion. He stood five feet ten inches tall and had dark blue eyes and red hair. He suffered a series of health problems after he enlisted, including compression of the brain, orchitis caused by mumps and pneumonia.

Once he completed basic training he boarded the *S.S. Olympic* in Halifax with his older brother Tim. They arrived in England on July 6, 1916. On December 13, 1916 Bill embarked for France and was "taken on strength" (a military phrase meaning officially added to the battalion) with the Canadian Light Horse. One year later Bill's health was precarious and on April 4, 1917 he reported to the field ambulance suffering from an inflamed mucous membrane and was invalided back to England and the Canadian Military Hospital at Eastbourne. According to Rice, Bill was gassed and soon after returned to England with trench fever. On May 31, 1917 he was discharged from hospital but, given his poor health, he was appointed a Sergeant instructor at Shorncliffe and spent the rest of the war in England. On April 18, 1918 he was hospitalized for six days with influenza.

On December 22, 1918 Bill was given permission to marry and on Christmas Eve he married Annie Edith Holland, a twenty-two year old "spinster" who was from Crabble Hill. The wedding took place at the parish church of Buckland in Kent in the presence of the bride's father, who was a customs house officer.

Bill never fully recovered his strength. He died of pleurisy and pneumonia in 1923, a death which Rice Sheppard attributed to the War.

\* \* \*

Rice Sheppard Junior (Tim) was thirty years old when he enlisted in February 1915. He was five feet seven and had brown eyes and black hair. He was married, worked as a cook and had served six years in the Alberta Dragoons.

After basic training he was sent to England on the same voyage as his brother, Bill. When he arrived in England, Tim was taken on strength by the Canadian Army Service Corps. On December 15, 1916, he arrived in France and a week later joined his unit, the Canadian Light Horse.

On July 4, 1918 he reported to field ambulance with what the medical files recorded as "PUO" an acronym for pyrexia (fever) of unknown origin. Rice Sheppard called it "trench fever". Morton and Granatstein described the conditions leading to trench fever:

> *Day and night, soldiers lived in the miasma of rotting corpses and latrines, turned acrid by the odour of chloride of lime. Rats patrolled the trenches and gorged on human flesh. Within a few days of reaching France, officers and men alike were infested with lice. Such was the misery that men woke up bleeding from scratches gouged to relieve the itching. In the foul conditions, infection often followed. Only in 1918 was trench fever… or "PUO" – traced to body lice.*

Tim was discharged back to the trenches after five days but continued to suffer from the condition. He did not return to England until March 3, 1919, five months after the Armistice. Six weeks later he embarked for Canada aboard the *S.S. Belgic*, arriving in Halifax on April 23, 1919. One week after that he was demobilized in Toronto. He had served four years in the trenches of France and one wonders how he fit back into civilian life.

\* \* \*

Jack Welsh was twenty-three years old when he enlisted at Niagara Camp on June 11, 1915. He was five feet four inches tall and had blue eyes and fair hair. His file reveals that he went AWOL less than three months later. There is no evidence that he ever faced a court martial and he simply disappeared from the Army records. I know that he later lived in Edmonton and worked with Grandpa as a carpenter but he never changed his name as he might have done if he had feared detection. This is a puzzle.

* * *

Alex Welsh, my Grandpa, enlisted in Edmonton on November 13, 1915 while his brother Jack was on the run. He was twenty-eight years old, stood five feet eight, and weighed 142 pounds. He was assigned to the 66th Battalion and after basic training boarded the *S.S. Olympic* in Halifax. Grandpa arrived in England on May 7, 1916 and was transferred to the 31st (Alberta) Battalion. On June 29, he embarked for France and two weeks later, on July 14, Grandpa and two hundred other ranks (non-officers) reinforced the 31st Battalion at field head-quarters at MicMac Camp near Ypres. For the next few days under cool and cloudy skies Grandpa trained in bayonet fighting and throwing live hand grenades and defending against gas attacks.

During August the Battalion continued training and made a number of night raids on the German trenches to capture German soldiers or to collect papers, maps, badges or uniforms to help identify the enemy units and their plans. These raids sometimes succeeded and often did not, but they produced a steady stream of wounded and dead. Bayonets and stick bombs produced gruesome injuries. Occasional artillery barrages collapsed trenches, completely or partially burying men.

On September 10th the 31st Battalion relieved portions of the Canadian Infantry Brigade at Pozzieres Ridge, the scene the previous month of vicious fighting and huge numbers of Australian casualties. The plan called for a counter attack by the Canadian forces on the night of September 15th to retake the ridge. Preparations proceeded despite intense enemy shelling. On September 12th a German plane was shot down and burned behind the Canadian lines.

On September 13th, 380 men, including Grandpa, were ordered to dig a trench to the rear of the front line in preparation for the Canadian offensive. Two men in the party were killed and sixteen were wounded, among them, Grandpa, who was shot in his left shoulder and suffered shrapnel wounds to his left thigh and knee. The medical records show that the shrapnel was removed from his shoulder without anesthetic. When I told my friend Alex Pringle about this, he said, "That was your blood flowing out of the wound." Perhaps that is why I was so affected by the dry account in the medical report.

Grandpa spent one day at the Australian tent hospital at Boulogne before being evacuated to the Military Hospital West Bridgford in Nottinghamshire on September 17. An x-ray showed that shrapnel remained in his left thigh. He was in generally good condition and though he complained of shortness of breath and pain over his pericardium, his heartbeat was strong. Grandpa was prescribed bed rest. A medical examination on October 24th showed that his left knee was continuously swollen and over the next two months bandages were changed daily and eventually the knee improved. He was sent for physical training to the Canadian Military Hospital in Hastings. It was then that another x-ray showed a small piece of shrapnel lodged in his left knee joint. The examining doctor advised against interference with the shrapnel, as he believed it wouldn't prevent Grandpa from carrying on with his occupation of carpentry after the war.

Grandpa returned to hospital to convalesce and he met and courted Grace Ellen East, who worked at a local boy's school. On November 6, 1917 he was granted permission to marry my Grandma Grace and eleven days later their wedding service was performed in the presence of Grandma's sister Dolly and her brother George at the Parish Church, Saint Mary the Virgin, in Mortlake in the county of Surrey.

This was fourteen months after he was shot. On December 12th Grandpa was awarded a good conduct stripe. As he was not fit to return to combat, he was detached for duty with the Egham police.

On September 18, 1918 he and my Grandma — by this time seven months pregnant – sailed for Canada, arriving in Montreal on October 8th.

On October 30th Grandpa was examined in Toronto and an x-ray showed a small fragment of metal in the left knee joint close to the articulation. The Board decided to discharge him as medically unfit for service. He was thirty years old.

Maybe he was lucky.

Two days after he was wounded the planned attack went ahead and the 31st Battalion suffered 350 casualties. The harassing patrols, artillery barrages, gas attacks and charges over no mans' land continued right up until the morning of November 11, 1918 and by that time some 4,400 men had served in the 31st (Alberta) Battalion. Of them 941 were killed and 2,435 were wounded: a casualty rate of 77%. They died at St. Eloi Craters, the Ypres Salient, Vimy Ridge (Thélus Village), Fresnoy, the Somme, and Passchendaele Village. The casualty rate of the 31st (Alberta) Battalion was almost twice that of the general force.

To look at this from a contemporary perspective, some 30,000 Canadians received the General Campaign Star for service in Afghanistan between 2002 and 2010. According to Canadian Casualty Statistics, 158 were killed in action and 2,000 were wounded: a casualty rate of 7%. One remembers the reaction of the Canadian public to each death in Afghanistan and can only wonder what the reaction would have been if the bodies of individual servicemen were returned from the WWI trenches of France. Given that the casualty rate of the Alberta Battalion in France was ten times that of the Afghanistan conflict it is hard to imagine, that but for stifling censorship, there would have been any enthusiasm for the gigantic meat grinder of that "war to end all wars".

Given those odds, it seems almost inevitable that Grandpa would have suffered a wound or worse. As it was, he escaped with painful, but manageable wounds that affected him for the rest of his life. He met my grandmother in England, which he would not otherwise have done, and they had my mother and she had me. As my mother said to me when I shared Grandpa's service records with her, "We nearly didn't make it – me or you."

Jack Sheppard was an eighteen-year-old student when he enlisted in July, 1916. He was five feet seven and had blue eyes and brown hair. Jack was assigned to the 218th Battalion and landed in England aboard the *S.S. Southland* on February 17, 1917. He trained at Purfleet until April 4, 1917 when he was hospitalized with parotitis, which progressed to mumps and ensured his stay in hospital for three weeks.

Two weeks after his discharge from hospital he landed in France and was transferred to the 13th Canadian Infantry Battalion. The Battalion was engaged with the British Forces on a push against the German troops dug in along the St. Quentin-Cambrai front. Morton and Granatstein observed that "the fight to capture Cambrai was the bitterest and most costly part of the long autumn struggle by the Canadian Corps." The plan called for the Canadian Corps to cross the Canal du Nord and capture the Bourlon Wood and the high ground east of it. On Sunday, September 21, 1918 Jack was promoted to Corporal, as the unit continued to train for the action. At 5:20 am on September 27, the order was given and the corps waded across the canal and encountered heavy machine gun fire on the other side.

The operation succeeded and Bourlon Wood was captured but casualties were heavy. The War Diaries record: "on [September] 30th further advances were made, but, as the result of savage counter attacks and a destructive enfilade fire, some of the captured territory had to be yielded again".

Jack was shot in the abdomen and severely wounded in this action – six weeks before the Armistice. On October 3, 1918 he was treated in the field and then shipped back to England to the West General Hospital in Manchester. On November 23rd, he was transferred to the Woodcote Park Military Convalescent Hospital in Epsom where he stayed until he was discharged on December 21, 1918.

On February 12, 1919 Jack was examined by a Medical Board, which recommended that he be discharged, as he was unfit for service. The Board found that "the bullet had entered the costal cartilage at the 9th rib and exited over the tip of the 10th right rib." This was a very lucky shot, for if the angle of entry had been slightly different, the bullet would have entered the chest cavity causing possibly fatal wounds.

Seven years later the *Edmonton Journal* reported that fears were entertained for the safety of the by now 28 year old Jack who had been missing from his parents' home for two days. The paper described Jack's physical appearance and provided details about his car and requested that any information of value be provided to the police. The next day the paper reported that Jack's body had been found in a farmer's field near Legal, Alberta. His car was parked on an adjacent road and a note found in the car was signed by Jack and gave his home address. The story noted that Jack was of a quiet and steady disposition and that he had been in poor health for some time. A full military funeral was held for Jack and the 101st Fusiliers band played to an overflowing crowd at the South Side Metropolitan United Church before interment at the family plot. The medical certificate of cause of death records that Jack died of "a gunshot wound in the head – self inflicted – suicide."

Jack left no spouse or children. Though Great Grandpa Sheppard did not mention in his monograph that Jack killed himself, Rice attributed Jack's early demise to the physical and spiritual wounds he had suffered in the war.

* * *

Stewart Welsh enlisted in Edmonton on October 12, 1916, one year after his brother Alex signed up, and one month after Grandpa was shot. Stewart was thirty years old, five foot seven and he had brown eyes and light brown hair. He was assigned to the Army Medical Corp Training Depot 13 at the Sarcee Barracks in Calgary until September 27, 1918, when he was transferred to the Canadian Army Medical Corps of the Siberian Expeditionary Force. On Boxing Day, 1918, six weeks after the Armistice, he embarked for Siberia aboard the British Steamer, *S.S. Protesilaus*, and arrived in Siberia on January 15, 1919.

Stewart participated in Canada's short-lived and unsuccessful military effort – "a fiasco," according to historian Benjamin Isitt – to thwart the Bolshevik Revolution.

Prime Minister Borden wanted to demonstrate Canada's enhanced international status following her participation in some of the major European battles. He believed that the Russian Revolution could be stopped, the "disease" of Bolshevism cured, and trade relations developed with the White Russian regime. The mission caused a furore in Canada and the union movement threatened a general strike if the Canadian troops were not withdrawn. As Isitt notes: "The general strike tactic which would erupt from Victoria to Winnipeg to Amherst months later – was endorsed as the means for forcing Canadian troops from Siberia."

It soon became apparent that supporting the White Russian General Kolchak was futile because the people supported Bolshevism rather than a return to an aristocratic regime. Isitt quotes a Canadian officer who said: "The people of Siberia resent the presence of the Allied troops ... they regard us as intruders ... they are all Bolshevists in the meaning of the word as it is used here. A Bolshevist, with them is one who wants a change." After four months in Siberia, Stewart returned to Vancouver aboard the *S.S. Empress of Russia*.

* * *

Sid Sheppard, the only one of my great uncles I met, was a character of legendary proportions. He was a prize-winning pig farmer, poet, and gambler *extraordinare*. I remember seeing him in his succulent garden in Penticton and being taken to his "digs", a little office decorated with horse racing forms, which he'd built between his house and garage. He put on a green eye-shade as protection from the overhead light and told me about his system for picking horses. Cigar smoke curled up to the light as Sid laughed and recited his poems and shared his secrets. We drank raspberry wine.

I was not really surprised to discover that Sid had lied about his age and fooled the naval recruiting officer. He applied on November 17, 1916 when he was sixteen years old and ineligible, but he lied and put down November 11, 1898, as his date of birth rather than the true date, which was May 28, 1900. I assume he moved his birth month from May to November as that made him eighteen on the day of recruitment. Uncle Sid was five feet six inches tall and claimed he could swim. One wonders what sort of discussion Grandpa Sheppard had with this son, but whatever it was, it did not prevent Sid from being assigned to the *Niobe* and a series of convoy and patrol boats and minesweepers which sailed out of Plymouth and Milford Haven.

Sid was a stoker Petty Officer when he was demobilized on January 4, 1919. He entered into a vigorous correspondence with the Navy over the next four years until he received his back pay, service medals, and his share of the prize money earned for service in "offensively armed sea-going ships of war between the 4th August 1914 and November 1918." Sid's share was one pound forty pence. His hand-written letters of request are earnest.

A few months after returning from the navy Sid, then twenty, took Miss Phyllis Burke for a cutter ride along Whyte Avenue in Edmonton. Without warning, a car drove at high speed into the back of the cutter sending Sid and his girlfriend many yards from the place of impact and completely demolishing the cutter. Only the horse escaped unhurt. *The Edmonton Bulletin* for October 28, 1919 reported that Sid lay in a precarious condition at the General Hospital, suffering from concussion of the brain. Luckily both Sid and Miss Burke recovered.

\* \* \*

Jim Welsh was twenty-four years old when he enlisted at Hamilton on January 2, 1917. He was five foot seven, with dark hair, brown eyes and teeth which needed attention. He was assigned to the 54th Battalion, (the Central Ontario Regiment) of the Canadian Infantry and arrived in Liverpool aboard the *SS Justicia* on July 5, 1917. While on board, on July 1, 1917, he signed his military will and gave the whole of his property and estate to his brother, Jack Welsh.

On the morning of July 20, two weeks after he arrived in England, Jim attended a physical training parade at the depot at Westenhanger, Kent. Staff Sergeant Hardie was in charge of the exercise and he noticed that Jim was not paying strict attention to the details that he was giving for the various exercises. Sgt. Hardie ordered Jim to come out to the front for the purpose of showing him the exercise. Jim replied: "I don't want to come out." When Sgt. Hardie repeated the order, Jim said, "I won't."

Jim was charged before a District Court Martial at West Sandling with "disobeying in such a manner as to show wilful defiance of authority of a lawful command given personally by his Superior Officer in the execution of his office". Jim represented himself and argued that he was doing the best he could and that the sergeant ordered him to be put in detention without asking for an explanation. According to Jim, the Sergeant had previously said that if the exercises were hurting anyone he need not do them. Jim said he was having some pain and was awaiting an operation.

Under a cross-examination conducted by Jim, Sgt. Hardie confirmed that Jim had objected to the exercise by refusing to come out to the front. The purpose for which Jim was ordered to the front was to go through the exercise. The Sergeant was not aware that Jim had a disability and did not recall him asking to be excused previously. He said that Jim was doing the exercises in a sloppy manner, that Jim did not tell him there was anything wrong with him, and that Jim did not ask to be paraded out to the medical officer. This cross-examination underlined all the main points for the prosecution and illustrates why a man who acts for himself has a fool for a client. It also shows that the twenty-four-year-old farmer from Owen Sound was no match for the practiced drill sergeants.

The Court Martial found Jim guilty and sentenced him to twenty-eight days detention and ordered him to forfeit forty-eight days pay, including the twenty days he spent waiting for his trial. The sentence was "promulgated" to Jim before a full parade, presumably to make an example of him, and he served his time at the Shorncliffe Detention Barracks in Kent. Upon his release on November 2, 1917 he returned to his unit.

This was two weeks before his older brother, Grandpa Alex, was married in Surrey. There is no record of his attendance at the wedding and, indeed, he may not have known of it.

On Valentine's Day in 1918 Jim was taken on strength of the 54th

Battalion in East Sandling. A week later he was placed under suspension of pay for four and a half days "to make good for a table knife lost by neglect". He received pay of one dollar a day; the knife was valued at $4.50.

Jim's war was not going well and it was about to get a lot worse.

On July 8th, 1918 his unit received orders to move into Garvelle-Oppy. This was a holding action, to maintain the line secured by the 94th Brigade at high cost during May and June. The Battalion's War Diaries report that the six-day tour in the front line was uneventful, except for a patrol's encounter in no man's land and a raid on an enemy machine gun post.

On the night of July 22/23rd the battalion was relieved and moved into divisional reserve. The War Diaries record:

> "A" Company was located in a railway cutting upon which the enemy opened up at about 10 am the next day (July 23,1918) – blue cross gas and high explosive shells mixed, while the men were, for the most part, asleep. One man was killed and two men wounded and a large number gassed to a greater or lesser extent.

Jim was the man killed – six days after his twenty-sixth birthday. It is not clear whether he was killed by a high explosive shell or if he died from gas. Having read about the effects of gas, I hope he was blown to bits as he slept. The other option is too awful to contemplate. As Tim Cook writes:

> The properties of [Blue Cross Gas] which was actually a fine dust, caused violent sneezing, vomiting, delusions and general weariness in the victim. The gassed men were, as one report noted, "the picture of utter dejection" and in extreme cases were "temporarily driven mad by their pain and misery" as the chemical attacked the nervous system and resulted in violent convulsions and the loss of motor control.

In a world without twenty-four-hour news coverage, it took four months for the army to inform my Great Grandmother of her son's death. Jim is buried at Roclincourt Military Cemetery.

He was killed while Grandpa and Grandma were celebrating the first months of their marriage in England. Grandpa would not have found out about Jim's death until he returned to Canada because his mother, Florence, would have received the notice just as Grandpa and Grandma arrived at her home in Owen Sound.

Grandma had had a difficult passage on the ship from England. One month after their arrival in Canada, on November 8th, a boy was born. Grandpa and Grandma named him James. One can imagine Florence's anguish and joy. I never knew before I found the records that my Uncle Jim was named after a twenty-six-year-old man who was killed in action at Oppy Wood.

The Memorial Plaque and Scroll, which were issued to the next of kin as a commemoration of the soldier's sacrifice in the service of the King, were dispatched to Florence on October 10, 1921. The files note that Jim was not eligible for the 1914-15 Star, the Victory Medal or the British War Medal. I have read the criteria for these medals and, while Jim was not eligible for the Star as he did not serve before December 31, 1915, he was eligible for the other two since he did serve before November 11, 1918, and indeed, died in the mud of France. I will be pursuing this matter. I would like the medals to go to my mother.

\* \* \*

On January 15, 1918 the Edmonton Women's Press Club held an afternoon tea in honour of the mothers who had given three or more sons in the cause of the war. Some seventy mothers were invited and nearly fifty, including my great-grandmother Elizabeth Sheppard, attended. She had contributed four sons but there were several women who had five sons enlisted. The story in the *Edmonton Bulletin* on January 16, 1918 lists the mothers and the number of sons each contributed. The writer gushed:

> *The drawing room, conservatories and tea rooms were delightfully cozy and inviting and the guests were charmed with the lovely home. Each mother was presented with a posy of pink carnation and fern .... Mrs. McLung in her bright, happy and spirited way spoke very happily ....*

Bright, happy talk was needed to keep upper lips stiff, but what was truly in the minds of the mothers? Many of them had already suffered deeply. They'd lost their beautiful sons and the promise of grandchildren, even support in their old age. Their futures were smaller and sadder as they worried how it would all turn out. Whether their sons were killed or maimed, dark thoughts must have hung in the air as the posies were handed out.

My Great Aunt Mildred wrote of her brothers (the Sheppards) in 1982, saying: "I had four brothers go overseas and all returned but not without damage. I remember the church put on a wonderful supper for all the boys when they came home." One can imagine the sad affair with Jack wounded, Rice estranged from four years in France, Bill breathing with difficulty, and Sid recovering from the concussion suffered in the cutter accident. It would take a master to put a positive spin on this misadventure.

In the beginning no one was a stronger supporter of the war effort than Rice Sheppard. Early on he advocated a farmer's militia to provide homeland defence and later he recruited a Militia of 800 men. He supported the war through the enlistment of four of his five sons. In the closing paragraph of a letter to the editor of the *Edmonton Bulletin* in March, 1916, in which he had set out the arguments in favour of the United Farm Militia, Rice Sheppard said: "I hope, Mr. Editor, this explanation of our movement will satisfy all that it is a worthy and good cause, that will help the Dominion and Empire. God Save the King." No one could question his dedication to the Dominion, the King, and the war effort.

By 1919 feelings had changed. Rigorous censorship during the war years prevented Canadians from learning the truth about the terrible conflict. Press reports were heavily censored to ensure no information that could be useful to the enemy was published. This meant casualty figures were not reported. Nor were the details of battles lost, nor the terrible conditions faced by the troops. For example, as Keshen notes, in reporting on the battle at Ypres: "Beaverbrook did not mention the 6,000 casualties, but emphasized that those who fell 'died the best way men can: full of vigour of life and inspired by the determination to succeed at all costs'."

Letters from the men serving on the front were also censored to prevent disturbing news from reaching home and discouraging recruitment.

> Soldier correspondence was checked by military authorities, but its sheer volume meant that some material painting a less than glorious view of war got through. [The Censor] warned editors they would be held responsible if letters they reprinted revealed military secrets or had the effect of discouraging recruitment.

By the war's end the extent of the sacrifice and the bungling was becoming apparent. As Morton and Granatstein observed, Canada had contributed 620,000 men to the war effort of whom 60,000 died and 155,000 were wounded.

> From mourning, it was easy to move to disillusionment. The pre-war pacifists had denounced the "merchants of death" as manufacturers of war but now their theories explained a terrible reality of profitable devastation. Krupp, Vickers, Schneider, and other vast armament firms had profited from the war. Generals, too, emerged with little credit from a war that they had seemingly prolonged. The same electorates that had accepted their genius in wartime now felt savagely disillusioned at be-medalled commanders who lived in safety while their orders sent hundreds of thousands of uniformed civilians to their deaths.

Rice Sheppard was convinced the old line parties had used the war to profit the monied interests at the expense of the common people. He advocated the end of the party system and the election of independent members, free from the influence of the banks and big business. In a stirring column written in *The Alberta Non Partisan* on June 19, 1919, he targeted the elected politicians.

> ... What an awful charge lies against the men who accepted the responsibility of representing the people [who] have neglected that duty. Do they realize that the blood spent by the nation is to a large extent upon them, for the reason that they who had the power to make laws that would bring about right conditions neglected to do so, and instead created conditions that brought great wealth to a privileged few, who have become so great a

*burden upon the masses of the people, that they cannot longer bear them. This class have oppressed the workers and done everything in their power to keep them from learning the truth, and discovering the real cause of war with all its suffering which falls principally upon the workers ....*

*Our governments have pampered and pap-fed the big interests, and made it possible for the banks of the Dominion to fill their coffers with millions of money that could have been saved for the people, they have allowed war contracts to be hawked around and millions made out of them .... They bartered away our natural resources, our timber, gas and oil lands, coal, water power ....*

*They cried for help to save the nation, and the world for Democracy, and we gave our boys and we gave ourselves, for we worked harder than ever before .... But we must take upon ourselves part of the responsibility of these conditions for we elected whatever was offered us, ... [and we] allowed ourselves to be fooled by the slick politicians, and now we are suffering the results. ...*

*Let us be free from all party ties and prepared to take a stand as men to work for the true interest of all the people. Our old system has failed to give proper results, only by Independent Action can the peoples of our Dominion rise to the higher plane of justice and freedom – a true democracy.*

Rice Sheppard's anger at the betrayal of the common people was not unique to him and the sentiment he expressed so forcefully fuelled the radical politics of the prairies for a generation. These words give vent to the feelings that brought the United Framers of Alberta and later the Social Credit Party to power in Alberta and the CCF to power in Saskatchewan.

I see his activism in politics as a form of grieving. He was keeping himself busy to stop thinking too much about his loss. This is a deliberate act of remembrance, for naturally there are few alive today who remember my Grandpa or great uncles, and fewer still who would know of their involvement in the Great War. I myself did not know these stories. This was a journey of discovery for me and I am frustrated that I cannot know more. I would give anything to sit down over a brandy with Grandpa and his bothers and Rice Sheppard and his boys. But all of them are dead and there is no one alive who can tell me more.

As I followed the individual experiences I began to see the devastating impact of the war on these families. There is no glory in these accounts. There is no joy at victory, no hatred or hunger for blood. These eight young men did their duty. They enlisted and some of them were comparatively lucky, but years were taken from all these men. One very young man died immediately. Two died of war-related injuries within years of the Armistice. The rest bore physical and psychological wounds and infirmities that clouded their lives. Similar stories could doubtless be told by all who served, and all who cared for them.

My generation never went to war. We were spared what my father and grandfather were not. Still, I recall as a young man that I had passions and energy that could have been whipped to a frothy enthusiasm for combat – the same drive that motivated Uncle Sid. I envied my dad's war experience. My brother and I fought for the chance to parade about the house wearing his navy hat. Watching war movies that glorified combat and promoted violence as a response to injustice, we hankered to give guns a chance. Our generation was lucky that no incident touched off a huge irrational storm because I fear we may have welcomed it, until we discovered too late that war is a grinding awful business – just as my grandfather and great uncles learned.

Now that I am a father and grandfather myself I can imagine the sheer terror I would feel if my son or grandson were called up, or signed up voluntarily in some rush of patriotic fervour. As an older man I see only downsides. I feel the despair of Rice Sheppard and I understand his anger at his loss.

In 1940 he erected a memorial for his sons. By then three of the four boys who enlisted were dead. Rice Sheppard put his considerable energy into supporting the war and recruiting young men to serve. He ended up surviving his own sons. That must partly explain his passionate commitment to politics. He was running for mayor as an old man and still trying to combat the forces which had caused the war. Rice wrote:

> *[The war was won] by the sacrifice of thousands ... of men who went over the top facing Hell in the shape of gas and shell that the day may be saved and as they hoped, the day of a true democracy might soon dawn. Four of my boys faced that Hell. One bled, another was gassed, another was struck down by fever, but all joyfully suffered and many of yours did the same.*

He must have been very lonely as he sat in his garden, wood-carving and reminiscing about what might have been, but for the war. The great reprieve he was given – an extra fifty years of life – was diminished by his sons' loss of vitality.

Rice died the week before my parents were married – a year and a half before I was born.

* * *

When I was a boy and we stayed with Grandma and Grandpa Welsh, I remember Grandpa sitting in his chair at the kitchen table and slicing a boiled egg in an egg cup. I had never seen this operation before and was amazed at how he could make the knife slice through shell. The yolk dribbled down the cup and he dabbed it with his toast. He sipped his tea and winked at me. His eyebrow was a bush and it bobbed up and down. I stood beside the table with my chin resting on my hand and admired him.

I learned later that his wounds bothered him all his life and that he suffered from flashbacks and terrible nightmares. He had trouble working as a carpenter because of the pain. During the Great Depression Grandpa himself became depressed because he had trouble finding work, and he decided that Grandma and the children would be better off without him. He slashed his throat with a straight razor and began bleeding to death. Grandma found him and tried to stop the bleeding and ordered my mother, who was then seven years old, to run for help. Mom felt frozen to the spot, eventually running, as if in slow motion, to the neighbours.

Grandpa was sent to the Ponoka Hospital (Asylum) for three years and Grandma had to support five children by cleaning people's houses and scrimping. Jack told Grandma she should leave the neighbourhood because it was embarrassing to have the family of a person who had attempted suicide living in the same district. This from Jack the deserter. Grandma never forgave him. Neither could she understand how Colonel Griesbach's batman, who lived down the street, was granted a full military pension, when Grandpa – who had been wounded – received nothing.

Grandma and Grandpa admired and voted for Rice Sheppard. They shared his disillusionment with the bankers and the leaders of the old parties and supported his call for the union of farmers and workers.

* * *

The other day I tried to drive by the little house Grandpa built for Grandma but it has been replaced by a freeway. The rose pink chair and the sepia photo are gone, and the people who lived and loved there are as far away as the war that brought them together in the unreachable, unchangeable past.

# Barnardo Boy

Henry (Harry) Thomas Jones: Dec 3, 1891 – Feb 22, 1919

*Ethel Edey*

### Carberry, Manitoba: February 27, 1919

It was an impressive funeral. Six of your fellow Carberry soldiers carried the coffin, which was draped in the Union Jack. Twenty-six returned men marched in the procession. A fourteen-member firing party and bugler from Winnipeg 16th Battalion, C.E.F. gave an exciting performance. You would have been pleased with the large crowd in attendance. I was so relieved when the military authorities took charge of the arrangements. I tried to be brave, as you always wanted me to be. Now, with John out for the evening and the children asleep I am free to let the tears flow. My dear brother, once again we are separated, and my only comfort is this tattered shoebox of keepsakes.

### Kidderminster, England: 1897

This family photo shows the five of us, Mamma, Daddy, you, me, and little Jack. Being only a year apart, you and I were good friends and free kindred spirits until Mamma and Daddy got sick with the consumption. Mamma died December 28, 1899 when I was nine, you were eight and Jack was five. When Daddy became too sick to work there was no one to look after little Jack, so he was sent to the orphanage. One night when Daddy was home from the infirmary, I overheard Grandma talking: "I went to the Meeting House to hear that kind Christian man, Dr. Barnardo, speak about the thousands of orphaned street kids he has rescued from a life of poverty and crime. He said the children were all taught a trade and there were wonderful opportunities for these children to work on farms in Canada – a land of plenty. With me working all day at the carpet mill just to put food on the table, Harry and Ethel are running wild like street kids." Daddy said, "No daughter of mine is going to one of those homes! But it might mean a better life for Harry."

## Kidderminster, England: 1902

Here is a photo of the two of us – you look smart in your new Barnardo suit. There were six hundred children at the Bernardo home in Stepney. After prayers and a breakfast of bread, porridge and tea you did household chores, and then had lessons in reading, writing and scriptures. In the afternoon everyone worked at a trade.

A few months later came the news that you were going with a large group of other ten-year old Barnardo boys, to Canada. I was inconsolable. Canada was on the other side of the world! I thought I would never see you again. You made me promise not to cry. I made you promise to write to me about your adventures and to never lose touch. Grandma took me to the docks to see you off on the *SS New England*.

Here it is, your first letter. I had waited so long I was sure you had forgotten your promise.

*Dear Sis: I am now in Canada. It was a long trip. After many days the ship docked in a place called Boston. It is a lot like London. Then we got on a train and after a long trip we got to Toronto in Canada. We walked from the station to the Barnardo home here. It is a brick building but much smaller than Stepney. I stayed there for 5 days. Then me and some of the other boys got on another train. Canada is so big. For 2 days all we saw was trees and lakes. Then the land was flat and there were many farms. We got off the train in Emerson, Manitoba. A Barnardo man met us and took us to different farms. I am living with Mr. and Mrs. John Smith. They are kindly enough but the work is hard. I get up early to feed the horses and milk the cows. It is harvest time. Mr. Smith is a good farmer and teaches me how to do the work. The food is good, fresh cream and eggs. I help Mrs. Smith digging potatoes and picking peas from her garden. Every night I am so tired I am asleep before I finish my prayers. I only have time to write today because it is raining. I so miss you and Daddy but I am being brave. Harry*

I kept all the letters you wrote about the different farms where you stayed. About snowdrifts and the biting cold in the winter. How you learned all the different kinds of farm work, from barnyard chores, to driving horses for ploughing, seeding and harvesting the crops. How the Barnardo boys would get together to visit and share stories. Of the new friends you made and how you now thought of Canada as your true home.

### Kidderminster, England: March, 1910

Here is the photo of me with my Bernardo charges leaving for Canada on the *SS Tunisian*. I was so very excited to be joining you in Manitoba. I saved every penny I could working at the mill, hoping to have enough one day to go to Canada. Then I heard Barnardo was looking for volunteers to accompany a group of children. This was my chance. You wrote that the Bradley's would let me stay with you at their home in Carberry, Manitoba, and I could get work looking after the neighbour's children. I hardly recognized you. You had grown big and strong – no longer the skinny boy I remembered. Life was good: we were together again. We both had jobs. We went to dances, county fairs, box socials. Cassie Bradley was like a sister to me.

### SS *Royal George*: December, 1913

We joined the Barnardo Christmas excursion to England. Here is the photo of me on the deck of the ship. It was wonderful to visit with Daddy and Grandma. They were so proud of the man you had become and could not believe the stories of our new life in Canada. After only three days I was ready to leave. London was so crowded and noisy, and the air thick with coal fog. We both were missing the blue skies, open spaces and solitude of farm life in Manitoba. More likely, we were missing my John and your Cassie.

### *Wellwood, Manitoba: October, 1914*

My wedding photo: There I am with my two favorite guys – you and John. You both look so very handsome. Such a happy time for us. We were hearing reports Canada was sending troops to England to help fight in the war against Germany, but it seemed so far away.

### *Brandon, Manitoba: September, 1915*

My, you do look official in your army uniform and new moustache. On the back of the photo you wrote: *"Hello Sis: Just to let you know I am still alive and well. Hope you are the same. Is it stopped raining down there. We had three days rain here last week but it is fairing up now. Have you thrashed any yet? How is the boy getting on? Hope he is well. There is some talk of us going away soon but do not know for sure. Write as soon as you can. B Company 79 Batt Brandon.*

The boy he mentions is my little Edward, who was born in May, premature and sickly. You were just as proud as John was when he was born.

I didn't want you to sign up for the army but you felt you should serve your country and the commonwealth, and all the local lads were signing up. You left your Attestation Paper with me for safe-keeping. *"Henry Thomas Jones, no. 150985; born in Kidderminster, England; next of kin: Edward Jones, father; date of birth: 3 Dec 1891; trade: farm labourer;*
*23 years of age, 5'8", ruddy complexion, brown eyes, reddish brown hair."*

*England: April, 1916*

*Dear Sis: I am now here in England. We sailed from Halifax on April 24. I have been transferred to the 16ᵗʰ Canadian Scottish Regiment. I had this picture taken in my new uniform when I went to Kidderminster to visit our father. He is well and was happy to see the picture of you and baby Edward. There is talk we will be going to France soon. Harry.*

This is when my worry started. Eagerly waiting for a letter, but dreading the news it might contain. Reading the horrible war accounts in the paper, scanning the lists of men killed or missing, praying every night for your safe return.

*France: August, 1916*

*Dear Sis: Arrived in France June 28. Our regiment was involved in heavy fighting in Ypres. The Germans started using poison gas so they gave us gas masks. But many of our men died or got sick from the gas. We spend days and nights in trenches. Sometimes the water is up to our knees. It rains a lot here. We are pestered by rats, fleas, and lice. We pass the time playing cards and sharing stories. I'm giving this to a wounded fellow who is being sent back to England. Hope you get it and that you, John & the boy are fine. Harry*

After so many months of waiting I was thrilled to receive your letter. Hearing of the poison gas gave me something else to worry about. I prayed more.

*France: November, 1916*

*Dear Sis: Having a few days furlough. Enjoying a soft bed and hot food in a small French village. After Ypres our Canadian troops moved to support the British for the Somme offensive. It started badly as many of our munitions were duds. In September we saw the first British tanks. Our troops moved fast and captured Courcelette ahead of the seven tanks we had with us. For the next two months progress was slow. Snow has brought an end to the fighting. It seems war is like farming: success or failure often depends on the weather. We have suffered many, many casualties. By the grace of God, I remain safe. Hope you are fine. Harry*

183

*Carberry: February, 1917*

Here is a clipping from the Brandon Daily Star, Feb. 14. *4,000 Barnardo Boys in Service: C. Bogue Smart, inspector of British Immigration to Canada, writing to the honorary director of Barnardo's Homes, says: "The conduct of your boys in Canada in this national crisis is wonderful. Just consider these young fellows, at one time almost forgotten, coming forward; voluntarily, leaving profitable situations, to the number of over four thousand, to answer the call of King and country!"*

*France: April, 1917*

*Dear Sis: Enjoyed your Christmas package. The lads & I ate it all before the rats could get it. Finally seeing some success with our capture of Vimy Ridge during a snowstorm. We spent the winter building miles of tunnels for our troops to pass through. Observation balloons gave us a good picture of German positions so it was a short battle. We still suffered many casualties. I was recommended for a commission but declined. Much yet to be done here on the ground and I don't want to leave the lads. Hope you and baby John Henry are well. Thrilled you named him after me. Harry*

I was not surprised that you declined an officer position. I knew the real reason was you would not want to leave your buddies. You were always loyal to your friends, telling stories, playing jokes.

*France: June, 1917*

*Dear Sis: Fought in the short Battle of Fresnoy in Scarpe. It was called off after two days due to heavy casualties. Here is a photo of me with my new Sergeant stripes. This is not a very good one but is the best I could get. Hope you get it alright. Harry.*

*France: August, 1917*

*Dear Sis: This war drags on with little progress and many casualties. Our brigade pulled off a successful raid on Hill 70 near Lens. Most others didn't fare so well when met with poison gas and flamethrowers. After 10 days of heavy fighting we are pretty well back where we started. So many good men killed, wounded or gassed for no gain. Hope it is a good harvest and you and the boys are well. Harry.*

It was always such a relief to receive a letter and hear you were still alive. The stories we read in the newspapers were so horrible I could not take it in. Cassie and I took comfort from each other but all we could do was continue to pray for your safe return. You had already been gone a year – how much longer could this war go on?

### *Carberry, Manitoba: September, 1917*

A clipping from the *Carberry News-Express*: *For conspicuous gallantry and devotion to duty during a raid near Arras, local boy, Sargent H.T. Jones was awarded the Distinguished Conduct Medal. His officer being killed, he took command of the party, put the enemy to flight, captured a machine gun, completely destroyed the enemy's position and safely withdrew his party, bringing back the officer's body and the machine gun. His courage and resourcefulness were responsible for the success of the raid.*

This story was the talk of the town. Cassie and I were both so proud, but it reminded us again of the great danger you were in every day.

### *France: November, 1917*

*Dear Sis: Survived the worst battle of the war. Huge amounts of rain since August turned the fields here into a muddy bog. Mud was so deep many men and horses drowned trying to get to the front lines. Most muck I've ever seen. Much worse than a Manitoba farmyard in spring thaw. Those of us left are exhausted from the heavy fighting and trudging through the mud. Now that Passchendaele has been captured we are on furlough to rest up. The poor farmers here. First we built trenches across their wheat fields, now the fields are totally destroyed. Happy to sleep in a real bed and eat hot food. Hope you are keeping well. Harry.*

### *Bexhill, England: September, 1918*

*Dear Sis: Sending this from England where I am taking an officer's*  185

*training course. This photo shows me in my new uniform. After the battle
at Amiens I was given a commission without option so here I am. Our
brigade fought well and the Aussies were a great help. The war seems to be
turning in our favour so I am hopeful it will be over soon. Visited Daddy.
He is well and sends his best wishes to you and the baby girl. Expect to be
here until November. Harry.*

## Carberry, Manitoba: November 11, 1918

The news of the Armistice spread through town like a wild fire. Everyone
was celebrating. Cassie and I hugged each other and jumped up and
down like schoolgirls. Our prayers had been answered! You would be
coming home safe and sound. We were hopeful you would be home
for Christmas, and what a Christmas it would be.

## Carberry, Manitoba: December 18, 1918

John and I bundled everyone up to meet the train. I knew you would
want to see the children. Cassie and Mr. and Mrs. Bradley also drove
down. There was a large crowd there to welcome you home. I think it
was the most excited I've ever been in my life. I could hardly believe
it was true that you were home. What a reunion – I could hardly take
it all in. The children were a little shy at first but you quickly charmed
them until they didn't want to let go of you. Of course, Cassie & I
didn't want to let you out of our sight either.

The clipping from *The Carberry News-Express*, December 19, 1918:

> *Wednesday night a large crowd was at the C.P.R. station to
> welcome two Carberry heroes who crossed the Atlantic on
> the new boat "Minnedosa" arriving in Winnipeg Wednesday
> morning, Lieut. H. Jones and Lieut. W.C. Lawson. Both these
> men left Carberry as privates and were recommended for
> promotion by their superior officers for good work and efficiency
> on the field. Lieut. Jones has probably the longest trench record
> of any of our boys and brought back with him a Distinguished
> Conduct Medal and advanced from a private to a lieutenant
> .... He was in all the big battles at Ypres, Somme, Vimy Ridge,*

*Fresnoy, Hill 70, Passchendaele and Amiens ..... Lieut. Jones brought back with him a large number of souvenirs .... The two boys were pleased with the hearty reception given them on their arrival.*

### Carberry, Manitoba: February 27, 1919

We had a glorious Christmas with you, the Bradleys, brother Jack, and John's family. We were well entertained with your war stories and the children's excitement. Life was settling into a new routine. Mr. Bradley was talking about retirement now you were home to take over the farm. Cassie was making wedding plans. The local folk were enjoying your souvenir exhibit in the jewellery store. The children loved Uncle Harry's visits; you always had treats in your pocket and tricks to play on them. Then suddenly you became so ill. The doctor said it was the Spanish 'flu, which came back with the returning soldiers. Cassie, Mrs. Bradley and I took turns at your bedside, but there was nothing we could do. What a cruel turn of fate, bringing you back safely from the war, only to take you away from us a few weeks later. We are separated once again. I have no choice but to try to be brave, as you always taught me.

I take comfort in the tribute from today's *News-Express*:

*CROSSED THE BAR: LIEUT. HENRY THOMAS JONES.*
*A peculiar sense of sadness crept over the people of the town and surrounding country when it became known, on Saturday after-noon last, that Lieut. Henry Thomas Jones had ended his last long earthly fight, a fight in which, be it said, he displayed that same courage and determination which made him a good soldier in the service of his King and Country. The late Lieut. Jones was a victim of the influenza epidemic which has prevailed for the last couple of weeks. He was well and favourably known in Carberry and district, and when early last week it became known that his condition was serious, inquiries regarding him flowed in from many sources. The interest, which was born of acquaintance with a genial soul, was intensified, as was the sadness surrounding his*

187

*death, by the fact that he had seen long service in the Great War .... The feeling throughout the entire community is that a MAN is gone out from amongst us.*

## Author's Note

One year after her brother's death, Ethel Jones Edey, died on March 11, 1920 of the Spanish influenza, leaving three children under five years of age. The eldest, Edward, was my father.

Between 1870 and 1930, approximately 100,000 children from the British Isles came to Canada from the streets of London and Liverpool. There are over one million descendants of these children in Canada today. Child migration was a way of populating the colonies with 'British Stock' and of providing a source of cheap labour. This immigration was encouraged by the Canadian government.

The Barnardo homes were started in 1867 by Thomas Barnardo who felt called to devote himself to helping destitute children. Barnardo's homes sent over 30,000 children to Canada starting in 1882. Barnardo typically received 12 applications for every available child. Barnardo's commitment to his children was genuine and their affections for him were deep and permanent. The Canadian government declared 2010 "The Year of the British Home Children". Canada Post issued a stamp with an image of a Barnardo Boy working on a farm in Russell, Manitoba.

London in 1900 was filthy. Coal was the main fuel, giving off clouds of noxious smoke. Children, ragged and filthy, barefoot and hungry, constantly struggled for survival. Hordes of urchins eked out a hand-to-mouth existence while their parents worked fourteen hour days in factories. In east London there was no clean water for washing and drinking, nearly 20% of children died before their first birthday.

Diphtheria, cholera and measles flourished. Rent, even for hovels, was so high that when parents were unable to work, they quickly fell into arrears and would be thrown out on the street. Children were often considered orphans if they had one surviving parent, had been abandoned by their family, or were forced out into the world because of overcrowding at home.

The Spanish Influenza was brought to Canada by soldiers returning from World War I. The greatest effects were felt between 1918 and 1919 but the flu epidemic continued into the 1920's, eventually killing over 50,000 Canadians. The virulent virus claimed more victims than the battlefields of Europe, killing over 20 million people world-wide. In Canada the population donned masks to limit exposure, public gatherings were cancelled and public buildings were closed. The medical system was overwhelmed and the deputy prime minister issued a plea for women to help care for the sick, no nursing experience required.

*Acknowledgements*

I am grateful for the family research documented by my late uncle, John Henry (Harry) Edey, without which, this story would not have been possible. Thanks also to my sister-in-law, Jo Ann Edey, who brought this research to my attention.

# "What War
# Really Means I Know Now"

## Dr. Norman V. Leslie, World War One Surgeon

### *Dr. Mary Anderson*

Dr. Norman V. Leslie (1883-1947) was a surgeon at the French Front during World War One. He was a good friend of the McQuesten family of Whitehern in Hamilton. He sent many letters home to Thomas Baker McQuesten (1882-1948) during the war about his service in the trenches, which he describes graphically. The complete set of letters is preserved in the *Whitehern Museum Archives (*www. whitehern.ca). The first is written on the ship going over to England when Dr. Leslie is in a buoyant mood. Following that are three of his many letters, describing conditions as experienced by a working surgeon at the front. The three letters appear here in their entirety since the complete letter best conveys Dr. Norman Leslie's personality and his relationship with Tom McQuesten. Square bracketed question marks indicate that words are illegible.

## To Thomas B. McQuesten from Dr. Norman V. Leslie

October 17, 1915, To: Whitehern, Hamilton
From: #2 Canadian General Hospital [France]

Cher T.B.

You cast dust on my name. I do write and have answered every letter
of yours. So Gordon Southam is a Major. Good. He will make good
no doubt, but one can't help thinking of the many captains and
lieutenants out since the first, who one would imagine would be given
the chance of promotion. This business is one of favor and interest
from top to bottom thru' and thru' [?] a pull; such is the [?] Are we
ever going to get a chance to sink somebody? You perhaps notice that
Hugh's son is a Brigadier General. Great! From Captain to Major (I
am not sure which), to Brigadier. Shades of Napoleon, and all in a year.

After the last big affair we were certainly busy getting very serious
cases and lashings of them. Poor devils. Such hellish injuries, bones
smashed to splinters, great chunks of flesh and muscle torn away, and
on top of that pus running from them: nearly all, and very frequently
gas-gangrene and infections which develops with great rapidity and
eats up and destroys good healthy tissue. The buglers of the camp
were busy calling the last post for a time. This is the hideous part. The
beautiful part is the way the Tommy takes his wounds – quite silent
in pain and facing a maimed future with cheery fortitude. They are
wonders. The stories they write about the soldier are very true. He is
working hard.

They like the Canadians very much, nurses and doctors. Their
superiors, many of them do not (we reciprocate) we are a rather
dreadful lot and cause them a great deal of worry about us and our
morals. We really are not so dreadful, but some of them are so smug
and so virtuous, and really cannot mind their own affairs. But I am [?]
[?] – so go buy yourself a drink with this. Write! Who am I going to [?]

Yours,
Norman Leslie

August 16, 1916
To: Whitehern Hamilton, Ontario
From: [France]

My Dear Tom,

Your letter to hand. I had not gotten your letter or tobacco or the tabac itself, but thank you just the same.

Well old dear, this is somewhat different from the base hospital. Of course the work in the hospital is far better every way. Here the opportunities for medical work are necessarily limited. You look at a man and send him out. But on the other hand are lots of excitements etc. The life at least so far is not monotonous; one sees all sorts of grim things and hears the most unconscionable rackets. The roar and bark of our guns is most annoying, and always jolts one considerably. It is so sudden and penetrating. The sound of the enemy shells is even more disconcerting as they have a very tangible bite to their bark to them. As for adventures: Well! A medical officer's life is not a patch on the soldier's who has to be in the trenches all the time but even tho' one has his narrow escapes. I have had two or three narrow ones, that is comparatively narrow where the luck broke my way, but they are really not worth recounting for so many others have had so many really narrow brushes and they say nothing of it. All the same the life is very wearing and men very soon show the strain tho' they stay with it just the same.

Am very glad George [Norman Leslie's brother] has done so well, and in a way am sorry to see him start for he is likely to get it. That is the usual outcome. Still that is what he has gone in for. He will get over I think.

[Baines?] father has certainly got the local touch down cold. His view and little bits of scenery are easily seen all over the place. He knows this life all right. It is a scene of utter desolation all right, wrecked buildings, dug outs stuck everywhere and nothing seen but soldiers. Grass and weeds grow everywhere. In the trenches you see blue cornflowers and red poppies sprouting up from the bags, a pretty sight in its way.

Then the rats. Their name is legion. You see grass stirring and a slinking form sneak along in the day. Then at night they become very bold. There are several devils that come into my abode every night. There is a sort of window. You cast your eye at this, and there are two or three peering at you, and when it is quiet they slip into the room. I hate them, but have been able to kill none yet. Occasionally you see a wild cat that has remained true to its name, but these cats don't seem able to handle the [question?]. They are very thin poor things. Truly this is a strange place, and it is going to be a great problem after the war. There is such ruin and there will be so many dead to dispose of. They are everywhere.

Well old top write again,

Yours,
Norman Leslie

October 15, 1916
To: Whitehern, Hamilton, Ontario
From: Dr. Norman Leslie, [France]

My Dear Tom,

Yours received and glad as always was I to hear from you. I have got as I remember one package – Bull Durham tobacco from you, but I have received one package not named, of pipe tobacco, and I have received two packages from Miss McMeekin's florist & Drewery's Drug Store. These as I infer are her own private gift to me (warn squalls) and I am taking them as such. So one of your packages has probably gone astray. But please have your card put in so you get the benefit of my prayers, not as unknown, so all will then be right and proper as should be.

As you say, I should get leave to Canada, and believe me I am going to have a try. As for resigning, I think I will stick it out though when I have spent six months or more up, I think I will have a try for England. I never have been there and should have little trouble in getting it as I have spent about two years in France. Still I don't know but what I like France and probably will be dead keen on getting back. My life at the Front I like. True there are certain times when one wishes he hadn't but those times are not frequent, and one has to take the thick with the thin, and at that my position is so much better than the first lines, that I really by comparison am quite safe. The recent fighting in which the Canadians have figured and that well has been severe but the losses compared with what was gained are slight.

I have gained a great respect for the Germans as a dugout builder. These dugouts are up to 30 feet deep, sloping shafts generally two, sunk into the chalk, and at its bottom generally a passage with small rooms cut out. These stairs at one time were away from the direction of fire, but as the dugouts changed hands, what were the back doors, naturally became the front doors, and as Fritz had the range of these dugouts the porch became a sorting place. Some casualties resulted from this, but down below, one was safe tho' alarmed for to have a shell hit above you or near you caused a disturbance which did not make for comfort. The dugouts themselves, some of the ones taken over were terribly dirty equipment British and German, and smell very badly from more horrible causes. The Germans had made bunks and on these were pillowcases. These often were blood soaked and horrible. Some did not have the dead cleared out till our own men did it. Some of the sights on the road and trenches recently taken were horrible. Seared themselves into my brain. I know dead in all sorts of attitudes and conditions. At that time it was impossible to clear them. We had enough to do with the living and it is not right to risk the living for the dead. But we clean up quickly and are decent burying as soon as possible so by now all will be gone and identified.

What war really means I know now. The sights, sounds and conditions are terrible; but shining through it all, the manly virtues; courage, steadfastness and self sacrifice. The officers and men hold and advance through hell and after it all as willingly risk themselves again to help the wounded. And the wounded themselves take their often heavy burden and bleak future with a bright courage that often is heart breaking. They are truly a fine lot. As for souvenirs, there are lashings of them and our men came out with a great many odds and ends. I could have got heaps but ongoing in and out; one if he is wise and of a prudent nature, travels as light as possible. There are sounds in the air which are the best physical stimulants I know of. One does not stand on the order of going, but goes. I am becoming agile and can hurl myself on my face with true circus like dispatch and neatness, and I have got much practice at that. So the less equipment one carries I find the better. I believe in burrowing into the breast of Mother Nature. So, few souvenirs for me but a whole skin.

But to go back to dugouts. Fritz wrought well but he left his card on many. After my first tour I itched in the wrists thru' the chest tummy and knees. Lord it was awful. I tore myself to pieces. The itch is back. I became almost naked and unashamed. I scratched in public and before rank. Ralph [?] came into my dressing station when his lot took over, and even in the face of [Christ?] and the Cloth did I undo myself and scrape, scrape. The Duke of Argyll was a truly great man and to be blessed. [The Duke of Argyll erected posts on his estate upon which the animals could rub and scratch themselves]. But the itch is now gone, praise be to perseverance and chirurgical skill and certain cunning unguents. Never did I know a better patient.

If you want to send me some tobacco as you hinted, send me some [Brahadhis?] Guards Mixture. Drewery knows the kind. A man here, like the sick, takes fancies principally because he pictures the place and the friends it comes from. I get lots of Colton here, the best, but like great desires for the kinds I knew. I can picture the places at home; not homesick now, but a sort of dream land where I was happy and did not know it. I am happy enough here all right, but it is different.

I guess old lad you are having a hard time of it running the whole ranch by yourself, but as you have a fair (not physically) head on yourself, you will do it properly I know. Am glad to hear Logie is doing well. He is a clever man. I heard from George. He sent me a pipe on my birthday, the first knowledge I got of him, and a pleasant one. He is doing well I think, and I am most glad. The old story about blood being thicker is most true I find, and I watch his progress with anxiety. He is showing his good qualities and a great deal of feeling and good sense, which makes him a fine fellow.

But I find I have written a prodigious long letter and most disjointed one I fear, and as the candle is down and as alas I now am like the early lark I will say goodnight.

Your old friend,
Norman Leslie

P.S. Please remember me to your mother and sisters.

Dr. Leslie's letters indicate the bravery and the stoicism that he and the Canadian soldiers displayed during the war. However, there is an indication in the Whitehern Archive letters that Dr. Norman Leslie suffered what was called "shellshock" during and after World War One. The condition is now known as PTSD or Post Traumatic Stress Syndrome.

After the war Dr. Norman Leslie and his good friend Tom often used to spend time together on a Saturday afternoon at the Hamilton Club or at the Thistle Club. Tom McQuesten had wanted to enlist in WWI, but his mother argued vociferously against it. Mary Baker McQuesten's violent opposition to the war is coloured by the fact that Tom wanted to enlist, just as his friend Leslie and his law partner, Chisholm, had done. They had great rows over this, and it was a protracted family crisis; but in the end, Mary Baker McQuesten, the Victorian Matriarch, won out and Tom did not enlist. Even his brother Calvin tried to intercede on his behalf but his mother was adamant. Calvin wrote brief prayers in his diary: "that Tom may go . . . that mother may tell him so." Mary did not favour the war and stated: "*We do not like the way men do things.*" She lamented: "*O dear Yes! The war is so terrible and all these young Canadians cut off in the prime of life and their mothers left to mourn them all their days.*" The widowed Mary Baker McQuesten feared losing her favourite son Tom and his salary. His was the only salary for the family since his sister Ruby had died; and he was the family's only hope for the future. They had made many sacrifices for his education. In spite of many arguments, Mary managed to keep Tom at home. However, receipts found in the Whitehern Museum Archives indicate that, despite her opposition to the war, Mary donated money to the war effort.

One wonders how Tom must have felt after hearing what Dr. Norman Leslie had endured and had reported for himself and for others. A letter dated March 26, 1947, from Mel Smith to Tom McQuesten, mentions Dr. Leslie in failing health: "*I have heard nothing further since I left Toronto as to the health of our friend Dr. Leslie, and I trust he is quite himself again. This also applies to many others of his type that we know in Hamilton.*" The phrase "*of his type*" may be referring to a "shellshock" condition that Leslie and others may have suffered during and after the war.

It is not known if Norman Leslie ever went back to medicine after the war experiences at the Front. A *Spectator* article dated July 13, 1938 states: "*Dr. N.V. Leslie fills in vacancy in Hydro body. Prominent Hamilton physician and war veteran to succeed John Newlands.*" Tom likely recommended Leslie for this position using his influence with government and with Hydro. Also, through Tom's recommendation, Dr. Leslie became a Niagara Falls Bridge Commissioner on July 22, 1941 until January 9, 1947. No doubt Leslie would have assisted in many of Tom's bridge endeavours. Rev. Calvin McQuesten in his diary mentions Dr. Norman Leslie as applying to be a Commissioner and as having received the position.

Tom may have been relieved that he had not enlisted after reading Dr. Leslie's letters and seeing his condition on returning. Tom went on to create wonderful benefits for Hamilton, Niagara, and all of Ontario. To name just a few: Gage Park; The High Level Bridge (later named for McQuesten); McMaster University; Royal Botanical Gardens; Queen Elizabeth Highway; Niagara Parkway and Gardens; Carillon Tower; many restorations; Rainbow Bridge; Blue Water Bridge; Thousand Islands Bridge; Northern roads, bridges and development. The three international bridges were part of Tom's efforts to cement the peace between nations. His grandfather, Rev. Thomas Baker, had participated in the war of 1812 on the HMS *St. Lawrence*. So Tom may have been greatly affected by his friend Dr. Norman Leslie and his war experiences, since ever after, he often spoke about the value of peace.

# Dad

*Sterling Haynes*

My dad, Nelson Willard Haynes, was named after Lord Nelson but his best friends on the baseball field called him "Boss Haynes" and sometimes "Nellie." When Boss was a sixteen-year-old farm kid his brother Fred and his many cousins played baseball for Fullarton Corners, a senior team in Ontario. In 1916 this was a true farm team from the sticks. Surprisingly, these young men won the Ontario Senior Baseball Championship, defeating Toronto in the final five-game playoff. His cousin, George Baker, a huge Ontario farm boy, pitched all five championship games, even the double-headers. Jokesters said, "That there Baker had a rising fastball."

Dad played shortstop and his brother Fred was the catcher. Baker was the captain but Boss Haynes ran the team. Boss was smart and tough, a red-headed guy who batted left and threw right-handed. He was good with the glove and a great bunter. His sixteenth summer was to be his last season with the Fullarton Corners Giants. He couldn't hit worth a damn but was a good shortstop. He could turn the double play with the best of players. The inside of his thighs were scarred from the spikes made by aggressive base runners as he blocked the bag at second base or tagged the runner with the ball.

In September, after the little "world series," he enrolled at the University of Toronto as a dental student. At the end of first year university, Dad enlisted in the Canadian Army Expeditionary Forces. It was 1917, and he had just turned seventeen. As a recruit at the Canadian Aldershot Camp in Nova Scotia he learned to shoot the sniper's gun known as the Ross rifle, and to handle explosives. While there, the commanding officer noticed that he had one year of dentistry training at the U of T. He was then transferred to the Canadian Dental Corp and shipped overseas to the British army base in Aldershot, England.

Dentists in general were in short supply then, but even more so in the Canadian tent camp in Aldershot. The Brits had their permanent wooden barracks. The 4,000 Canadians were billeted and had a tent camp with six to eight men to a tent and no heat. I can remember my Dad saying that for the cold winter months he slept with his toque on and wrapped himself in his greatcoat to keep warm.

During the days he worked long hours in the Canadian surgical tent field hospital. At first he followed and assisted the dental surgeon, but soon he was on his own and took charge of serious jaw injuries. Because of his work he was promoted to sergeant.

His time off was spent studying the anatomy of the head and neck and reading up on methods of treating broken jaws, maxillae and facial bones. At work, the wounded came in vast numbers after the Battle of Vimy Ridge and soon he became competent at dealing with facial trauma. He turned to sports to help him deal with the ever-increasing daily surgical problems and became a very good soccer player. The soccer and football games helped him relax and sleep at night.

I can remember him telling me that a few German soldiers on the battlefield would look into the mouths of the allied wounded. If they saw any gold fillings or gold crowns they would kick them out with their boots and leave a mess of broken cusps, teeth and even jaws as they harvested the gold. Eventually the wounded were evacuated back to Aldershot, England.

These violent crimes and war injuries kept Dad busy fixing soldiers' broken mouths and applying arch wires to their remaining teeth. Immobilizing the troops' broken mandibles for eight to ten weeks produced good functional results. All the dental work was done under local procaine anaesthesia nerve block. This is how my father became an expert dental surgeon.

As a sergeant he was paid a dollar a day. He knew that dental school at the U of T was expensive and he saved every penny for his tuition. On November 11, 1918 the war was over and Dad was repatriated to Toronto. On January 3 of 1919 he entered second year in the school of dentistry at the U of T. He received his DDS in 1922 at his formal graduation.

During the summers from 1919 to 1921 he cleared land on two farms in Alberta owned by his brother, Wesley. Each farm was 320 acres, one at Irma, the other at Killam. He worked by himself with a team of horses, a double bitted axe and a grub hook. Knowing how to use explosives from his war years was a great help, as he could blow up large stumps or massive rocks. His weekends were busy, too. He'd play baseball for the town's local teams and help his Russian farm friends and neighbours blow up their stumps, too. He told me that he was amazed to see Russian women, harnessed in groups of six, pulling "breaking" plows to break up the rich prairie soil. Dad himself was tough as a pine knot and made a lot of money doing this rough work.

He married my mother, Elizabeth, in 1923 after they had graduated – Dad in dentistry and Mother with a BA in English and drama.

He initially practiced dentistry in Carleton Place, Ontario and was even elected Mayor there. But he longed to go back west and so he settled in Edmonton, Alberta, in 1923. He opened an office downtown in the Empire building, suite number 214, for general dentistry. He started playing baseball for the Edmonton Arrows and was their shortstop for the next twenty-five years. In the winters he played handball at the YMCA every day at noon.

In 1925 he went to Chicago's Northwestern University and studied and wrote the examination to become a dental surgeon, eventually receiving a Master of Dental Surgery [MDS] degree. With his war experiences he was well qualified to deal with maxillo-facial injuries and broken jaws. When he returned to Edmonton, he purchased the first dental x-ray machine that was operational in Alberta to help treat the large number of facial fractures.

As an Edmonton high school student in the 1940's I was elected to become his first assistant at night in his office. A badly broken mandible or a Lefort #2 maxilla fracture could take up to three hours to do: administer a nerve block, then reduce and immobilize the break. It was during these times that Dad taught me the surgical anatomy of the head and neck. A few years later this knowledge would help me study anatomy and surgery at the University of Alberta's medical school.

When Dad died in 1958 I found his strong box full of useless Alberta's Prosperity Certificates in $1.00 and $2.00 denominations. This so-called Alberta "Funny Money", produced by Bill Aberhart and the Socred government in 1936, was declared illegal tender by the Supreme Court of Canada in 1938. The hundreds of useless bills were supposed to pay for all the difficult surgery he had done in the depression years for Albertans. Propped in his office's corner cupboard I also found his sniper's gun, a Ross Rifle, wrapped in oily rags.

Dad was a compassionate man full of humour. His Canadian army service provided the money and training for him to proceed to his career in operative dentistry. Throughout his life, his major motivations were altruism and understanding the problems that faced him.

# Janus's War

*Carol Leigh Wehking*

There were parades.

In the early days, starting that very August of 1914, in towns all over the Dominion, each time a contingent of young men who volunteered for the war went off for their training and deployment, the town would turn out as if it were a holiday.

Just before our last year of school started in September, 1915, my friend Abigail and I went to the city for a short visit with Uncle George and Aunt Mary. As we walked from the train station, we encountered head-on an orderly but high-spirited assemblage of young men, marching towards us to the station. People were crowding the streets, and there was a festival air – with a strange thin cloud of doom, which most people disregarded, casting but a narrow shadow on a few. The young men (some of them *so* young) were full of zeal to kill for our faraway King. "For freedom" and "to stop the Hun."

My family had been horror-stricken when we learned that the Dominion of Canada had entered the war in Europe, at the time only three days old. War! Were countries to send off their young men to kill one another because governments could not agree? Was there no other way to solve the problems? But young men the country over flocked to sign up and fight!

"My brothers are all afire to go," Abigail said. "They mean to sign up the very day they're old enough."

There in the midst of the eager crowd, Abigail was very animated by the excitement around us, and seemed almost as if she would join in were she not with a sedate Quaker companion. I was more than a little overwhelmed, and found myself almost cowering against my friend. The crowds jostled and shouted and sang, feverish in their cheering of the men, who were strutting and grinning as if they already felt themselves to be heroes.

"How can they?" I asked Abigail once we had gotten past the crowds and were walking along the quiet street where my aunt and uncle lived. "How can those boys be so eager – don't they have any idea what it means, what they will be required to do?"

Though she and I had known one another all our lives, and Abigail was quite familiar with our Quaker ways, she looked at me as though I had lost my mind. "But Helen, who will stop the Germans if someone doesn't fight?"

"But war is wrong!" I blurted, saying what I had always understood in my Quaker faith.

"What choice is there?" Abigail replied. "Belgium and France have been invaded, and Britain has declared war – what on earth should Canada do but join, when such aggression cannot be countenanced?"

The aggression was wrong, I did not disagree with that. But was declaring war truly the best anyone could do?

Yet I could see that Abigail had a point – who will stop them if someone isn't prepared to meet them on the very terms they have established: fighting with armies?

I felt perplexed and ill-equipped to think about what was happening. Yet I knew in my heart that young men shooting at one another and even killing civilians had nothing to do with whether democracy or tyranny would thrive.

Abigail and I put this conversation behind us, but it was impossible to ignore the war when it was the topic of every newspaper and on everyone's mind. Public support for the war was very strong at first, when those early volunteers in 1914 marched proudly away, believing it would "all be over before Christmas."

Each time I encountered a parade – which was not often, as I was mostly home at the farm – I looked into the faces of the mothers who were sending off their sons, their boys, to fight in a war that would make them into killers. Those boys they had nursed at their own breasts, sung    203 to sleep with lullabies, taught manners and gentleness, praised for their schoolwork, their kindness to their sisters, their attendance at Sunday School. These were sons who might be shot down, who as likely as not would never return. Or who might return, having seen, endured, and even perpetrated unspeakable horrors. Who might return maimed, blind, or missing arms or legs or faces. Or simply "missing" – their fates never to be known. What was in these mothers' eyes? Pride? Usually. Fear? Sometimes. Most often something like a fébrile combination of patriotic passion, pride, and ... what? Joy? Could it be? Or perhaps it was terror behind a brittle show of joy?

I thought of Julia Ward Howe, who wrote after the bloody American war in which brothers killed brothers over the issue of enslavement, "We will not have great questions decided by irrelevant agencies; our husbands will not come to us, reeking with carnage, for caresses and applause. Our sons shall not be taken from us to unlearn all that we have been able to teach them of charity, mercy and patience. We, the women of one country, will be too tender of those of another country to allow our sons to be trained to injure theirs." This seemed to me the only rational stance a wife or a mother or even a sister or daughter could possibly take.

Yet even within the Society of Friends, there were young men who chose to enlist, who saw no other way of stopping the outrages but to fight them where they were, just as Abigail had proposed.

Could that be right? As the sister of two gentle young men, cousin and neighbour to countless others, I could not see how the killing of young men could solve the issues. Wouldn't it in the end merely establish who was strongest, rather than most right? There were some in these parade crowds – there *were* some – who saw beyond the "courage and glory" to the horror and the killing, and whose faces showed it. Their eyes were filled with sorrow and foreboding. Tears were visible, or hidden behind a mask of composure which required stern discipline to maintain.

At the train station once, I saw a young wife, her apron bulging, her eyes red with unabashed weeping, clinging to her husband as he struggled not to break down himself. And there on the public platform with crowds of people around them, he placed his hand upon her swelling belly and caressed the child he might never see.

These men were on their way to Quebec for training, after which they would be sailing over the sea to join the fighting. Some of these were teachers like my brother Edwin, or farmers, or industrial labourers – all sorts of men who knew how to do all sorts of things; but most of them did not know about killing other men. Most of them would have to be carefully trained to be capable of overcoming their natural humanity in order to take another man's life.

Later, when the wave upon wave of volunteers had reduced to a trickle – all the volunteers willing to go without being asked having been used up – and Borden had introduced conscription, the men did not depart with such cheerful optimism. There were fewer expressions of pride and more of fear and reluctance. By the time Edwin went to France in 1917, Canadians had been hearing for some time of the conditions in the trenches. Thousands and thousands of young Canadians had already died, and volunteers were no longer so plentiful. The men went with less willingness; the crowds were thinner and less hearty.

There was no parade when Edwin left. He, like the volunteer soldiers, was full of ideals and energy for the coming work. He, too, felt that he must make a contribution. He was young and strong and healthy and capable, and enkindled with a sense of purpose. When the Americans entered the war, he was one of the first one hundred men who were accepted to do relief work with the Friends War Victims Relief Committee. He left his teaching position at Sidwell Friends School in Washington DC, and went to Philadelphia to be trained at Haverford College, by the newly-formed American Friends Service Committee. The FWVRC would be under British Quakers and the International Red Cross. He wrote to us all through the training, fired with inspiration for whatever lay ahead, knowing it would involve hard work, a creative mind and a stout heart.

Our own mother was both proud and anxious. We had no idea where he might be sent or what might be demanded of him, but we all knew that soldiers were not the only people being killed.

Edwin explained to us that in the U.S.A., this service is acceptable as Alternative Service to military duty for Conscientious Objectors, and since Edwin had been living in the U.S., it counted as his service; at twenty-five, he was able and willing to do what he could. Here in Canada, once conscription came into effect in 1917, it was still possible to receive official status as a Conscientious Objector, but it was difficult. Men who did not want to kill other people, who did not believe "might is right", were not likely to be granted Conscientious Objector status and exempted from fighting – unless they were Quakers or Mennonites or Brethren. It amazed me that even members of the Peace churches no longer had automatic exemption, but had to go before a tribunal.

COs were given a hard time. Sometimes they were put in jail. Often they were snubbed or criticized by their colleagues and neighbours and sometimes even their own families. My friend Martha's brother, who is not a Quaker, went to jail rather than to war. I knew for very certain that it was his deep personal religious belief that "Thou shalt not kill" was not meant to have man-made exceptions; yet his own father condemned him and called him a coward. It takes a great deal of courage to stay firm in one's own convictions when the tide of public and private opinion is against you. The COs in jail did not get kind treatment. Raymond was beaten by other inmates for being unpatriotic and cowardly, neither of which he is. The guards stood by and did nothing. They felt he deserved what he got.

I wondered how anyone could feel more pride in a man who is willing to obey orders without considering his own morals, willing to make widows, and fatherless children and sonless mothers, than in one who obeys the Commandments, respects his fellow-man, and understands that sacrificing a whole generation of youth for greed or politics at the command of a government which has no sympathy for its own people, is not a cause of honour, but of shame. Martha's peaceful brother was in prison, and men who wanted to kill were celebrated. The world seemed two-faced to me.

I thought of the two-faced Roman god, Janus, who looks forward
and back at the same time. Janus was also the god who presided over

the beginning and end of conflict, and hence over peace and war. The doors of his temple were open in time of war, and closed to mark peace. I could see the doors gaping open. I could not reconcile the conflicts in my own mind.

Janus was everywhere.

*Rochambeau*, the ship that was to take Edwin and the other relief workers to the war zones of Europe sailed from New York on the same day as troop ships taking soldiers to wage war. Edwin left in high spirits, writing us one last letter, mailed in a dash ashore before he sailed. In it he reiterated his eagerness to meet whatever challenges were before him. He seemed full of purpose and determination. Ready and well-trained to wage peace.

He wrote to us during the journey, as well, as he was sad that he had not been able to come home to Ontario for a farewell visit before departing. He wrote from the ship: "... [We] will always be where we can see the same moon and the same familiar groups of stars. They will always make us at home no matter where we are." All the time he was away, I found comfort in that idea, and thought of Edwin every time I looked up at the night sky. I thought this true for soldiers, too, and hoped that they and their families found comfort in the stars, as well.

Letters from Edwin had come fairly regularly while he was training at Haverford, but once he reached France, it took a long time before we had any real news of what he was doing there, or any address to which to write. He was sent to a little village near the River Somme, where that terrible battle had taken place just the autumn before, when so many men died, and when the German army bombed and burned every French village through which they withdrew. I wondered what the men thought as they died in their trenches. Did they believe their deaths would solve something? Did they think of their families? Did they die with the King on their lips, or their loved ones? Did the man beside the dead man weep for his companion? Was he glad the bullet or bomb was not for him? Did the men who bombed the villages close their minds to compassion, and merely follow orders? Was it with vengeful purpose, or with remorse? My mind filled with unanswerable questions.

Edwin said that the earth all around was devastated, that the Germans destroyed the farming villages wantonly, and the crops and orchards as well. Gruny, where he was posted, had a few buildings still partially standing, only because some of the fuses failed when the Germans were trying to blow up the village as they departed. But the few people remaining were without hope, and did not even try to keep up their homes any more; they had given up. Everything was in a state of chaos, dirt and forlornness.

Edwin had to wait a long time for a letter from us. When it arrived, he was mending a rooftop, and someone brought the letter to him, climbing the ladder to deliver it, as they knew he would be eager for it. He read it sitting astride the ridge pole. I loved this image: Edwin high up in the sunshine, looking over the French farmland as he read our words of love and encouragement, and of the mundanities of life on the farm.

It was a long time before I put together the other details of this picture: that the farmlands all around were ruined, that from this perch he could see other ravaged villages and the black billows of smoke from the fighting at the front, less than two miles distant.

We had had only a few letters from Edwin since he had arrived in France, each detailing his work and his impressions of the place where he was stationed, when at last a letter arrived that told us something that was nothing to do with France or rebuilding or the war. Even before Edwin went overseas, Mother seemed for a time a little different after one of his letters. I noticed this, though my younger brother Russell did not. It was as though she carried a secret. A Janus secret with two faces, one of which made her joyful, the other caus-ing sorrow, but – a secret which she both cherished and longed to share. And I thought perhaps Father might know it, too. Then, at last with this letter the mystery was solved. Mother and Father revealed that indeed they had known the secret for some weeks: Edwin had a sweetheart! A fiancée, in fact! I was filled with excitement. Her name was Marion, and she was a Friend from Philadelphia. So that explained both the joy and the sorrow of it. Joy that Edwin had found his soul-mate, and though from the city, she was a Quaker. That she was American was the sad part, for then we felt that Edwin truly would never come back to live in Ontario, and I am sure that in her heart Mother had kept alive a hope that Edwin would not stay away forever, though she would never have said so. She and Father must surely have resigned themselves before then.

But I was very happy for both Edwin and Marion, and I imagined that having a new love blossoming in his heart must help my brother through the loneliness and the difficulties in France. At home on the farm, daily life was not so terribly different from before the war. Edwin wrote that he was glad that he was brought up on a farm, as he had many skills that were very useful in the work he was doing. I wondered if Marion was afraid for him. I knew that I was, and I suspected this was so of Mother and Father as well, though none of us spoke of it, for fear of bringing one another distress. Edwin wrote lovely things about how Father and Mother had always been a perfect model of married love, and that he hoped that he might create such a family, with the same foundation of love and respect, and the same Quaker values to guide them all.

Another letter from Edwin filled my heart with sorrow for the children of Belgium. Edwin wrote that hundreds and hundreds had been orphaned and displaced by the war, and some of these were "repatriated" to France. In three villages Edwin helped to build schools for them. They built the place, helped to equip it, and then he lived with the children and taught them as well. He has such a quiet and rather solitary nature; it must have been very demanding to be surrounded by crowds of lonely, sad children. But here is the most heartbreaking part: these children did not know how to play. They were scarcely children! Many of them found work to do when they had time to themselves. Imagine, picking up a broom and scrub brush and cleaning out the dormitories because it is a school holiday! It was good that they were willing workers, and especially so for the garden, in which they hoped to grow some of their own food to help bring the children back to health. But sad, very sad indeed, that they did not know how to play.

Edwin took it upon himself to teach them to be children again. He said they did not even know how to throw or catch a ball. ("Not even so well as thee, Helen," he wrote, attempting to lighten the story by teasing me about my lack of skill.) He was teaching them games. He said they learned the skills pretty quickly, and he hoped yet to see them choose to play spontaneously. He said he looked forward with an eager soul to seeing them smile and hearing them laugh.

Children in Ontario still laughed and played, though not so merrily as they once did. Most only barely got enough to eat, though we were surely better off than the city people, where rationing meant a great deal if you didn't grow any of your own food and could only buy what your ration-card allowed.

Spring of 1918 was on its way at last, and Father said it would be right for maple syrup making any day. The snow was very deep, and the days bright and clear, and he and Russell had already been into the sugar bush on snowshoes to check the trees. There were a few with some branches down from the ice storm the previous month, but not much damage else. No split trees, so if the weather held it should be a good year. Mother said we would not waste any syrup this year in making snow candy. I wondered whether there were maple trees in France and whether Edwin would have maple sugar or syrup.

We so greatly looked forward to hearing from Edwin. His letters were usually very interesting with information about what he was doing, the conditions, and so on, but sometimes it was long between letters. If he answered immediately, it was still six weeks from the time we posted a letter until we received his response. But he worked so hard – long hours sometimes seven days a week. And of course he also wrote to Marion. His letters to us were always addressed "Dear Home Folks" or "Dear Folks at Home", and we passed them around the family. We tried to have several of us write letters to go in one envelope, so that he had lots of word and love from home.

The previous fall, though, when he first arrived at Gruny, he'd written: "Dear Folks at home in Comfortable Houses," as there was not one complete house still standing in the village, and he slept with no shelter and the constant sound of bombers and artillery. Gruny was first taken in September of 1914, and by the time the Germans withdrew, there was almost nothing left. He wrote, "The destruction is so complete that there is not a can or a bucket but what has a hole shot in it." He did everything from building to cooking to doctoring to making hay. And he was admired. One child told another, "He's a teacher, a doctor, a roofer, and an acrobat!" The lads called him "Monsieur Victor," though he never knew why.

When we had gathered in our apples that autumn, it was sad to read in Edwin's letter that the Germans had cut down every tree in every orchard. We sent apple butter in one of the parcels. It took months to arrive, only reaching him in February. He wrote, "You haven't the least idea what you put in. You probably know what it contained when it left Canada, but those same things assumed an entirely different value over here in France …. Never have I been more of a little boy than when I sat on my bed and unpacked each package, reading between each morsel the love that prompted you all to send it."

Edwin and the other workers went to the abandoned trenches and pulled lumber and metal from the dugouts to use in the village. Edwin managed to make a snowplough of sorts out of bits of metal and an old high, two-wheeled manure cart. He wrote, "It is a pleasure to be able to put some of these machines of war to a practical use for the sheltering of civilians." When there was too much snow to get on with roofing, they wrapped their feet in sacks and went out to cut wood for fires by which to keep warm and cook. He said he remembered Grandfather teaching him how to split wood. (He didn't know yet that Grandmother had passed away.) The fruitwood from the orchards, seasoned for a year, at least must have made good sweet fires. He said, "The trees were covered with snow and heavy frost, so for once the ugliness of all the destruction around here was disguised by nature."

We received a letter from Marion, which was thoughtful of her, I felt. I was longing to meet her in person, but I knew this was not possible yet. She sounded so lovely; it would be a pleasure to welcome her into our family. If she was Edwin's choice, we all knew she would be very special indeed. I wrote back to her, as did Mother and Father. Hearing from her, instead of merely about her, made her more real for me, and I could not help but think about their wedding, whenever that might be. That she and Edwin would make their solemn vows to one another before gathered Friends, and that I would gain another sister, were happy thoughts during sad times.

By that spring of 1918, Abigail's twin brothers were both in France, at the front. They had indeed signed up on their birthday, trudging through the February snow to the recruitment office in town. They were a few years younger than Edwin, and I knew them a little. Frederick was bold and adventuresome, so I was not surprised to learn that he had volunteered, but it shocked me to hear that quiet, gentle Martin had signed up, too. Did he go out of pressure from Frederick and other young men? He was honourable and would never want to be thought a coward, or unwilling to do his part. Perhaps it was a sense of duty. But then Abigail explained that Frederick was a private in the trenches and Martin a stretcher-bearer. It made sense to me that Martin would not be willing to take a life, but was willing to risk his own to save others.

Abigail acknowledged that she was afraid for them both, but it was obvious she was proud of them as well. We talked of Martin and Fred for a time, not without a little tension between us, and then she asked me about Edwin. She knew that he had been teaching in the States for some years, and wondered what he was doing in the war. I told her that Edwin was in France in the uniform of the relief workers, which was embroidered with the 8-pointed star of the Friends Service Council, very near the front lines, working in profound deprivation and hardship to help the civilians whose lives and livelihoods had been ruined by the terrible fighting there. That he was building and rebuilding homes, bringing in the harvests with the women – since there were no men to do the heavy work – teaching children, building schools.

She could see the value of this work, work that is based in love rather than in hate, and which brings life rather than takes it, yet she repeated the question she had asked when we were caught in the parade three autumns before, "Who will stop the Germans if someone doesn't fight?"

I still did not have an answer. I explained to her our 250-year-old conviction that fighting is wrong. The words of our Peace Testimony came easily to me: "We utterly deny all outward wars and strife and fightings with outward weapons, for any end, or under any pretence whatever: this is our testimony to the whole world." These words were as familiar to me as my family name, and I had never doubted their wisdom. Yet I had never before had to measure them against any actuality of "wars and strife and fightings". Was it enough to *deny* war? What about, as Abigail said, an aggressor who was already fighting with outward weapons?

I had no doubts at all that killing is not the way to establish moral ascendancy, governmental superiority, or philosophical rectitude; yet how to stop what is wrong, if fighting is what is happening? I had no solution to this enigma.

I took this question away with me, and pondered it deeply. I asked Mother and Father what their answer might be, and we talked long and earnestly, about cruelty, hatred, greed, evil, and immorality, and about our Quaker testimonies and the principles that have guided us for centuries. I never doubted that what Edwin was doing was right. I could not imagine him taking up a weapon or trying to kill another person, yet he would never shirk his duty. I knew that he would always choose the way of peace, and his actions would spring from love and humanity. But Abigail's question remained in my ears. In Meeting on Sunday mornings, I would wait in the silence for light to shine on this darkness. If someone spoke in ministry, I hoped his or her words would enlighten me. It felt as if I were carrying an extra load upon my shoulders, but answers did not come, and the heaviness did not lift.

There had been an article in *The Canadian Friend* around the time Edwin left for France that lamented the "widespread misconception that Friends are primarily objectors taking a negative position instead of a positive one." Refusal to shoot "makes way for active, positive service." Friends, it said, are called "to bind up the broken in heart and to rebuild the waste places, to comfort those that mourn and to prepare the way for the longed for peace."

Engaged in this very work, Edwin tried to write once a week, though several times there were longer gaps. Since he was so near the front, these gaps were frightening; he was not by any means away from danger. He never complained of hardship or deprivation, but we knew he faced them. Mother had written about the price of butter and eggs, and his response was very poignant, as he had had neither butter nor an egg in months.

As well as letters, we sent him parcels, always putting sweet things in, though we tried to write neutral descriptions of them on the label, so that the packages would not be plundered before they reached him. He, of course, always shared whatever we sent. He had made many hints about maple sugar, and we managed to get some to him, despite the unlikelihood. He said there were no maple trees in France! Few trees of any kind left standing near Gruny.

We also sent clothing and blankets, quilts, linens, and so on, for the people of ravaged France. Every piece of clothing that was outgrown but still serviceable went into boxes, which were sent every few weeks by way of the AFSC or the Red Cross. I thought of some orphan child in France learning to play ball, wearing Russell's outgrown trousers and sweater.

We read in *The Canadian Friend* that Toronto Meeting had a sewing and knitting afternoon every Tuesday, and we began hosting a similar gathering each week at our home. At Wellington Quarterly Meeting, we suspended all programme and business, and everyone – even the men and the children – knitted and sewed. The AFSC listed what things were needed most, and we tried to send as much of each as we could. I used to be such a reluctant knitter, but when I thought of the listless, hopeless people in the devastated villages, and the Belgian children who didn't know how to play and had nothing, I knitted with great hope in my heart that each thing I created would help someone through the winter to come. Each item had a little prayer for the wearer knitted into it; we all did this.

The socks and mittens and scarves I knitted later were not nearly so nice as the ones I made at first. This was because at first, I gathered up all the ends of wool left over from various projects over the years since the beginning of Mother's married life. It was fun to knit things in many colours, and to think of each length of wool, "this is from the little suit Mother made for Russell when he was newly born," or "Edwin had matching mittens and a hat from this," or "Father wore this sweater, knitted by Clara, until one day it was so threadbare that it fell off his shoulders as he was heaving hay down for the cows," or "this is left over from the very first thing I ever knitted: a scarf for Edwin when he went off to George School."

Things were not so grim in those earlier war days; everyone still thought the war could not go on and on. But by the spring of 1918 there was less of everything, and we worked with wool practically straight off the sheep. It had no colour at all, so it would not help to cheer up the refugees or those whose homes had been destroyed, but it still had all the lanolin in it and would be warm in rain and in wet. Edwin had been very happy to receive the thick knitted gloves I made for him, though of course most of what we made went to strangers. Sometimes I fancied they were friends – that there was a connection between us now, though we could never acknowledge it personally.

Edwin's letters to the family continued to tell of his relentless work, the trials and the small triumphs. I realized that what he was doing would have lasting importance to countless people, and my heart glowed to think of how his young manhood was being spent. They had completed the second school, and they had some men helping them who were in the army and had been in the midst of the fighting. Someone had suggested that there be military training for the boys, but these army men were strongly against it, saying, "If an army is made, a war will result." Edwin remarked that, "It was one of the strongest peace meetings I have ever attended. ... What a strange and comforting experience to find so many Pacifists among these men who are normally soldiers."

Sometimes his letters spoke of Marion (who, I suspect, receives letters a little more regularly than we do!) and his joyful love for her. But in February he expressed a heavy concern for her. She was gravely ill and had been hospitalized. I prayed for her return to strength and health. What sorrow it must have been for them both that she was so sick. Edwin should have been by her side, but instead was far away, nurturing others.

I confess that I continued to imagine the wedding, and how full of joy and love it would be, after all the hardship and sadness. I thought

215

what sort of dress Marion might wear, and what flowers might adorn the Meetinghouse. Mother said, "Thee must not hope too much to be a part of it, as they will naturally marry in the Meeting where they will be living, and that will be in Washington. Travel that far, for our family, is not likely." I was cast down, but then I thought, it is only imagination anyway, and if it lifts my heart from the grim particulars of daily life, then such a fancy is a good thing, and it need not be a thing that will bear real fruit.

I wore mended dresses and aprons by then – everyone did – and many evenings were spent darning stockings, turning sheets, making repairs, so that we might make do. We were better off than countless French and Belgian people. At least we had sheets, if they were threadbare. We had food (though Edwin said that the women in rural France grew, harvested, and milled their own wheat, so that they had plenty of unrationed bread, at least). We also canned and preserved what we could and sent it with the clothing, to France. But in France, they also needed money for rebuilding, as well as everything else. There were so many children who were orphaned and displaced! I was glad that some of them had Edwin to help look after them. As others were doing all over, we held concerts at the farm to raise money for reconstruction, and sent that to the AFSC as well.

Before too much longer, Edwin would be back in North America to bring attention to the reconstruction, and raise funds. He said that if the war ended right now, Friends would have at least another five years' work in France alone. On his birthday, he wrote a most heart-warming letter to Mother, thanking her for the way she brought him up, and the sort of mother she had always been to all of us. I had never thought to thank her for her mothering, but I agreed with all that Edwin said.

We were given more to fear when we learned that the disastrous influenza that had nearly wiped out an army training camp in Kansas had now been identified in France and in Boston. It was a terrible flu, and seemed to aim itself at healthy young adults, as if nature were telling us we are not in control, that we must not waste life, for we never know when it may be taken away. The secret fear that ate away at me was that Marion would succumb, because her health was so taxed already. Or that Edwin would be taken. Perils seemed to be all around, and yet I lived safely and well-provided for. What a strange unbalance the world was in!

The war went on and our life on the farm went on and still I carried my toppling burden of concerns: Edwin and Marion's safety and health; collecting and making things to send to France; making do at home; and – most troubling of all – my inability to reconcile Janus's two faces of peace and war. Abigail's question would not leave me, but nagged at my heart, waking and sleeping.

One day as Abigail and I walked home through the woods still patchy with snow, I felt an idea growing, and felt at last I had, not an answer, really, but something to say in response to her question.

"Imagine," I said, "an enormous army of people as willing to die for their ideals as all those soldiers, but who will not fight. A disciplined, well-trained army of thousands and thousands who are willing to go and speak to the aggressors, to speak to that of God in each of them, to start from the place George Fox calls 'the virtue of that life and power that taketh away the occasion of all wars', and to try to reach a place of understanding. Thousands would die in this effort. Perhaps even as many as are dying now. But they would be carrying love in their hearts, and peace in their words, and their shield would be that of compassion. They would not spread hatred, and divide people into warring sides, but work to unite people with a kind of love that would transcend the differences and acknowledge our common humanity. We Quakers believe that each person has an Inward Light, that there is 'that of God' in everyone, and that is what we must address and answer in everyone."

"Do you really believe there is 'that of God' in the Kaiser, Helen?" she asked me.

"Surely there must be!" I replied, but inwardly, I own, I felt a shivering sliver of doubt.

Abigail and I talked for a long time; I was not only trying to explain the Quaker point of view to her, but to understand it better myself. Her question, "But who will stop the Germans if we don't fight?" had never ceased to trouble me, though my conception of an army of peacemakers seemed as if it might be an achievable alternative. Yet how would that be accomplishable? The wider society does not see things in this way, and it would mean changing the whole culture of Canada to make the formation of such an army even remotely possible to contemplate. It is something I can imagine, but is it something that could *happen*?

And the question of "that of God" in the Kaiser ... I now had new doubts growing in my mind. Can there be such a thing as pure evil? But surely Kaiser Wilhelm could not be, even if such a thing exists! He has a wife; he has children. He must have known tender moments, moments (at least) of gentleness and peace, that betoken a kindliness or humanity, channels through which one might reach the Inward Light. Unless it *is* somehow extinguished. Could it be that that of God *can* be obliterated in a person? Could a person choose impulses to evil over impulses to good long enough and consistently enough that he might no longer hear the voice of goodness in his heart?

Or could it be that his enmity with the British, when Queen Victoria was his grandmother, and his cousins and aunts and uncles all over Europe, many on the Allied side, was comparable to the Quaker boys who, despite our testimony, have joined the army to fight – a difference of opinion, and a departure from values, even though the love of family is still there?

So, *is* there that of God in the Kaiser? If so, can it be reached? If not, is there no other way to stop him than to fight with weapons? The men who give the orders are not the ones who pull the trigger or take the bullets. The men who stand in front of the bullets are not the ones who make the plans or the decisions. The men behind the decisions are behind the safety of walls, but the ones whose lives are at stake have no say in the matter at all. It makes no sense. Playing chess with bits of ivory hurts no one, but pushing markers around a map, when it represents thousands of real people – how can that be conscionable? *How can men in braided uniforms with shining buttons and medals on their chests send innocent boys at the beginning of their lives out to kill each other?*

I could not answer these questions for myself. I became deeply troubled, and at last I wrote a letter to Edwin that I sent separately from the family's, asking his thoughts on these perplexing contentions. Somehow he found the time to write back to me separately, to help me

try to weed the thorns from my path:

*Dearest sister Helen,*

*I, too, have wondered, seeing the ruination left behind by the retreating army, how men could bring themselves to ravage other humans in this heartless manner. I, too, have wondered whether there is indeed 'that of God' in these soldiers.*

*But I have then thought about my training to come here and do what I am doing. (Thee does know that we were trained as long as a soldier trains before being sent to the front?) And thee and I have been brought up from our cradles to think the way we do, and believe what we believe.*

*The soldiers in the enemy armies may have been brought up with very different beliefs and values, and trained under a very different system. Their own natural Inner Light may have been smothered or at least covered over until no light shines forth.*

*Thee must remember, though, that the armies of both sides have perpetrated as well as suffered terrible things. The soldiers have had to endure horrors and follow orders that perhaps their spirits reject. Neither thee nor I knows what each one may have had to overcome in himself in order to follow the orders he has been given. And as to those giving the orders: I have, like thee, suffered much more doubt on their account ... But I think that without the gentle upbringing and the firm convictions of which thee and I have been the beneficiaries, and with another set of convictions ruling their development, and clouding their hearts, that they must still have at least begun with the same Inward Light. The soldiers have been trained to obey without question; deep under the covering of brutality and cruelty that have been taught them, however dim, that Light may still be alight, though guttering. I do not give up hope that it may be possible to find and answer that of God in these apparently godless enemies. Surely they think that 'our' side is godless, too. Both sides believe and pray that God is with them. I wonder whether God might be weeping in sorrow.*

*We and our faith are on trial. We are being tested as never before. Remember that Rufus Jones said, 'There are other paths to victory besides those of destruction and death.' And as Christ said, 'He that takes the sword shall perish with the sword.' These are not thoughtless men, but wise and respected. Why are their words not heeded at this time?*

*But that is not my work here. My work is to help the helpless, befriend the friendless, and put my own Light and strength to good use in bringing back life to people and lands that have been so far put down as to have lost all hope and will. It is enough to do; I cannot also wrestle with the dark angels of doubt, when there is so much need for hope.*

*In hope that thy faith may remain strong, thy always loving brother,*

*Edwin*


It comforted me to know that Edwin had suffered the same doubts, and had retained his faith despite being faced daily with the results of the hardened hearts of men. I kept this letter by me and read it over again many times. When next I encountered Abigail, I was ready to speak again on the topics we had debated already, but in the end, I did not.

When next we met, Abigail was in a state of great suffering and grief. Both Frederick and Martin were in the battle of Amiens. I knew of it, of course. There were terrible casualties on both sides. My heart broke for Abigail and her family when I heard what she had to tell me: Martin was killed carrying a wounded soldier off the battlefield, and Frederick was now in hospital with a shattered leg. And he was shell-shocked.

Abigail felt not only sad, but bitter as well. Her fears had come true: one brother dead, the other never to be the same again. Martin would never return. Fred would come back disabled both physically and mentally. Would he be able to work again? What sort of life would he lead? Would the brothers' sacrifice make any difference to anyone but their families and themselves? The one who would not kill was now dead. The other must live a life much diminished, with indelible memories of all that he had seen and done.

Abigail spoke bitterly of her brothers' high hopes when they departed for the war. Then she said, "What is the good of it? We – the Allies and others – fight the Central Powers to prevent them taking over other countries because we believe it is right. That the Central Powers are wrong. But what if 'we' lose? Then will wrong be right? Or will it prove us wrong? Or will right be subsumed into wrong? And then what will the fighting have been for? And even if 'we' win, does that indeed prove that we are right? I see now why you and your people cannot countenance war or fighting. What is the point of it?"

I could give her no answer. I longed for clarity, and I prayed for my faith to be strong enough to bring me to a place of clear vision.

I thought again of two-facing Janus, not as the two-sided secret that Mother had had, nor Janus, god of beginnings and transitions, which I felt applied to Edwin and Marion, but Janus the god who presided over both the beginning and end of conflict, the god who presided over war and peace. I knew that hearts were broken all over the western world, and that many things would never again be the same. Many doors would be forever closed and many unknown doors now stood open. I felt that good and evil were no longer separate things, but tangled and overlapped, and I longed for the simplicity of distinguishing right and wrong. This has been called a war to end wars. Oh, that this may be true! Surely the horrors, the devastation, the savagery, brutality, and barbarism, and the suffering and death of so many have taught us all that war is only a way of inflicting agony and sorrow on everyone!

Can we truly now be content that war will not come again?

Janus, close the door and let us live in peace.

## Author's Notes

Edwin Zavitz was twenty-five years old when he went to France in the autumn of 1917. Edwin came from a Quaker farming family in Middlesex County, southwest Ontario. He had two sisters, Clara (older) and Helen (younger), and a younger brother, Russell. Edwin was educated at the (Quaker) George School in Philadelphia and at University of Michigan, and had been a teacher at Sidwell Friends School in Washington, DC for some years before volunteering for oversees work when the U.S. entered the war. Edwin returned to North America before the war ended, made a slide show of his photographs and sketches, and lectured in Philadelphia and on tour, raising funds for the rebuilding of France. He and Marion were able to visit his family for Christmas that year, and in January were married in Washington, D.C. Friends' Meeting. Edwin returned to Sidwell Friends School where he taught for some further years. Later he was head of University School in Cincinnati, Ohio, and then at Baltimore Friends School as head until he returned to Sidwell in 1942. Edwin and Marion had two sons. After World War II, AFSC sent Edwin to France to check on what aid was needed because he spoke French so well and understood service work. Edwin died of Leukemia in 1950, and Marion died later the same year.

Helen was born in 1898 and married another Quaker (who had been imprisoned in Canada as a Conscientious Objector) in 1921. She and her husband had seven children and farmed in and near Poplar Hill, Ontario. At her death in 1966, the procession of cars from the funeral home to the cemetery at Coldstream Meetinghouse was nearly a mile long.

The characters of Abigail and Martha and their brothers are inventions.

The Archivist for Canadian Yearly Meeting of the Religious Society of Friends, Jane Zavitz-Bond, most generously provided me with Edwin's letters and with microfilms of *The Canadian Friend* (the national Quaker publication in Canada) from the war years. I thank Jane profoundly. She has been generous with her time, her knowledge, and her expertise. I am gratefully indebted to her for her help and for her friendship.

# My Shadow

*Barb Rebelo*

Annie stood on the railway platform clutching her wide-brimmed hat, which the gusts of November threatened to blow away. She waved her arm at the dim shape of her brother Alf, pressed against the window of the coach. His earnest young features faded with each second that passed, as the troop train left the London, Ontario Station, bound for Halifax.

Her father stood beside her and she could feel his anguish, as his stooped shoulders shook. *This is really happening,* she cried inside. *He is going to the war in France, and Dad and I are here watching him go. How can he be so excited when we are so afraid for him?*

She watched the train pick up speed. It got smaller in the distance, then shrank to a dot. *That dot is taking our Alf away from us,* she thought in sick wonderment. She knew that when he arrived in Halifax, a troop ship would bear him away to join with the 1$^{st}$ Battalion, Canadian Over-Seas Expeditionary Force. She felt a rush of grief, pride and unreality. Such strange emotions that she hadn't felt since her brother Reg left the family to work on electrical systems for the mines in Northern Ontario.

Annie's dad grasped her hand. Turning to him, she realized that he looked older. She put her arm around his shoulder, and led him to the bench on the platform. They sat down, holding hands, squeezing tight, both waiting to choke down overpowering emotions.

"I'm glad your Mother didn't come," he whispered. "She couldn't bear it."

"I know, Dad. That's all right; she said her goodbyes in her own way. Let's just rest here awhile until our train comes; then we'll go home."

With a nod, he folded his crooked hands over the top of his cane, and rested his chin on them. With sorrowful blue eyes he stared down the now-empty track. Only in his late 50's, he was already crippled with arthritis.

Annie reflected how Alf had wanted to join the Canadian Forces so badly, twice attempting to enlist while underage. He turned eighteen while working in Flint, Michigan as a foreman in an automobile plant, and shortly afterward enlisted in London, Ontario. They took him right away, and he had time only to send a letter home to Brantford to let the family know when he was to leave. Annie and her Dad had decided to take the train to London to see him off. This fever to go to war was not his alone. In the past three years since 1914, thousands upon thousands of beloved sons, brothers and husbands had gone – many never to return. The world had begun to refer to them as the Lost Generation.

*It's what he wants, thought Annie, shaking her head. We've all tried to talk him out of it, but it's of no use. It's all he can think about. My Shadow – he's always followed me everywhere. I will miss him so.*

She realized that if she had been born a boy, she would want to go, too. She and her four brothers had grown up together, sharing everything. She loved each one of them, even though they were different. But her love for Alf – the youngest – was fierce and protective. She ached inside, for there was a feeling in her heart that Alf might not return to them.

\* \* \*

As days turned into weeks, the everyday routine of home life brought diversion to the family. Annie found that her job at the ticket office of the Brantford-Hamilton Railway kept her occupied and helped keep her thoughts and fears for her brother under control. She joined the local Red Cross group who rolled bandages and knitted socks to send to the soldiers overseas. Not only did Annie write to Alf, but through the organization was given the name of a pen-pal, a young Belgian soldier who had no family. She found it a pleasure to do something for a boy who was so alone.

Christmas was difficult for everyone. Her mother set a place at the table for Alf, as if he would walk through the door and join them. "It's only right," she said. "He is here in spirit, and we must have a place for him."

In January, a letter from Alf arrived for Herb and Millie, Annie's oldest brother and his wife. Herb brought it over to the house, and everyone gathered to hear the news. Alf was still in camp at Bramshott, England, but was leaving for France within a few weeks. He was well and full of enthusiasm about having applied to work with motor maintenance, writing, "My favorite thing is tinkering with motors." He was waiting to hear whether he got the job, and would let them know.

In May, Annie received a postcard from him. It was a lovely thing, trimmed with lace, and the embroidered words read, 'A Kiss From France!' She was proud of the postcard. She framed it and set it beside her bed, where she could see it as she was falling asleep and waking.

\* \* \*

The August night was oppressive – humidity hung in the air like a blanket. Annie sat at her dressing table and put down her hairbrush. She gathered her damp hair in a twist, and pinned it up, unable to tolerate the feel of it on her skin. She wiped her face and neck with a cloth, and headed toward the front hall.

She pushed the screen door open and stepped out onto the verandah. The rich aroma of tobacco drifted in the air, and the glow of a pipe revealed her Dad's presence in his battered wicker chair at the far end of the porch.

"Dad, you're still up!" His usual habit was to go to bed at ten o'clock and it was nearly eleven-thirty.

"I don't think I'll be able to sleep, Annie. I'm restless tonight, and

I don't want to disturb your mother." He puffed on his pipe in the darkness. "It's so warm in the house, you know. Not much better out here."

Annie settled onto the top step, and hugged her knees. At first, the night air felt heavy and quiet; then she became aware of the chirping of what sounded like thousands of crickets. The bullfrogs in the ponds blurted out to each other in their own language. It seemed to Annie that they were saying *groink*, like the sound of someone plucking broken guitar strings. She and her Dad sat in comfortable silence in the darkness for a while; then he stood up. Heaving a sigh, he emptied his pipe into the ashtray.

"That's it for me; I'm turning in now, Annie. You should get to bed too, my girl." He passed behind her, and rested his hand on her head for a moment. "Good night."

"Good night, Dad. I'll be in shortly." The porch door creaked behind her as he pulled it shut. Resting her chin in her hands, her mind drifted. She loved the darkness and solitude. At time like these, she pretended that Alf was beside her. It was a habit she had formed over the months since he left, and it was her own precious secret – a way of coping with her loneliness for him.

*Alf, I know you are far away, but we see the same moon at night. For now, that has to be as good as being together. Sit here beside me, My Shadow, and I'll tell you some stories.* She lost herself in her own imagination, and more than an hour passed before she went to bed.

\* \* \*

The night had deepened. The stickiness in the house was so close Annie was restless. She fell into a fitful sleep and entered a place where reality and dreams tangled.

*"We're going on a picnic, going on a picnic!"* Alf sang out, flipping his nickel in the air, and catching it. They were on an open-air streetcar, on their way to the Sunday School Picnic in Mohawk Park. Mother and Dad had given the five of them a nickel each. What a treat!

Annie laid her hand on her little brother's arm and said, "Put your nickel in your pocket before you lose it." The next moment, his fist hit the nickel in mid-air, and it bounced over the edge of the streetcar platform, onto the road. He began to wail, "My nickel, my nickel! I lost it!"

Older brothers Herb and Reg turned around to quiet him, but the volume of his cries increased. Neighbouring passengers, having heard and seen what happened, passed a straw hat around the streetcar, and a lady sitting behind them gave it to Annie. She looked in the hat, and counted forty-five cents! Her other brother Vic, who was sitting beside her, hissed in her ear, *We can't keep that money – Mother and Dad would have our hides!* But Alf had stopped crying, and was smiling now. He climbed up on his seat and turned around to the people behind him. *"Thank you – thanks!* He called out, an endearing grin on his face.

Annie's dreams flashed to another scene. She and her brothers sat on a blanket in the grass at Mohawk Park. The picnic basket was open, and everyone was enjoying the lunch. The sky darkened overhead, and it seemed to be night. From far above, she heard whistling shrieks, and dull booming noises. The sky and horizon flashed with red-white images. Could it be fireworks, this early in the evening? She could not remember ever seeing firework displays at a Sunday school picnic! Annie looked around at her brothers. They ate and laughed as if they didn't see or hear the noise and flashes.

Another deafening whizz, then a sharp crack. *"Look out, Alf! Look out!"* She could not see her brother anywhere.

Annie sat up in bed, drenched in sweat, and gasping for air. The blast still echoed in her ears. She put a hand to her head as she lay back down. A terrible dream – that's all it was. But that shot was so real. Annie realized tears were running down her face. She gradually became aware of a presence in the room, as if someone was trying to tell her something. Her body went rigid, and she lay in the dark, all her senses alive. Then she heard Alf's voice:

"Don't worry about me, Sis. I'll be all right."

*How could this be? He's on the other side of the world!*

"Alf, is that you?" she whispered, scrambling backward on the bed, her ears straining. She heard the hammering of her own heart, nothing more. Reaching to her bedside, she turned on her lamp, glancing around her room. "Where are you? I heard you speak to me!"

There was no answer.

She sprang from the bed, and ran down the hall to her parents' bedroom. She shook the knob and banged on the door. "Dad, wake up!" she sobbed, collapsing against the wall.

She heard her parents' muffled tones, and the door opened. "Annie, what on earth is wrong?" Her Dad pulled her to him, and wrapped his arms around her. Her mother stood behind him, shrugging into her robe.

"What is it, Annie? Are you ill?" she asked.

Annie looked at their concerned expressions, and covered her face with her hands. How could she explain to them what had happened – what she had heard? They would think she had had a nightmare, and it would only upset them to hear about it.

"I … I heard a gunshot outside. Didn't you hear it? It was so loud it woke me." She could tell that neither of her parents had heard the noise she described. They looked at one another, shaking their heads.

Her mother led her to the kitchen, and sat her down at the table. "You've had a bad dream, Annie, nothing more. Sit a few minutes and try to relax."

Her father went out into the back shed that connected to the kitchen, returning a moment later with a lantern and his rifle. They watched as he lit the lantern. "I'll just go round the yard, and have a look."

"Be careful, John!" Her mother called after him. They followed him as far as the porch, watching the light from the lantern bob away in the darkness, until he rounded the corner of the house, out of sight.

"Come back inside," her mother said. They went from room to room, watching her dad's progress around the yard. Fifteen minutes later he mounted the porch steps and came inside, extinguishing the light.

"There is not a soul out there, my girls. And if someone was there, he's long gone. I think we should go back to bed."

The remainder of the night was agony for Annie; sleep would not come. She opened her book, but after reading the same paragraph a few times, she realized that she hadn't comprehended a word. The ordinary night sounds of the house unsettled her nerves.

*I can't tell Mom and Dad that Alf spoke to me, but I can't keep it to myself, either.* She debated with herself, wondering what to do. As the dawn approached, she found an answer. *I'll go and see Herb tomorrow, and I'll tell him about it, all of it.* She knew she could confide in her eldest brother. Most of the time he teased her about things, but this time she knew he wouldn't.

When daybreak came, Annie slept. Her mother opened the bedroom door at breakfast time, and peeked in at her. She shut it quietly again, leaving her to sleep.

* * *

Annie boarded the streetcar for downtown. It was still early enough in the day that she had a seat to herself, and she was relieved. She didn't want to be obliged to make small talk to anyone, because her mind was filled with the terror of the night before. It seemed her stop came up suddenly, and she descended the steps onto the sidewalk. Herb's street was just around the next corner, and she hastened along, searching for the words she would use to tell him. She hoped Mill would be home as well.

From the sidewalk she saw Herb through the open doors of the garage beside the house. He stood at his workbench, busy with tools, his cigar clenched between his teeth. At her approach, he looked up, his thick glasses glinting in the morning sun that shone through the window of the garage.

"Sis, what a surprise!" He reached for a cloth in his back pocket and wiped his hands, walking toward her. "What's new? Have you come for lunch? Mill's in the kitchen ... " His voice trailed off when he got close enough to see the expression on her face.

"Herb, let's go inside, please." Annie's voice wavered, and she fought the burning feeling that started to fill her throat.

"Sure, kid." Herb hugged her and guided her into the house and down the hall into the kitchen, where her sister-in-law was washing dishes.

"We've got company, Mill." Herb gestured for Annie to sit down. He pulled out a chair, turned it around, and sat with his arms on the back of it.

"Annie! How lovely to see you." Mill wiped her hands on the dishtowel, and approached. She took off her apron and sat down beside Annie, taking her hand. "What is it, dear? You look as if you've seen a ghost."

Annie wiped away tears, then poured out the events of the previous night.

When she was done, her brother looked out the window, his mouth set in a hard line. "I don't know, Annie. I don't know what to think. I do know that Mother has seen and heard things in her lifetime that cannot be explained. But this came to you, not her. You may have some of her insight, I suppose. Maybe something happened to Alf and your intuition sensed it. He's always been closest to you."

Annie nodded, biting her lip.

Mill, still holding her hand, gave her fingers a gentle squeeze. "I think Herb is right. Some things can't be explained between two people that are close – when they are far apart in distance. You were right to come here and tell us what happened, but I think we should keep this between us for now."

Annie felt as if a heavy weight had been lifted from her. Herb stood by the table looking down at his sister. "We'll find out soon enough if Alf is in trouble. Until then, we'll carry on as usual. We won't say anything to Mother and Dad. Agreed?" He bent to kiss her on the cheek. "And stay for lunch. I've got to go out and see Dad later this afternoon, so I'll go back with you."

\* \* \*

Annie sat on the old swing that hung from a shady maple tree in their side yard, facing the road at the front of the house. Glancing up, she noticed that the leaves above were starting to turn yellow. *It's mid-September*, she realized. *Where did the summer go?*

It was late afternoon, time to get ready for her shift at the railway ticket office. She slid off the swing, and was walking to the house when she noticed a boy on a bicycle riding down the lane towards their property. She shaded her eyes, murmuring, "Is he a telegraph boy? Please, dear God, let him pass by our gate – keep going, keep riding!"

The boy stopped and checked their house number. He leaned his bicycle against the fence, and opened the gate to the front sidewalk. He disappeared from her sight, but she heard him mount the steps to the front porch. She gathered her skirt up and ran. She could not let her parents answer the door. At first, her feet felt heavy, as if encased in cement, but their voices seconds later shook her out of her slow-motion nightmare.

She rounded the porch. Her mother sat forward in the rocking chair, sewing things abandoned in her lap at the telegraph boy's approach, her eyes on her husband in his wicker chair.

"Here," he asked the boy, setting aside his newspaper, "what's this, then?"

The telegram informed them that their son, Alfred John Harding, had died at Amiens, France on August 16, 1918, wounded from stray shrapnel, they were told later, in a letter from his commanding officer. He was hit during battle while tending the motor brigade vehicles – a job he had wanted to do; he was taken to a field hospital where he died from his wounds at dawn two days later. Given the time difference, Annie knew it was the exact hour she had woken to hear his voice with its message of love.

\* \* \*

The tiny white-haired woman in the hospital bed was weary. Annie was eighty-six years old, and during her lifetime, she had seen plenty of good and bad things happen to people. She had given of herself all that she could, and didn't ask for much in return. But she was of an age that she didn't want to worry about others anymore, and she didn't want anyone to fuss about her, either. She just wanted to rest. Her family had all gone before her, and she was the last one. It was time to go.

Annie closed her eyes. *There, that's better,* she thought. *Now I can picture whatever I want. I can be that young girl again. The girl that nobody now can believe ever existed. The light-hearted girl of so many years ago.*

"Sis, will you come with me?" Her brother Alf spoke to her with gladness in his voice. "Here, take my hand."

Annie opened her eyes, and saw him standing beyond the foot of her bed. His thick chestnut hair shone, his blue eyes twinkled and he wore his special endearing grin. He was holding out his hand to her.

She rose from the bed, rather amazed that she could. She drifted toward him, her arms outstretched, her heart swelling with happiness. She looked over her shoulder just once, at the tiny figure on the bed.

"Was that me, Alf?" She turned and looked into his soft eyes in wonderment, and he hugged her close.

"Just your shell, Sis. The real you is here in my arms, young and strong again like me!" He laughed, putting his hand around her back, and taking her other hand, as if to dance. He dipped her down low, lifted her up and spun her around. They were overjoyed to be together again.

"What's your dearest wish?" he asked, smiling down at her.

"If you let me be *your* Shadow," she said, I'll be happy forever."

They left the hospital, holding hands. They never looked back, as they talked and laughed. It was November, and snowing outside, but they took no notice. They walked down the street, arms entwined, and blended with the swirling snow, were soon lost to sight.

### Author's Note

"My Shadow" is a true account from my grandmother's life, told to me in my youth, and it has always haunted me. It takes place during the Great War, and relates her uncanny link with the supernatural – a bond of love so strong that it defeated death's separation from one last contact with her youngest brother, killed in Amiens, France.

# Blame

*Barbara Hudspith*

Blame the Great War or the wife's reproach
or the churlish father,
it will not alter the fact that
Reg is rent
and dies at Vimy.
Shipped home are a mud-caked pipe,
a spattered watch
and the lock of hair
he had pinned to his pocket.

*France, Spring 1917*

Shifting his weight from foot to foot, and insensible to the rain coursing down his neck, Reg paces in agony. He has foregone lunch and now supper in an attempt to inch his way up the queue to the infirmary. Lifting his eyes again to the tent, he groans audibly and shakes his head in disbelief. A hand has emerged from behind the flap and then vanished. The sign, that held every hope of deliverance from this infernally throbbing molar, is no more. The medics have gone. The clinic is shut. And this is the last of the last straws.

He wants to beat his breast, tear his hair and curse the day, but there is no one to blame and no one to listen.

Languidly, he retrieves a packet from his pocket and appends his last letter home. He adds a brief account of this final jab and hopes that someone someday will care enough to read it. Absently he strokes his jaw, and with the wool sock bunched up in his palm, attempts to cradle and soothe it. The futility of his wait now depresses him as profoundly as his growing suspicion that the officers in charge of this campaign care nothing for their men and send them as blithely to the slaughter as the horses that stumble hourly beneath their packs. He has known for days that they are nearing the line and in a private moment, has taken pencil in hand and begun his goodbyes.

He has been under no illusion on either front.

Now acutely aware of the price he has paid, Reg senses the heaviness of his fatigue. His calves cramp and his feet, once numb, now burn with the damp and the standing. If only he could toss these loathsome boots, soar above this infernal ooze and trip the light fantastic. If only he could don a suit and tuck a rose into his lapel. If only he might leap from the train and sweep his girls up and onto his shoulders. Baby would run pell-mell but Judith, he smiled ruefully, would need some coaxing. Always the cautious one, she would surely make strange after this agonizingly protracted absence. No matter. He would win her over – having all the time in the world.

And then he catches himself.

"It will be better for you when I'm gone," he has written. "I know you've never been happy and this way you'll have my pension and be taken care of. Give my love to mother, hug the little ones tight and add a great big kiss for Baby. Know, above all, that I love you."

Snow is beginning to dapple the Ridge, and at dawn, with his abscess still searing, Reg is hit with both barrels. Dying but not yet dead, he is strapped to a stretcher and delivered to the dressing station. His molar remains stubbornly intact.


*Canada, Autumn 2006*

"I remember walking down to the station with him in his greatcoat, and he was carrying this enormous pack on his back," Mona recounted in her later years. "We were going to say goodbye, but Mother wasn't with us. She refused to go. Refused to forgive him for leaving her. I had just turned four and Judith would have soon been six but even at that age we understood. It wasn't about the war, you see. It was about him leaving her with two little ones, and she wouldn't speak. Not a word to him. She was that hurt and angry.

"Mother, you see, had lost a younger brother, and he had been blown to bits. Nothing came home. Only the telegram. So distraught was our grandma that she took a steamer back to England in the middle of the war. She needed to be convinced – to confirm the story first hand. It was madness, of course, for her to risk herself like that but we all understood. She had sent him, at twelve, to be a drummer with the Grenadier Guards on the advice of a well-meaning captain. 'The Guards will never see combat! Mark my words,' he'd assured her. But her Harold had seen action as soon as the war broke out. One minute he was in training at Purbright and the next he was gone. There was only time for one letter to slip through and one cheery little post card.

"Though an indomitable woman, Grandma could not live with that horror. Harold's cronies had given her conflicting accounts, and she knew they were trying to spare her. Mother would often find her, with her Bible on her knee in the evenings, just crying.

"She blamed herself, of course, for trusting, for being so gullible, and who knows what else. Harold had planned to follow them out to Canada, you see, and was just about to purchase his passage. He was twenty-four and hoping to be in the reserves.

"And so on that day in early winter, my mother sent us to the station with her youngest sister, Ott, because we couldn't go alone, of course. And if she had forced herself to see Father off, she would have had a migraine. Even poor Harold had been subject to migraines, and he would often faint in the sun still standing on guard at the palace. But no one would come to his aid. They were cruel to their men in those days. Not an ounce of pity. To his shame, they would just leave him lying.

"And so, we got to the station and there were hordes of soldiers milling about getting ready to board. It became a miserable long wait, and Judith and I began hopping around the platform to keep our legs from freezing.

"Then Papa took a cookie from his pack and held it out to me and said, 'Would you like it?' I took it from his hand, and he smiled and watched me bite into it as if time were suspended and the clock would now stop until I had finished every morsel. Then the whistle blew and he found a seat and tried to wave, but we could barely see him as the cars thundered past and left us in their wake. When he was out of sight entirely, Ott took our hands and we started for home.

"But before we'd gone half a block, Judith shook herself free and grabbed me by the shoulders. Spinning me around so that she could look me right in the eye she began to shout, and I could feel her spit on my cheeks.

"'You shouldn't have taken that cookie!' she shrieked. 'That was a bad thing to do. You took part of Papa's lunch and now he'll be hungry and it's all your fault!'

"I felt desperate and cried all the way home and I couldn't erase it from my mind – that picture of Papa sitting famished on the train because of me. I went to bed in torment. I was only little. How could I have known? And I dared not bother Mama. She was already in bed nursing her head and if I had gone weeping at her door, the blame would have fallen on me.

"He hadn't wanted to go to war, you know. He was hounded. There were catcalls every morning when he walked down Barton St. to the Westinghouse, and then again inside the plant. Even the men he thought were his chums berated him.

"'Why aren't you in uniform, fella? A coward, are yah? A strapping young man like you. Yah oughta be ashamed. More than fit to go. Don't care about your country, eh? Don't know how yah can hold yer head up. If you haven't the decency to sign up, you're not wanted here!'

"Finally he confessed to Mama that he couldn't bear it one more day. So he had gone to get it over with, and missed his lunch to stand in the line and enlist.

"It broke her heart – that final letter – tortured her ever after. She always believed it was a bayonet that got him, though there was no proof. She'd seen it at the pictures, you see, how they were trained to eviscerate, and it preyed on her – that particular horror.

"He still called me 'Baby' – even when I was four. As soon as he came through the door, he'd yell, 'Come 'ere, Baby!' And I would run. Not Judith though. She would hang back behind Mama and watch.

236

I don't recall her having a pet name like I did. Just Judith, I think. Just Judith. But me. Well ... I loved to ride on his shoulders!"

## Canada, Spring 1917

Though dying by inches in the Vimy rain, Reg had lingered long enough to make contact. Penetrating the intimate ether of her sleeping place, he had come for one last longing look. Charlotte had woken with a start and marked the very moment of his passing. No one could disabuse her of the fact. No one cared to.

> Blame the hectoring mob
> or the pain in his eyes,
> it will not alter the fact
> that when the telegram came,
> she fell to the floor in a heap.

Charlotte is wrapped in darkness pitch thick. Tea and biscuits slip through the door on invisible hands, but no one dares enter. Suffice it to say that her bed and her dreams are punitive. It is not the curtains that fight back the light.

Grief is now called for, and she will wear its weeds openly, but it is a private pain that pierces her soul. For the words she last spoke were curt, if not cruel, as he marched himself doggedly to his doom.

## England, Autumn 1896

> Blame the philandering father,
> the persistent lover
> or the depths in the mother's eyes,
> it will not alter the fact
> that in the fall of 1896,
> Reg is plucked from the nest
> and sentenced to a stretch
> at Grays.

In an alien hall, a boy fidgets. He is in shock. The massive clock above his head bongs incessantly and causes him as much agitation as does the interminable wait and his urgent need for the loo. He has been told to stay put until the prefect arrives, and overwhelmed by the enormity of the school and the stentorian tone of the headmaster's voice, he fears to twitch so much as a muscle. If only he could loosen this cursed tie or wriggle free from these chafing cuffs, but there is no hope. Just as there is no chance of climbing again with the girls in the garden. Not now. Not ever. And definitely not here.

Even if his father had had the kindness to linger, he would not have felt so abandoned. But abandoned he is, and seeing the smile on the man's florid face, he'd intuited that his pater felt well rid.

Then a terrifying thought begins to niggle and he wonders, just wonders, if this is the punishment for all of his sins. It is his weakness to tease their Dorrie – make no mistake – but he means no harm. Without her, his big sister, he would surely perish. There are so many pitfalls, so many ways to offend and she has been his rock. And now here he is alone at Grays with no one in his corner. Has he brought this upon himself?

His ears begin to ring and his hands to tremble and buffered no more by the tenderness of sisters, the boy has come entirely unglued. Then, raising his eyes, he spots the prefect prancing menacingly towards him, and a trickle begins to dribble down his leg.

### England, Spring 1904

The drawing room has now emptied of guests, and Reg alone remains. While couples linger along the strand hoping for a sunset, he gazes at the sea from his perch and loses himself in a reverie. His school tie lies crumpled at his feet, his green cap thrown hastily in the corner. Leaning heavily against the sill, he cups his chin in his palm and sighs.

"What are *your* plans for tonight?" pipes a perky voice behind him.

It is Miss Inch who manages the lodging house in which he now dwells and, knowing her intentions are well meaning and her interest genuine, Reg shakes himself from his stupor and attempts to meet her eyes. It is a tender subject she is broaching, and he fears that his voice will betray him.

"Going to bed with my book," he returns lightly. "Not much else to do, is there?"

"Surely your father has a plan! No one should be stuck in on a night like this!"

"Not a plan that includes me," he replies offhandedly. "I saw him leaving an hour ago with a young woman on his arm and some champagne tucked under his coat. They were heading towards the motor."

"Never!" she challenges. "Who was it then? Not Mrs. Gates, our newest lady? I just can't imagine that he would ..."

"No, no. Of course not. It was her daughter who has come to stay for the week. The smart young lady with the yellow curls and the pretty laugh."

"Well I think it's a disgrace," she retorts and, settling into the chair at his side, she takes time to ruminate upon this unexpected revelation.

"A lad like you with a father who should be enjoying his company and taking him out in the motor, sitting here on the finest of spring evenings. Perhaps he's planning to take you out tomorrow on one of his famous drives up the coast? Did you ask?"

"He would only say what he always says when I'm back from school: 'Why are you always around when you're not wanted?' My father, you must have gathered, has never been one to tolerate the company of children."

"But your mother?" she prods hopefully.

"Oh, she has no interest in me at all. She has a new gentleman and a new infant son. I can't even say that I know where she is. Perhaps she's returned to France where she once was so happy. My sisters were sent across to live with her family, but according to the postcards they send me, it has been a miserable failure. They will soon be sent back in disgrace and expected to go to our father's sister in London. Not that I'll ever see them! Though Philly is considering the girls' academy at Grays. I do so hope she comes."

A long silence fell between them and, wagging her head in mute protest at the boy's lot, Miss Inch remained for some time keeping him company. When the light faded and the promenade emptied of strollers, the boy reached for his book, pressed it tightly to his chest and rose to go. Turning towards the stairway that led to the upper floors, he bent low and offered her a peck on the cheek.

"What a terrible shame," she mused to herself. "What a terrible shame. What could be worse for the poor lad than that?"

### Canada, Summer 1910

Reg is pacing the platform. He has taken the trouble to conquer his forelock and iron his shirt and now the cursed sun is causing him to sweat. A fine way to greet your beloved, he grumbles to himself.

"When *will* that train arrive?"

He has seen her only once in all the five years of his exile and even then he had noticed a change. It was the dainties and creams and puddings they were spoiling her with at the Inn, he imagined. She was beginning to resemble a butterball!

She was family, after all, and her aunt and uncle did treat her as one of their kin. Her letters had been all about parasols and boat rides on the river on Sundays – if she were to be believed – and he had to admit that he had been genuinely jealous. One minute she sounded like an indentured servant, and the other like a pampered young niece.

And yet, he smiled to himself, in spite of their wretched separation, what he feared most had never come to pass. With all of those pompous, flashy toffs frequenting the place, she might well have forgotten him. Or worse still, been preyed upon by a cad like his father who went on holiday not so much to fish as to flirt. At the mere spectre his lips curled in disgust and he began to stomp noisily down the platform.

Some days he thought he'd go mad with the waiting. If it hadn't been for the lads on the floor telling their jokes and spinning their tales, he couldn't have borne it. So many times he had wanted to throw up his hands and go for a farmer. All that lovely fresh air and sun and the smell of the hay after harvest. No dark dungeon of a plant to toil in. But he had made her a promise.

The factory lads had become his family in an odd sort of a way. He had to admit that he had grown fond of them in spite of the boredom and the wretched sameness of the assembly line day after deadening day. Who else did he have on this soil? Just his landlady when it came to that, and she was a regular peach. Charlotte would love her.

Did they have any notion, back home just how humble his circumstances were? Fancy Aunt Ada scolding him for referring to his "job."

"Never use that word again in front of the servants!" she'd hissed. "What will they think of us? You have a position, not a job."

A position indeed.

How will Charlotte take it, he wonders, when she realizes just how far he has fallen – or rather, how far *they* have fallen, for they will be in this together now. She must know that his grandfather is the richest man in Nottingham. Will she be expecting an inheritance to come their way? Heaven forbid! He will need to disabuse her of any such notion, but all in good time and definitely after they've wed.

How fortunate it was that her grandma had furnished her with a trousseau, for he could not even afford the suit he was standing up in. Would she mind that it had been borrowed from a pal just for the day? It had been either a smart suit for him or the fee for the license and a posy for his girl.

It has not been a whirlwind romance, he reflects, nor a serious case of calf love – on either side. Far from it. And his face begins to redden and his breath to come in puffs at the mere memory. His pater had strolled into the parlor that night and, perceiving him to be at a loss for occupation, had lost his rag. Grabbing him violently by the shoulders, and thrusting him through the scullery door, he had thrown him down at Charlotte's feet. Literally.

"If you have nothing better to do than hang around me all night," he'd bellowed, "let it be known that you're not wanted here! Why don't you go to the pictures or to the skating rink for heaven's sake! There's Charlotte right in front of you. If you don't want to go alone, take her, but get out of my sight."

Mortified, he'd picked himself up and out of the corner of his eye, caught the look on her face. Was it pity? Affection? Fellow feeling? He did not know and had never asked, but it was the catalyst, and lonely as he was, a great and lasting solace.

It had all hung by a thread. If Charlotte's mother had not been still in his father's employ, and if Charlotte herself had not been filling in for the kitchen maid, he would not be standing there today wrestling with such stress and delightful anticipation.

*England, Spring 1905*

"I think it is time for you to fend for yourself," his father had begun, one evening, rapping the stem of his pipe against the paper. "The colonies would be the best place for you. They are apparently hungry for immigrants, or so it claims in this article, and with an excellent education from Grays – like your own – and a good family name behind you, I believe it to be your best course of action. As soon as the spring term is over, you could be on a ship steaming to Canada. What could be more adventurous than that!"

Reg's mouth had dropped. He was not wet and knew full well that this was one of his father's ruses. Chances were, his pater had been orchestrating this for months and had simply decided on this particular moment to pounce. Chances were, he had already purchased his passage.

Silence hung heavily between them. Terrified of what might come out of his mouth, the boy leapt from his chair, bounded up the stairs, and shut himself into his room. What was it that he had done now to ruffle the patriarchal feathers? He would probably never know. Was he so seriously flawed that his father had to put the breadth of the sea between them?

He would become an entrepreneur and set up his own empire of lace like his grandfather or go for a soldier and march smartly on parade. And he would never ever come back ... well, never come back to see his father.

Insensitive to Reg's impetuous exit, his father had called for a second tumbler of scotch and continued to peruse his paper.

*Canada, Winter 1913*

> Blame the threat of war,
> the fractured family,
> or the young man's naivete,
> it will not alter the fact
> that the marriage was fraught
> and the larder often wanting.

Desperate to better himself, Reg studies by night to be a draftsman, but no position presents itself. When his grandfather dies and leaves him a small inheritance he thinks it wise to invest, but the budding new firm he has chosen soon collapses and he loses half of his legacy. Charlotte's family follow her to Canada. With eight under one roof, all hope of intimacy evaporates. Charlotte cooks and chars for the lot, but she is serially pregnant and forever weary.

Reg purchases a plot of land in Florida – sight unseen. To his horror, it is nothing more than swampland. Gone is the other half of the inheritance.

Shamefaced, he attempts to economize. Turning a deaf ear to Charlotte's pleas, he engages the services of the cheapest midwife in town. Trusting the advice of his pals at the plant and not considering first his wife's welfare, he has made a costly mistake. Charlotte's births are complicated and her deliveries unnecessarily grueling. While her incisions gape and her stitches fester, pain assaults the new mother on two fronts. She will not easily forgive or forget this blatant infraction of the marital code, and she will never again trust herself to the hands of that wretched woman.

Two babes have arrived in rapid succession – first Judith, then Mona. Reg has been seen to dance around the kitchen. He is now the head of a bona fide family of his own. He chooses a riot of flowers for his wife and cheap cigars for the lads. He is learning.

There are bollards and bumps along the way, but nothing so dire that it cannot be mended. It takes time to read the other's heart and patience to plumb the height of its depths. Reliable cartographers do not run in the family – on either side. They have set off to sea with no compass.

## Canada, Summer 1927

Charlotte and the girls have enjoyed a holiday at the beach thanks to the YWCA. It has been a relief to flee their tiny closet of a flat where the air remains stale and dank and the leaves on the houseplants wither and shrivel.

But Mona and Judith are not content. Eager students with great promise, their wishes have been disregarded. Matriculation is out of the question. Filing and typing will be their lot. The rules are the rules, and the Women's Guild insists that they now earn their way. The canning factory and the stenographer's pool hire them immediately.

The matriarchal mantle is quietly slipping from Charlotte's shoulders and coming to rest on her eldest girl. Judith does not welcome this shift in management, but it is clear that their mother has fallen into the morass of melancholy and someone needs to be steering the ship.

While Reg's sisters remain attached to the struggling little three-some, the family patriarch, when he writes puts distance into his voice.

The Military Cemetery at Bruay is a brief boat ride away, but no one – on that side of the Atlantic – visits the grave. No one speaks the name. Is this is an unspoken pact? An agreed-upon silence? No one knows.

Charlotte rocks and repeats her mantra: "If only he'd come back, I'd have nursed him his whole life through. Poor Reg. Poor, poor Reg."

Money is scarce and in the winter months, the flat is cold and bare. Bulky wicker furnishings have been ordered to mitigate the impression of poverty, for the girls are now entertaining suitors.


## Canada, Summer 1932

At nineteen Mona marries. Her curls are yellow and her smile bright and with a chasm where her father should have been, the daughter becomes fair game. She is conspicuously naive and woefully vulnerable. In less than a year, the fellow has vanished, taken a mistress and remarried. But the knave has not yet dissolved his union with Mona.

She is burdened, not only with the rent and a heavy heart, but with nine torturous years of litigation. Private detectives are hired and papers served. Bigamy is a criminal offence and the rogue and his lady are on the lam. Shamed publicly by the judge for her poor taste in husbands, Mona is stunned. Discovering that the details have been reported in the local paper, she breaks down entirely.

The judge knows nothing about the telegram nor the mother's melancholia. He is not inclined to delve. Doesn't even ask. Their significance pales as does the Great War, the family's shame, and the opportunistic rogue.

### Canada, Autumn 1944

Reg has appeared once more to Charlotte in the genetic makeup of a newly born granddaughter. Her hair is fair and her skin is as pale as her mother Mona's. Charlotte is exuberant. Is this a sign that Reg has forgiven her?

Mollified, she becomes fixated upon the child's welfare.

### Canada, Summer 1955

Charlotte has experienced her first heart attack. Living still with her daughters and unabashedly unwilling to keep a separate domicile, she becomes obsessed with her illness. Refusing to strain herself by walking, she orders a wheel chair to be delivered, but when a dog sees fit to bark at her wheels, the chair is sent back. Confining herself to the indoors, she agrees to make necessary forays into the wider world only if the car can be brought within inches of the door and the day is warm and still.

### Canada, Winter 1960

Judith turns fifty and is diagnosed with cancer. A mastectomy is booked. Charlotte rocks and moans incessantly.

*Canada Summer 1962*

> Blame the six-year-old sister, the Great War,
> or the train crouching on the tracks,
> it will not alter the fact that in the summer of '62,
> Mona tries to strangle a woman
> who lies sleeping across the hall.

Mona is sitting upright – her gazed fixed. While July, like a hot-iron, scorches the city's streets, the windows on the ward where Mona dwells remain tight shut. Not a whisper of a breeze slips through.

Then at nightfall, as if on cue, she mounts a raid. Tearing off the sheets, she strides with purpose across the hall. Peering slyly into the doorways, she selects a room and enters. Her view being blocked by the curtains that cocoon the bed, she twitches the obstacle aside and sidles up to the sleeping enemy. Sliding the tips of her fingers around the thin neck, she begins to press with the heels of her palms on the larynx.

Coughing and spewing, her foe flies upright. Writhing in terror, the woman breaks her assailant's grip, and for one long minute the trench falls silent. By the time reinforcements arrive Mona is already in retreat. She appears, in this singular suspended moment, to be walking in her sleep. Groggy and mystified, she casts about for something to hang onto – something to recognize.

Her doctor is enraged. Has he been bested by a duplicitous patient? Misdiagnosed this cunning charge? He retaliates by prescribing a round of shock therapy and the introduction of a feeding tube that is to be inserted and removed at each and every meal. The nurses are appalled and balk at the barbarism, but their chief stands firm. Fearing the whispers already circulating, he thinks to redeem himself by hitting her with both barrels.

The psychiatrist knows nothing about the war train pawing at the tracks or the offer of a cookie. Doesn't even ask. That humble confection was of course the catalyst and the crux, but in the mind of a distinguished man of letters, its significance paled as did the Great War, the frantic sister, and the family's obsession with blame.

*Canada, Autumn 1974*

Judith loses her battle after enduring endless attempts to halt the enemy's progress. Mona, now heavily medicated, steps into her shoes.

*Canada, Winter 1982*

Charlotte has chosen to closet herself. In the tiny room in which she now sits, two windows give onto the yard. Their sashes remain painted shut. Not the whisper of a breeze slips through. Now terrified of drafts, she hangs a massive velour curtain across the door. Is it just the wind that she fears may find its way through?

*Canada, Spring 1982*

After a brief stay in hospital, Charlotte, now in her 95th year, succumbs to pneumonia.

*Canada, Winter 2006*

"They wedged something between my teeth," Mona would recount in the winter of her 94th year, "so that my jaw wouldn't break or my teeth shatter, and they strapped me to a gurney. Then they wheeled me into that horrid room day after terrifying day, and I don't know why I tried to kill her, that poor, poor woman. But I did, you know. I did!"

She blamed herself, of course, for the cookie. For his going away. For her mother's migraines. For the shame she brought and for her girlish gullibility. For Judith's breast cancer and her mother's entrenchment. For her unspeakable crime and for not knowing why.

*Canada, Spring 2007*

Mona receives a vision the night before she dies. Papa will come for her at the moment of her passing. With clarity and conviction she shares this with her daughter and with the nurses that are still on shift. No one disabuses her of that notion. No one cares to.

Old sins may cast long shadows
but old joys
can rekindle the light.

There is now a notable exhilaration in Mona's mood and a breathless quality about her voice. In the hour before dawn, her eyes begin to brighten and she hears a distant call for ... "Baby".

Opening the door,
he sweeps her up
and holds her high
and places her snug
on those
most beloved
and oh, so familiar
shoulders

*Author's Note*

The story told in "Blame" has been etched in my memory since childhood, as I heard it often repeated by my mother and grandmother. In the fall of 2006, I felt an urgent need to visit Vimy and to search out my grandfather's grave. Coming face to face with the cross that marks the site was a liminal experience. I left with a deepened awareness of his presence and his impact on all of the family.

# Mind Fields

*Michelle Ward-Kantor*

*Toronto, 1920*

I was not looking forward to returning home. It had been a difficult day with John. He had survived his battle with influenza several months ago, but the illness had weakened his already poor heart. Although I cared for him and did all I could to take the load off his wife, lately I found myself wishing he would die quietly in his sleep. It was unfair for him to have to live this way, with his wife worrying over every sigh, every grunt of pain that suggested a new affliction. She'd looked almost as gaunt as he this last month and I worried she herself might soon need home care.

My head throbbed as I boarded the streetcar, thankful to be out of the icy December wind. I kept my scarf wrapped tightly during the ride, trying to rid myself of the damp chill, one that buried itself in my bones. I hardly noticed the other passengers as I worried about what to say to Mum that night at dinner. The conversation I meant to have was long overdue. Although I usually didn't like it when Patrick wasn't there to eat with us, I hoped tonight would be one of those times.

Patrick and I returned from the war just over a year ago, within a few months of each other. Dad had died eight months before the war started. When I first left for France, I worried about Mum being alone, until the things I saw made it seem as if home was on another planet, in a different time. When I did return home, I was happy to see that

Mum seemed to have carried on fairly well, although she had aged terribly. Where Patrick was concerned, she tried to be optimistic. He walked with a limp, but that wasn't the wound that concerned us.

"He'll get better, don't fret," she would tell me.

Mum had no way of understanding what Patrick might have gone through during those terrible years. He wouldn't speak to her about it. Granted, I hadn't spoken much about the war either, but now I thought maybe if I told her what I had seen it would help her understand, although I suspected she really didn't want to know.

As the streetcar hummed along, I found myself remembering the Christmas of 1915. I had been working in a hospital in France for several months by then, yet I still hadn't gotten used to the idea that there were some men I couldn't help.

The other nurses and I did what we could to make Christmas a cheery affair. We made gift bags for each of our 600 patients. The men were so grateful and I remember feeling teary-eyed as I watched them open their presents. We had a carol service and that, too, put a hot lump in my throat. It was lovely and the men appreciated it very much. In my bed afterwards, I wrote a letter to Mum, telling her how much I missed her, but I said little about what I had seen and heard during my time there so far. Tonight I felt I needed to share some of that.

I disembarked from the streetcar and walked the short distance to the small brick two-story. Dad's law firm had done very well in the years before he died and the house was paid for. I could smell meatloaf as I entered. I removed my boots and mitts and hung up my coat and scarf. "How was Patrick today?"

"Not too bad," said Mum, as she worked. Her cheerfulness sounded forced. "He slept late, and was pretty quiet through the day."

I glanced at the table. It was set for three.

"He's not coming down, says he's not hungry." She glanced at me. "No matter, I guess meatloaf isn't one of his favorites."

"Don't worry, Mum. I'm sure he won't miss Christmas dinner." I smiled, wanting to give her something to look forward to. I carried the meatloaf and potatoes to the table.

Once we had started eating I began. "Maybe it's just as well Patrick isn't hungry. I've been meaning to talk to you about something anyway, and it's probably best if we talk alone."

She looked startled. "Is anything wrong? Has Mr. Porter gotten worse?"

We both knew that without my job with Mr. Porter, things would be a little tight. Mum had her part-time job at Dr. Donnel's office, the dentist Patrick and I had gone to as children. She enjoyed answering the phone and scheduling appointments, but he was due to retire soon. With jobs so scarce, we had often talked of what we would do when that happened.

"No, Mr. Porter is about the same." I hesitated, took a bite of meatloaf, chewed and swallowed.

"I wanted to talk to you about Patrick, and what he might be going through." My stomach felt queasy. I realized how many things I had kept hidden since arriving back in Toronto.

"Do you remember the letters I wrote to you while I was away?"

She was quiet for a minute. "How could I forget?" she said softly. "I missed you both so much, especially at Christmas."

I reached across the table and covered her hand with mine. "I didn't tell you about the things I saw, the stories I heard."

She listened then, her face looking sad and worn.

I told her how I had treated men with trench foot, how their feet were sometimes black with gangrene. I told her the stories that some had confided to me, or ones I had overheard, how one soldier had lain dead next to men in the trenches, while Germans hovered nearby, how rats ran over them, how they scratched and scratched but could do nothing about the lice, how they listened to each other, coughing violently as they sat in the muck. I told her how these brave men tried to laugh off their wounds.

"It's nothing," they would say; yet when I pulled off the field bandages, I would find their wounds had festered. I described the men who had lost legs or arms, and the stench of infection.

I told her about Frederick Arnold, a man about the same age as Patrick, with the same blue eyes and blonde hair. He arrived just after the New Year, with an affliction that caused him terrible 251 headaches, yet he had no outward injuries. It was my first experience with this. He rarely spoke and his hands trembled violently. While I had been trained to administer ether for surgery, change bandages, apply solutions for infection and all manner of treatments, I had little inkling of how to help this poor soldier. I did what I could, tending to his feet, blistered and swollen like so many others I had seen, though I was happy to see they were not gangrenous.

For the first few days he lay motionless on the thin cot, sitting up only when I assisted him. His hands shook badly when he tried to feed himself, so I often held the spoon to his mouth. The doctors suggested rest and a diet rich in foods that contained milk.

One of the nurses who had experience with massage worked every day on his hands and arms, and soon I learned the techniques. It took weeks before we saw some improvement. When he sat up, he often stared straight ahead, as if looking for something in the distance. This man's anxiety followed me as I dressed wounds, changed bandages, and soothed the other patients as best I could.

I told Mum about the fatigue and sadness I often felt, how there was never enough of me to go around. But I felt it must be nothing compared to the men who lay there, row upon row in their cots. Sometimes they grumbled, but often they were cheerful, even in their discomfort, content to be in a bed, with access to food and clean water. We nurses did our best to remain positive, and I thought so often of Patrick, somewhere out in this madness. For me to complain would be ungrateful.

On night shift sometimes, I heard Fred – as we began to call him – moaning, often yelling in his sleep. Once he half sat up, looked around wildly, his eyes searching for something, someone. I reached out to touch him, to reassure him so he would lie back down, but he lashed out at me. His face was dimly lit by the moonlight coming through the thin curtain and I saw the sweat on his forehead. When he finally lay back down, I put my hand on his back, rubbing it gently until his breathing became even. This became routine.

"You see Mum, I hoped if Patrick was hurt, someone was tending to him this way. I couldn't bear to think of my little brother somewhere out there, with no one to watch over him."

Mum was chewing slowly, her eyes watching me. I couldn't stop the words. They were desperate to get out, to be heard. I had forgotten that, although it was my release to be heard, for her it must be an onslaught, a look at a world that up until now, she had been unaware of, a time that she had never asked about.

"Are you okay, Mum? Should I stop?"

She shook her head. She had put down her knife and fork and had stopped eating.

I told her how I assisted the doctors by holding Fred's arms to stop the tremors. Several times, the doctor suggested to Fred that he was well and the movements would stop, told him it was a physical ailment from which he would recover. Some of the other hospitals used electric batteries and such to treat shaking limbs, but our doctors didn't like them.

One of the doctors thought Fred was a shirker and must leave the hospital in short order. I sat in on one session where he chastised Fred. He suggested others might think him a coward. He should return to where he belonged; he should be helping his fellow soldiers fight the Germans.

"And Mum, two months after he had been admitted, he told me what haunted him, 'Sister,' he said, 'I can't escape the pictures in my head, the rifle jamming, John beside me yelling, the rain pouring down, and then, the shot, and it was quiet, half his face, gone …

"'And the rain kept coming, and I tried to bury John, dug with my hands, but then there was another one, another body, buried in the trench walls; the rats had eaten half his face …'

"He paused then, and I sat down on his bed, waiting quietly. And all the time he talked I thought with despair about my brother, wondering what he was going through, thinking, surely, he wouldn't get out of this alive.

"And then Fred used some awful language! 'Those f'ing bastards,' he said. 'They sent us out with rifles that didn't work! And we told them … over and over we told them.'

"He apologized for his language then. I was so startled, not only by his words but by what had happened to him. How those men carried on with those terrible images in their minds, I don't know.

"What if Patrick has something in his mind like that? He won't tell me, even though I ask, and you … never ask."

I stopped then. My mother's eyes had filled with tears. She was nodding. "I've thought of that, Anna. I think often of what he might have seen."

This confession surprised me. All this time I thought she went through each day as if nothing was different. She sighed then. "I pray that one day he'll sit down and tell me what has hurt him so. But he seems to respond better to you than to me."

She chewed silently for a moment. "Your patient in France, did he get better?" The hope in her eyes made my heart ache.

I told her how his concentration became better, the headaches and the nightmares lessened.

"And then they discharged him, Mum, just like that. Sent him back into that horror.

"'It's been so nice here,' he told me. 'Comforting, sort of like home. It's a sad state, when this feels like home.' He even laughed when he said it. 'I leave this afternoon. They say I'm better.' But I remember his face, and how he looked like an old soul. The way Patrick's face sometimes looks.

"He thanked me then for all I had done for him. I told him he would be home soon enough, to give us both hope. He was from Cleveland, Mum. Said he thought it would be a big adventure, coming to fight with the Canadians. Thought it was the right thing to do. He said it was a hellish adventure.

"I never saw him again. Of course, there were so many soldiers I never saw again, but thinking of Fred kept me awake at night. Was he back fighting while his hands trembled? Did he ever cry out at night?"

I stopped talking and began to pick at my lukewarm dinner.

"But Patrick has no tremors," Mum said. "And his leg seems not too bad. He gets around pretty well."

"I know Mum, but do you realize he still has nightmares? Still wakes up screaming sometimes?"

Mum had no hearing in one ear. She usually slept with her good ear down on the pillow. Perhaps she had never heard her son's cries. I stood then, put my plate on the side-board and gave her a hug.

"Are you finished eating? I'll stoke up the fire again and boil some water for tea."

There was more I needed to tell her. When I thought back to my time at London's National Hospital for the Paralysed and Epileptic, I became fearful for Patrick's future.

I had been transferred there a year or so after Frederick Arnold was discharged. This hospital had many wards set up just for the treatment of patients with shell shock and other nervous conditions. It was there I met Dr. Lewis Yealland – a man whose treatment methods I did not always agree with.

My first training session was with a group of other nurses. Here we learned to use a machine that discharged electric currents. Dr. Yealland often used it, together with "re-education", to help cure a patient's affected limbs. We had many patients with leg and arm tremors and loss of sight and hearing. Re-education was making the patient believe he could be cured, or, if he had had several sessions, had already been cured.

I assisted Dr. Yealland in all manner of cases and I was glad when electricity was unnecessary. Once with a mute patient, he simply tickled the back of the patient's throat with a tongue depressor and there was no need for an electrical current.

"It was really distressing to me to hurt a patient, Mum, but Dr. Yealland assured me it was sometimes necessary."

I recalled a case where we had to use electricity to help a man regain his voice. Tickling his throat did no good. The current was so strong that the man jumped back, detaching the wires from the battery.

Yet the treatment I most strongly objected to was isolation. This was sometimes used for men whose limbs jerked excessively. Dr. Yealland believed that leaving these men alone was necessary, to make them see that their illness was not something to be proud of, as if they could shame the men into being cured.

I recalled one session with a man whose legs jerked excessively. Dr. Yealland told him, "If you recover quickly, it is due to disease. If you recover slowly ... I shall decide your condition is due to malingering.

You must behave the way I want you to. You must be a hero."

I stopped talking and found myself remembering the one and only time Patrick had seen a doctor about his nightmares once he had returned home. I was relieved that he agreed to see someone, and was glad he asked me to accompany him, "so you can ask questions in case I forget," he told me. He was very reserved around people since his return from France, and he didn't open up to anyone. The doctor poked his head out the door after examining Patrick, and at Patrick's request, called me inside.

"When did your nightmares first start?" he asked. "Were you treated for this while you were still in France?"

"No, sir," Patrick answered quietly. "I was fine over there. It's only months after I got home that it started."

"Would you know if Patrick qualifies for any pension, Dr. Galloway?" I asked. "He has difficulty with people since his return, and is having trouble finding a job."

"Well you can apply." He looked at Patrick. "But I'm not sure you'll get anything. Have you been actively looking for work? That would be in your favour if such is the case."

"Yes, sir, a bit, sir."

"Let's give you a few months. Why don't you come back and see me then if the symptoms haven't gone away. I can recommend some talk therapy in the meantime."

The problem was, Patrick didn't want to talk. He told me, "No matter what I say, I have to get on with it. They'll think I'm malingering, after all."

He never did apply for a pension and that's when I knew how deeply concerned my brother was about the perception of others.

"You see, Mum … " My thoughts returned to our conversation. "Even with the treatment methods used by the doctors, many of the men couldn't return to fight because they didn't recover. Sometimes I think even being back home isn't enough for recovery. I've tried to make sense of what I've seen and heard." I felt tears well up and over-flow. "I know Patrick is trying to make sense of it, too."

"You're doing a good job, Anna." She surprised me then, praising me for all I had done for my brother and for the family since the war ended. "You see, when you both came home I didn't know what to do. It's hard to explain how you feel when your children come home after so many years away, and you just keep hearing how so many have died. Your dad was gone, and then you were both gone, too." Her tears came. "When you returned I was so anxious to pick up where we left off before the war. Sometimes, even now, I have to see you and touch you to reassure myself that you're actually here."

She told me how distant we seemed, even months after the war ended, and how – even though I had found a job as a nurse and was still patient and kind – something had changed in me.

"A mother knows when her children aren't right, and I knew neither of you would ever be the same again. I've wanted to ask you about the war so often, but I thought bringing it up might be too painful for both of you. Maybe I was wrong. I'm so glad you opened up to me tonight, Anna."

I felt selfish now; I had been so worried about Patrick's mind and, if I was honest, about myself, as well. Yet, Mum, too, was having a difficult time.

When the Christmas season came, Patrick spent many dinners at the table, much to my delight. He even came to church on Christmas Eve with Mum and me, and made an effort to talk to people in the parish who had known him since he was a child.

But as January came and went, he seemed to withdraw again. In early spring, I chanced to hear from a nursing friend whom I had confided in about Patrick. Her brother had received land compensation and was going to try farming again. He needed some help with the animals he planned to buy. The job wouldn't pay much, but she said she would wait to hear if Patrick might like to offer his services.

My heart soared as I remembered how my brother had loved spending summers as a child, helping our grandfather on his small farm outside Toronto. I knew they had often sent men to farms to recover from various mental anxieties during the war years. Animals have such a calming effect.

I was thrilled when Patrick agreed to try working there. Mum and I were ecstatic the weekend he decided to stay overnight to help with the new calves, even though we wondered if he would be okay, away from the sanctuary of his room.

I could only hope and pray that Frederick Arnold, too, had gotten a second chance at life.

## Author's Notes

Frederick Stanley Arnold was shot for desertion on July 25, 1916. The following note was sent to his mother:

To: Catherine Arnold, Cleveland, Ohio
From: Canadian Records Office
August 22, 1916

*Madam,*

*With deep regret, I have the honour to inform you that a report has been received to the effect that the soldier marginally noted [Frederick Stanley Arnold ] was tried by Field General Court-Martial at Boulogne, France, on the 5th day of July, 1916, on the charge of "When on active service deserting His Majesty's Service" and was sentenced by the Court: to suffer death by being shot". The sentence was duly carried out at 4:37 a.m. on the 25th of July, 1916.*

*I have the honour to be,*
*Madam, Your obedient servant.*

Because I could find no record of the hospital Frederick Stanley Arnold was treated in, I have based his treatment for shell-shock, using accounts of what was done at the time. Arnold was treated (and later executed) before the battle of the Somme, after which several hospitals were set up to deal with the thousands of shell shock cases. In the absence of recorded details, I created the circumstances around why Arnold had shell shock, as well as the symptoms he might have had.

## Sister Anna and Patrick

Sister Anna is a fictional character, however, her demeanor, the experiences with patients, Christmas festivities, and the incidents with Dr. Lewis Yealland, are taken from real accounts.

Patrick is also a fictional character but his experiences both during and after the war would have been typical of many soldiers. Public perception of soldiers suffering from "war neuroses" was not always favorable. While Canada eventually developed a pension and benefits scheme for returned veterans, those who had suffered mental trauma often had trouble convincing pension adjudicators that their symptoms were war-related.

# The Frozen Goose

*Margaret Lindsay Holton*

The black ice was treacherous and they were lost. Annabelle clung to Lachlin's little hand and tried to reassure him, "Don't worry Lory, we'll be home soon." The wind howled and the snow was blinding. Lachlin's tear-soaked face was contorted with fear and Annabelle knew that if they didn't find land soon they would be goners for sure. The howling drew nearer. She pushed on against that wretched wind, dragging her little brother behind her.

She had been wrong, she would now admit, though at the time she was convinced that she had been right. Her step-father had entered the kitchen with his butcher knife. Her mother was beside the stove. He had said that there was no work in town after the war and it was time to cut their losses and move on. He put the knife down on the table and went towards the fire. Her mother was silent as she continued to stir the soup. Finally she turned to him and said, "You know we can't go, Daniel. The children are settled, and we must make a life for them here. To go again would only make things worse."

He pulled off his wet boots and then his wet socks. His bare, wrinkled feet were turned towards the hearth. "There is nothing here, Helen. Nothing that a man can do. Nothing that a man can become."

She went to him, placing her hand on his shoulder. "We will manage. You will find something." Their stoic silhouette was framed by the glow of the fire.

Annabelle well remembered that day a year ago when Daniel had arrived in his uniform, cap in hand. He had told her mother that his best friend, her husband, had been lost at Passchendaele. Her mother had not said a word. Daniel and Helen had just stood silently staring at each other.

It had come as no surprise to Annabelle that their fractured union two months later had been the only way they had known how to fill the void of her father's loss. Daniel had solemnly promised Helen that he would protect and provide for her and the children. Annabelle had listened quietly as her mother had promised that she would nurse that broken man back to health.

She watched as he took her mother's hand in his at that fire and said, "You are a good wife, Helen, but it's not enough. I just can't do it. I'm just too tired."

Annabelle's mother kissed him gently on the head, withdrew her hand, and returned to the stove. "Here, have some soup. You'll feel better soon." As she laid out the soup bowls she turned to Annabelle. "Go get your brother, Bella. We'll eat now."

Annabelle left the kitchen and went up the back stairs to Lachlin's room.

He was sprawled across the bed reading a book about wolves.

"Listen to this Annabelle, 'A wolf can smell fear from another animal up to a mile away.' Imagine that!"

"Come on, Lory. Supper's ready. Daniel is in a mood, so be careful what you say."

Lachlin made a face and slid off the bed in his floppy socks. He shimmied across the wood floor to the closet and pulled out his worn slippers. "What are we having tonight? Soup and bread again?"

"Sshh. Don't say that. You know there is no money. We have to eat what we can get."

"If we need money, I could deliver the *County Review* again. I fixed the flat on my bicycle."

"Don't be stupid. It's the middle of winter. How could you manage snowdrifts and ice on your dumb bike?"

"I could do it. I could be the man of this house."

Annabelle quietly considered his puffed up defiance and softened her tone. "Don't worry, I will work. I will go to Uncle Charlie's store and see if I can do the check-out."

"How are you going to get there? Do you want to use my bike?"

"I'll walk. Come on, silly. Let's go eat."

During the meal Annabelle kept looking at her mother. The older woman was worn out and listless. The air in the kitchen was filled with foreboding and despair. Annabelle knew she had to get the job. She was convinced it would save her family.

The next morning she told her mother she would walk to Uncle Charlie's store to get some work. Her mother looked at her long and hard, then said, "It's too far in this weather to walk. It's over five miles. It's too far."

Annabelle said she could manage. She put on her toque and scarf and wrapped her warm overcoat around her. Her boots were dry and warm, her hands well-covered and cozy. "See? Snug as a bug in a rug."

Her mother said, "I will come with you."

Annabelle shook her head, comforting her. "I'll be there in no time. You'll just slow me down. I'll be back before dusk." With that, Bella opened the kitchen door and stepped out into the day.

The air was crisp and bright. Not a cloud in the sky. She began the long crunchy march down the country lane towards the store. She hadn't gone more than half a mile when she heard Lachlin yelling from behind. "Annabelle! Annabelle! Wait for me! I'm coming, too. Daniel said it's okay."

She stopped and turned around. Lachlin was storming up to her with his scarf flying behind, his mitts dangling from their strings. His head was uncovered and his coat unbuttoned.

"We aren't going anywhere with you dressed like that. Come here and let me straighten you out." Annabelle slipped off her mittens, tucked his scarf around his neck and quickly buttoned up his coat. She pulled up his hood. "There. Now maybe you'll make it."

He slipped his hand into hers, "Let's go this way! I know a short cut!" He pulled her towards the side of the road, "If we cross McCormick's Pond we'll be closer to Uncle Charlie's."

"No, Lachlin." She pulled her hand away from his. "Not the pond. It's too big and I don't know my way around in the woods."

262    "I do. It's easy. Follow me!"

"No, Lachlin. We're going by the road." So, on they went.

It took them just over two hours to get to the store. By the time they entered the premises, their ears were near frostbit and their noses were dribbling goop into their mouths. Their eyes, too, were streaming from the bitter cold. The wind had started to come up.

Uncle Charlie gave them cups of hot chocolate and listened quietly to Annabelle's plea for work. When she had finished he stood and went into the back room, returning with a twelve pound frozen goose. "Here, Bella, take this home to your mother. Say it is a Christmas present from me. And you can start work here in the New Year."

Annabelle hugged her uncle while Lachlin jumped with joy at the prospect of real food on their table. Uncle Charlie said, "Now off you go. Get yourselves home before this wind really starts blowing. The wolves are out and we don't want to lose one of you to the pack!" Lachlin howled for fun and then barked like a dog. Annabelle cuffed him playfully on the back of the head as Uncle Charlie put the frozen goose into a burlap bag. He handed it to Annabelle. "Can you manage this Annabelle? It's not too heavy?" She took the sack from him. "I can manage."

The children left the store around noon. They had only walked about two miles down the road when the wind whipped up out of nowhere. At the first gust Lachlin was almost hurled to the other side of the road. He quickly rebounded and clung to the side of Annabelle's flapping coat. "This wind is too strong! We should go through the woods," he shouted.

Annabelle looked down at his torn jacket. Buttons had popped. "Alright, but stick with me. No horsing around."

They stepped down from the road and cut into the sparse woods in the direction of the pond. The wind played tricks with the snow. First it was coming from this direction, then from that. Annabelle had trouble seeing her way forward. Lachlin started whining, "My feet are cold."

She put the burlap bag in the crook of her other arm and took his hand again, "Come on, Lory. We'll be home soon." They trudged on.

Within half an hour, they had reached the pond's edge. Annabelle knew that if they kept bearing toward the old willow on the far shore they would be close enough to the house. The old willow kept appearing and disappearing between the snow squalls. She had to keep a straight line. They started the march across the wind-swept, frozen pond.

And that's when they heard them. At first she thought it was only the wind, but there was no mistaking the murderous yap-yap of the on-coming pack. They were close and closing. Annabelle frantically yanked at Lachlin's hand, "Come on, Lory!" They began crossing at a run and were two-thirds of the way across when the ice cracked, trembled, then banged, like a gun shot. The surface split open two inches to reveal the freezing black water beneath. They skidded to a stop and tried to listen to the ice through the whistling of the wind and the swirling of the snow.

Lachlin began to cry. "I heard the wolves. They're coming. They're going to eat us!"

Annabelle snapped at him, "Stop it. They aren't interested in us. They want the goose. Just follow me." She took a step over the large crack and then another step forward and waited. She could see the old willow ahead on the far shore. She took another step, then waited. She took another, listening to the ice. Lachlin stepped gingerly into her windswept boot prints. They had made another twenty yards in this way when the ice shot and cracked again. Annabelle froze in fear.

Lachlin howled behind her, "Hurry up! They're coming! They're coming!"

She dropped down onto her hands and knees and pushed the goose sack out far in front of her. "Follow me, Lachlin." She crawled towards the sack. She shoved the sack ahead again across the patchy black ice, then crawled towards it. "Lory, do what I do! Do exactly what I do!" She shoved the sack and crawled slowly forward. She could feel Lachlin push into her boots from behind. The snow blinded her vision. She pushed on. She shoved the sack again then crawled towards it. She put her hand out again to shove the sack. But it was gone. She inched forward slowly sweeping the ice with her damp mitten. The ice was wet. She groped at the air. The sack had disappeared into that blinding white-out. Tears filled her eyes. They were lost.

Suddenly a familiar black warmth surrounded her. Astonished, she felt herself lifted up from the ice. Daniel's grizzly beard gently brushed her cheek as he swung her around onto his back. He bent over again and picked up little Lachlin, tightly placing him in the crook of his right arm. The burlap sack with the frozen goose hung from his other hand.

Turning back to the willow tree, Daniel trudged slowly home, towards the hearth, and dear Helen. Relieved, Annabelle snuggled her tear-streaked face down into the warmth of his broad neck and knew, with absolute certainty, that they would all be fine.

There were no wolves, the war was over, the winter would pass, and spring would come again soon.

# Authors' Biographies

**Mary J. Anderson** has a PhD from McMaster University. She has written two books, two plays, numerous articles, and a website: *Whitehern Museum Archives: www.whitehern.ca.* Dr. Anderson's books are: *The Life Writings of Mary Baker McQuesten: Victorian Matriarch* (WLUP 2004); and *Tragedy & Triumph: Ruby & Thomas B. McQuesten* (Tierceron Press, 2011).

**Alexander Binning** has lived in many parts of Canada and now lives in Parksville, Vancouver Island, where he reads and writes. He has worked as a librarian, teacher, heritage consultant and public historian. In 2004 *The Devil's Chair: A Novel of Lake Superior* was published by Bayeux Arts, Calgary. Two collections of short stories are in progress: *Bureaucratic Tales* and *Bush Tales.*

**Timothy Christian** is a retired Professor and Dean of Law from the University of Alberta in Edmonton; a former Chief Federal Negotiator who represented both the Liberal and Conservative Governments in negotiating a number of agreements with First Nations' peoples; and a labour arbitrator and mediator. After years of writing legal articles, briefs and decisions he has returned to his first love, which is history. He lives in North Saanich, B.C. with his wife, his dog and his boat.

**Vicki Delany** is one of Canada's most prolific and varied crime writers. She is the author of 16 published novels. *Under Cold Stone* is the seventh book in the Smith & Winters police series set in the British Columbia Interior. She also writes the light-hearted Klondike Gold

Rush books and novels of gothic suspense. Her Rapid Reads book, *A Winter Kill*, was shortlisted for a 2012 Arthur Ellis Award for best novella. Her newest Rapid Reads book is *Juba Good*, set in South Sudan. Having taken early retirement from her job as a systems analyst, Vicki enjoys the rural life in bucolic Prince Edward County, Ontario. She can be found at www.vickidelany.com

**John Dickenson** was formerly a geography professor at the University of Liverpool. In retirement he has been researching Canadian Home Children who were killed in the First World War. He is married to a Canadian and lives in Liverpool, England.

**Ethel Edey** enjoyed a career in healthcare administration. Introduced to writing through the Writing Certificate program at McMaster, Ethel had an essay published in the anthology, *In the Wings: Stories of Forgotten Women* (Seraphim Editions, 2012). She lives in Burlington, Ontario and winters in Florida.

**Sterling Haynes** is an octogenarian freelance writer of poetry, mostly Haiku and creative nonfiction. He's a retired rural doctor who now writes humour for newspapers, journals and magazines. His first book, *Bloody Practice* was on the BC best-seller list. His second was called *Wake Up Call*. Both were published by Caitlin Press and are available as E-books. He is working on his third, *Where Does It Hurt Now?* "Dad" is about Haynes' father, a talented dental surgeon, a soldier and a great guy.

**Linda Helson** lives and writes in Dundas, Ontario. Besides being included in *In the Wings: Stories of Forgotten Women*, she has had stories published in *The Hamilton Spectator*, *Ten Stories High*, *Hard Boiled Love* and *Nine Modern Muses*. She has written articles for *Country Connection* magazine and is a prize-winning poet.

**Frances Hern** has written three titles for Amazing Stories, a series about Canadians and Canadian history. The titles are *Norman Bethune*, *Arctic Explorers: In Search of the Northwest Passage*, and *Yip Sang and The First Chinese Canadians*. She also writes for children and has had poems published in numerous anthologies and magazines. For more information go to www.franceshern.ca.

**Pauline Hewak** is a high school English teacher born and raised in Hamilton. She has been writing poetry since her childhood and more recently, short stories, one of which was published in *In the Wings*. When she isn't marking papers she is working with her Poetry workshop group, pulling weeds, shoveling snow and dreaming about her next trip. She lives with three cats on a long street under the escarpment.

**Margaret Lindsay Holton** is an award-winning novelist, poet, and short story writer with ten titles published under her own artists' imprint, MLH Productions/Acorn Press of Canada, based out of Waterdown, Ontario. When not writing, Lindsay is very active in the Golden Horseshoe arts scene. Learn more about her work via her art blog: http://canadadaPHOTOGRAPHY.blogspot.com

**Barbara Hudspith** was born and raised in Hamilton and now resides in Grey County, where she offers retreats on the farm she and her husband, Bob, run.

**Lise Lévesque** is a Montreal-born writer whose career meandered through the fields of travel, communication, education and mental health. A graduate of McMaster University's Writing Program, she thrives on travelling, researching and writing. Two of her short stories have been published in *Main Street* and *In the Wings*. Under the pen-name, Ibu Lise, she is the editor of Harland John's *Soft Targets: The Bali Bombings*. She took a tour of China in 2012 and is incorporating this experience into a memoir.

**Cara Loverock** works in communications for the Government of the Northwest Territories. She is also a writer and former journalist based in Yellowknife, NWT.

**Todd McKinstry** lives in Hamilton, Ontario. He worked in the service industry for many years and is now a Licensed Paralegal. He received a degree in History and a Certificate in Creative Writing from

McMaster University and has published several short stories. That elusive first novel still inches forward.

**Bruce Meyer** is professor of English at Georgian College in Barrie where he teaches in the Laurentian University BA Program and at Victoria College in the University of Toronto, and St. Michael's College Continuing Education Program at the University of Toronto. He is author of over forty books of poetry, short fiction, non-fiction, pedagogy, and literary journalism. He is the inaugural Poet Laureate of the City of Barrie.

**Katharine O'Flynn** is from Montreal. Her work has appeared in several Canadian journals and anthologies. Another story from her unpublished collection of stories about her mother's life is to appear in *CommuterLit*'s second anthology, in the Summer 2014 edition.

**Barb Rebelo** is a former student of both McMaster University's Creative Writing Program, and the Pearls Writing Group in Hamilton Ontario. Crafting stories of suspense and the uncanny is Barb's delight. Her short stories have appeared in McMaster's *Main Street Anthology* (2005), and in the collection *In The Dark: Stories from the Supernatural* (Tightrope Books, 2006). In August 2009, Barb completed her first novel, *Wye Villa*, a mystery set in 1899 Somerset England; this novel is with Acacia House Publishing in Brantford Ontario; her agent is Bill Hanna. Barb is currently writing a sequel set in Port Dover Ontario. She lives in Flamborough with her husband and daughter.

**Bernadette Rule's** most recent poetry collection is *The Literate Thief: Selected Poems* (Larkspur Press, Monterey, Ky. 2007). She edited *Remember Me to Everybody: Letters From India, 1944 to 1949* by Frederick Gower Turnbull (West Meadow Press, 1997) and *In the Wings: Stories of Forgotten Women* (Seraphim Editions, 2012). Rule hosts the weekly arts-interview program, Art Waves (archive.org/details/artwaves).

**Jean Ryan** was born in Brooklyn when New York had three major league baseball teams. Upon completing McMaster University's Certificate in Creative Writing in 2008, she received the Award for

Academic Excellence. She is a professional storyteller whose memberships include the Storytellers of Canada/Conteurs du Canada, the National Storytelling Network (U.S.) and the Transformative Language Arts Network.

**Susan Evans Shaw**'s passion for history, be it family, local or Canadian, has generated newspaper articles, contributions to a number of anthologies, and two books from well known publishers. Her father (little Eric in the story) and her husband were both geologists. Their influence nourished her fascination with the past.

**Al Straitton** is a retired Hamilton high school teacher, having taught English and Drama for more than thirty years. He and his wife have four adult children. He invented a board game called "Stare!" which has sold almost 300,000 copies, mostly in the U.S. His writing experience has been limited to writing scripts with and for drama students and inspiring Writer's Craft students with small samples as models for proposed projects.

**Michelle Ward-Kantor** holds a journalism diploma, a Bachelor of Education degree and a certificate in creative writing. Her poetry and travel stories have appeared in many journals, both print and on-line. She is a contributing author to the following anthologies: *MainStreet*, *In the Wings: Stories of Forgotten Women* and *The 40 Below Project*. She has lived in Calgary, England, Australia, Vancouver, and southern Ontario. She currently lives in Edmonton with her husband and three daughters where she teaches creative writing. Visit her at michellewardkantor.com

Having written most of her work in the last twenty-five years for performance as an oral storyteller, **Carol Leigh Wehking** is accustomed to the research required for contextual and narrative integrity. She enjoyed delving into private letters, publications, and oral history for this story. As a Quaker, Carol Leigh takes a pacifist perspective on the war and its effects on both participants and victims.

**Anne White** is a recently retired professor of Medicine. She trained and taught at McMaster University until the millennium. She then followed her itchy feet to work abroad for eleven years both in the Middle East and then the Caribbean. Born and raised in England, she started travelling in her 20's, spending four years in Zambia with her husband and three very young children, before she finally arrived in Canada in 1972. Her main interests are primitive and comparative mythology, early Mediterranean history, languages and scuba diving. She lives in Hamilton as the hired help for two Devon Rex cats.

**Stan White** has written non-fiction all his life. More recently he has written short stories and poetry. Besides his collections of poetry, he has been published in many anthologies and literary journals. He is retired from a career in photography, and lives with his wife in Brantford. The poem, "Cold Front" was originally published in WITNESS, an anthology of poetry, edited with an introduction by John B. Lee (Serengeti Press, 2004).